Creating Commitment

Creating Commitment: How to Attract and Retain Talented Employees by Building Relationships That Last

MICHAEL O'MALLEY

WILLIAM M. MERCER, INCORPORATED

John Wiley & Sons, Inc.

New York • Chichester • Weinheim • Brisbane • Singapore • Toronto

Published by John Wiley & Sons, Inc.
Published simultaneously in Canada.

This publication is designed to provide accurate and authoritative information in regard to the subject matter covered. It is sold with the understanding that the publisher is not engaged in rendering professional services. If legal, accounting, medical, psychological or any other expert assistance is required, the services of a competent professional person should be sought.

ISBN: 0-471-35897-5

Printed in the United States of America.

10 9 8 7 6 5 4 3 2 1

Dedication

*To my life-long role models of commitment, Tim and Candy,
and to Stephanie, Kathryn, and Ryan, with whom I experience
the joys and responsibilities of commitment each day.*

Acknowledgments

*Also, I would like to thank Henning Gutmann, Renana Meyers,
and John Thornton for believing in this project;
Howard Blechner, Linda Culliton, and Pat Shannon
for their comments on earlier versions of this book; and
Marlene Brask, Mary Schnabel, and Trey Parker for
preparation of various elements of this manuscript.*

*Finally, I am extremely grateful to all of the companies
that have graciously invited me in over the years and openly
shared their thoughts and ideas with me.*

CONTENTS

INTRODUCTION

Business is beautiful because it packs all of human emotion into an eight-hour day. In business, people are let down, left out, given up, or passed over. They are also befriended, helped, encouraged, and celebrated. Human passions and needs do not mysteriously dissolve in the corporate parking lot. People don't forget what it is like to be a person when they arrive at work. They hope for the same considerations and are guided by the same expectations—and so it is with commitment.

Discussion of commitment need not be arcane and mysterious. Commitment in organizations shares many of the same elements that we find in other relations with which we are familiar, such as friendships and close relationships. With the exception of certain expectations around intimacy, many of the same underlying understandings that pertain to these latter relationships apply between coworkers, employees, and managers, and, more abstractly, employees and their organizations.

I have tried wherever possible to ground discussion of commitment in organizations on the everyday experiences we have in other social arenas such as close relationships. The emotional overlap among a wide variety of relationship types makes the exegesis of commitment more intuitive. The comparisons between employer-employee relationships and other forms of social interaction are instructional but not perfect—and I try not to overdo them. However, in our frenzied search for answers to relationship breakdowns, we ought not dismiss our everyday observations and experiences in understanding what it means to be committed or not.

The most common questions I receive from employers concern the efficacy of particular solutions to commitment problems. Do I think more training will work? What if we put in a day care center? Will telecommuting and travel vouchers be effective? There is no easy answer to these questions, because there is no one solution. There is no single corporate act that can reconcile all of people's wants and needs. Neither is there one multifaceted set of contemporary corporate actions that will cement a relationship for a lifetime, as if time were frozen. Commitment is complex and continuous, requiring employers to resolutely find ways to enhance or mend the psychological work life of employees. In the end, what a company hopes to achieve through its ongoing interactions with employees is to change the employee—the way he or she thinks, feels, and acts toward the company—so that the relationship is more sound and the work effort more persistent and complete.

There are volumes written on commitment in a variety of disciplines (e.g., economics, philosophy, psychology, sociology), offering wonderful insights on the topic. In writing this book, I have joined some of the major conclusions from all of this literature with 20 years' consulting experience, applied research, and thousands of discussions with managers and employees. My hope is that I have distilled a knotty subject into a straightforward and practical presentation. Throughout, I have had two aims in mind: first, to provide you with the means to self-assess your company's standing on commitment by furnishing a comprehensive definition; second, to offer you concrete approaches to building commitment in your organization.

I have tried to avoid the superficial abstractions that plague the area and to challenge the cursory assumptions that are often made—stated beliefs that seem detached from both research and experience. I also have attempted to sidestep the pedantic and the trivial, however stimulating these matters might be. The remaining middle ground is a discussion of the universality of commitment: of its basic nature and of people's fundamental needs irrespective of relationship type. My analysis draws on our personal experiences with commitment and gives them a structure we can use to discern the essence as well as the possibilities of employer-employee relations.

I concentrate throughout the book on how employers can create commitment with employees fully recognizing that commitment is a two-way street. Any one-sided relationship sooner or later tips over from its own weight. The dialectic of commitment requires employees to do their part: as such, I periodically mention employee behaviors that serve either to enhance or undermine commitment, although this decidedly is not the book's focus. The onus of a good start lies with the employer who, like a good host or hostess, invites the employees inside. It is largely up to the employer to make sure the right mix of people is present and that the right atmosphere and nourishment are provided. Success, then, depends on the quality of the social interactions that follow.

1

THE NEED FOR COMMITMENT

It is rare to have a discussion with corporate executives without the topic of commitment eventually arising. Many executives appear to be genuinely "shocked . . . shocked" by the exodus of their most esteemed employees, often noting a similar thinning within their own ranks. An employee's corporate life is a flurry of activity punctuated by offers, counteroffers, and job moves. Commitment appears to be waning at every institutional level. In fact, a recent survey conducted by the Hudson Institute found that only 42 percent of employees believe that their employers deserved their allegiance.[1]

The decline in commitment comes at a time when employers need employees more than ever. About one-half of all employees once again own the tools of their trade—their knowledge—which they can readily pack up and move from employer to employer. The days are gone when workers showed up, were handed their implements, and were told what to think and do. Today, companies' success depends on having a stable, talented workforce whose ideas coalesce into productive group actions. What they often get, instead, are collections of individuals, each of whom is prepared to walk out the door and through someone else's.

There are two reasons for the rebirth of an old-fashioned value—commitment. First, commitment is perceived as a business necessity. Worker shortages are seen as a barrier to growth among fast-growing companies. Figure 1.1 illustrates the increasing need for companies to find and hold

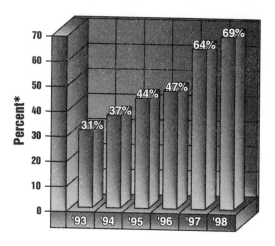

Figure 1.1 Employees wanted. The asterisk represents the percentage of America's fastest-growing companies that view worker shortages as a barrier to continuing growth.

Source: *Time* (June 22, 1998).

onto their talent. Put simply, without people, these companies will not be able to keep pace with demand and their growth will stall.

Indeed, a recent survey of executives across industries indicates that skilled-worker shortages are now having a pronounced effect by limiting sales by as much as 33 percent.[2] The demographics aren't favorable for improvement. There is a year-2001 problem upon us: In 2001, the baby boom generation will come of age for early retirement. There will be roughly 2.75 million Americans who will turn 55 in 2001, and the number will increase to 3.75 million in 2002—and gradually, the number will rise over time.[3]

Some companies and plants could lose more than one-half of their workforce to retirement over the next five years. The average age in many organizations, particularly within manufacturing, is relatively high: Layoffs pruned the younger, lesser-tenured ranks, and new technologies replaced the need to hire as many young employees. One could optimistically presume that many of the employees who will be eligible for retirement (and, in many instances, full pension benefits) will elect to postpone. Without further inducements, that may be unlikely. Nevertheless, even with the most advantageous assumptions, many in this age group will be lost to the workforce, because retirement often isn't a matter of choice: Many people will retire for health-related reasons. What actually transpires will have enormous consequences on both the economy and the financial markets.[4]

Senior management and executive ranks are not immune from the changing demographic landscape. Coincident with an aging population, there is a projected 15 percent decline in 35- to 44-year-olds over the next 15 years—the traditional reservoir of future management talent.

The second reason why commitment is back in style is because it is becoming very hard to replace workers—and not just because they are hard to find. Employees' knowledge and skill sets are more refined. Today, the work of organizations requires more intimate knowledge of the industry and of the specific company, as well as constant skill renewal and updating. If Betty leaves, the company has to find another Betty to maintain performance; an Al or a Pamela won't do. The learning curve is long and the ranks are thin: When an employee leaves, it really hurts.

I can see desperation setting in by the lengths to which companies will go to attract and retain people. I have seen prospects promised trips for two to Hawaii upon joining a company, and the employee with the most company referrals given a brand new Ford Explorer. Then, of course, there are the lavish sign-on and retention bonuses.

Where will the replacements come from? We can make the traditional appeal to liberalize immigration laws and import skill sets. Indeed, immigration already is at its highest levels in over 50 years; today, roughly 1 in 10 people in the United States is foreign born. Yet, there is increasing demand for skilled talent from overseas. The 1999 allotment of 115,000 H1-B visas, which admits temporary, nonimmigrant workers, was used up in just eight months. Currently, many companies are lobbying to raise the H1-B cap to 200,000, readily acknowledging that this is an incomplete, short-term solution to a much bigger problem.[5]

We also can recruit more actively from our high schools and colleges and hope that our schools, in turn, will provide a more prodigious supply of talent. Certainly, local and national politicians are trying to shore up our educational system and deal with the social problems that spill into our schoolyards. However, the prospect that companies' demands for skilled workers will be adequately supplied through our current educational system is not good. For example, the number of jobs requiring two- or four-year degrees is projected to rise by 20 to 25 percent over the next five years. The bachelor's degrees conferred, however, continue to fall in key areas such as engineering, mathematics, and computer science.[6]

Mostly, replacement workers will come from you. You have trained, knowledgeable employees who can be plugged into another company quickly. This other company won't have to spend as much on remedial education and training—you've done that for them already, where it was needed. This other company won't have to go on a far-flung, global search for talent when its employee base largely sits in its own backyard.

A new division of wealth, a new set of haves and have-nots, may well develop in business: those companies that will attract and retain the best people and those that can't—forcing the latter to retrench, relocate, redefine, or board up the windows. Companies that can't get and keep the people they want will be unable to conduct business as they had before in the days of employee bounty.

Finding and keeping good employees in this environment is imperative, but it's not going to be easy. According to a recent poll of American workers conducted by Louis Harris and Associates, over 50 percent say they will voluntarily leave their jobs within five years.[7] There doesn't appear to be much that will stop them, either. Human resource professionals claim that most efforts to keep talent have been unsuccessful.[8]

These failings frequently are attributed to the usual suspects: We either blame the people themselves or the vast and impersonal economy. Therefore, we affix labels to entire generations and ascribe a new human nature to them. We believe, for example, that Generation X'ers are less serious about their careers and are more inclined to have fun: As long as we can entertain them, they'll remain true to the organization.

We bless and curse the robust economy that has given us so many good years of growth but has made it exceptionally hard to find and keep good people. Unemployment has hit historic lows; small businesses continue to burgeon and flourish; and our schools are unable to turn out students at a rate at which their skills are needed. What person could possibly resist the temptations of an alluring economic climate combined with the bounty of opportunity and a willingness to pay?

Intractable mercenaries in a seductive land is a poor mix for commitment, so the argument goes. I see it much differently. For a brief moment in time, the historical veil has been lifted and we are permitted a glimpse of the truth. Companies are horrified to see that suitors can so easily swoop in and steal entire departments. They are so appalled by the loss of executive talent that they threaten lawsuits against recruiters and encroaching employers. They are stunned by the stampede of early retirees who snatch up offers to separate. Companies who once congratulated themselves on low turnover during poor economic times have been humbled by mass defections—it seems their employees really didn't love them as much as they thought.

Either we can comfort ourselves by thinking that the times and human nature are different and that there is nothing to be done to change that—that we must live with the consequences of our conditions—or we can admit that many employer-employee relationships are flimsy and that it is up to the companies to demonstrate, once again, that they are serious about their workers.

Managing People

The use of physical and investment capital has always been prominent in discussions of corporate success. It mostly has been recognized that these investments are embedded in a firm-specific productive capacity that requires, minimally, the operational excellence of people. The knowledge economy, however, has alerted us to the growing import of people's mental endowments, or human capital, in building organizational wealth. That creates problems for companies who depend on the power of people to excel. Unlike other forms of capital, people cannot mechanically be manipulated or fine-tuned to work at capacity; human capital have ideas of their own.

It is difficult to contemplate achieving the proper blend of effort, artistry, and intellect required for corporate success without commitment. Indeed, there are three things that companies have to do well in managing human resources, and commitment is an essential ingredient to each as depicted in Figure 1.2. To achieve success in the marketplace, organizations must successfully do the following:

○   Capture talent

○   Develop the talent they secure over time

○   Use, or convert, that talent to satisfy organizational aims

Let's consider these three things and the relevance of commitment to each.

Capturing Talent

Companies need necessarily to establish a reservoir of talent. The depth, breadth, and quality of this reservoir depends directly on the company's ability to attract and retain the best people. This ability partially reflects how appealing an organization is as a mate. How many unsolicited resumes do you receive? What proportion of people reject your offers to join? Of the people you hire, how many stay? Are you able to keep your best performers?

There is surely a technical component to doing these things well, but the reputation of the company is equally vital—to those outside as well as inside the company. The reputation of your company says

Figure 1.2 The role of commitment in managing people. *Note:* Commitment is the common theme that enables companies to realize the potential of people.

something about who you are, what you stand for, and how you relate to others including your employees, all of which partially are formed through your commitment to employees and vice versa. One good index of how well you are doing is to determine how eagerly people want in and want out of your organization.

A large part of being one of America's most admired companies or best places to work is showing unwavering respect for people.[9] The philosophy is simple: If a company treats employees well, employees will give back as much or more in mental and physical effort. Corporate respect toward employees is realized in many different ways: through growth opportunities, ability for self-expression, a clean and safe environment, and evidence of compassion. As one employee aptly put it, "Being a good company is like having a good wife [spouse]."[10] A good relationship is exciting; it develops and grows. There is camaraderie around shared values and interests, and there is the enduring sense that the other will "be there" when needed. One might speculate, for instance, that John Chambers' (Cisco Systems) or Gordon Bethune's (Continental Airlines) reaction to tough times would not be to squeeze the employees. They, and other similar CEOs, have worked diligently to create environments that demonstrate genuine appreciation for employees.

One company recently came to me asking if I could help them make it onto one of the premier lists of employee-friendly places to work, sponsored by the business press. They were rightly aware of the public relations coup this would entail and the related utility of attracting a larger pool of candidates. This company believed that by offering employees a smorgasbord of popular options, they would be publicly recognized for their largesse. They just needed a little help designing and communicating the nouveau programs. Whether their plan would succeed, of course, depended on whether the goal was to get on a list or to create employee commitment so that more people would actually want to work for them. It's possible to get the former and not the latter.

Companies that are able to create commitment realize that commitment ultimately is personal. This is the hard part of commitment that has profound implications for corporate conduct. It requires being consistent in what one does even though there may be short-term costs attached; it requires being flexible and making exceptions; and it requires making choices about what employees are prepared and unprepared to do—and providing reasons. Commitment is not created through a grab bag of trendy corporate goodies. It requires the patient and concerted attention of the whole organization.

To build commitment, you have to communicate with employees, assess their capacity to engage in various initiatives, give honest feedback, make decisions, spend money, take chances, and so forth. Like any relationship, there is a very big social component to success. If you want to throw your money away, institute new programs without being able to perform basic social/managerial functions well. Nowhere in this book do I say that building a quality relationship is easy, nor do I suggest that poor relationships can easily be salvaged by new programs.

Indeed, I have heard many reasons why companies *cannot* build commitment and why, therefore, they must be content with so-so experience in attracting and retaining employees. These reasons can be grouped into one of four categories:

1. *Too hard.* This is the self-condemning belief that management is too awful to pull it off. This is a more common justification than you might think, given how troubling it is. In essence, it is an admission that the company is incapable of running itself.

2. *Too costly.* Any time a company considers changes that might improve employees' lot, it immediately focuses on the costs that will be incurred as opposed to the human and economic benefits that will be obtained. The company engages in a cost-benefit analysis without ever considering the benefit part. If it costs money and is not related to physical or financial capital, the answer is "no."

3. *Too different.* Business is supposed to be "hard," but treating people with compassion and respect is "soft." Human resource professionals genuinely worry about how they will be perceived by their peers. If an initiative fails, one not only has to endure the spotlight of failure, but fend off smug glances that one is a

marshmallow. Doing things a bit differently involves risk (as well as courage and imagination) and, ironically, the risk is normally seen to be in the direction of greater commitment toward employees. Business as usual is assumed to be the safer option and the one to which many employers default.

4. *Too hopeless.* Some companies are in industries in which it is more difficult to hold onto people, such as retail sales. The problem is that these companies then tend to make the generalization that nothing can be done because of the nature of the industry and the jobs within it. The assumption is that companies in similar businesses necessarily have similar experiences in capturing human capital—but they don't. In addition, informed employees *do* care for whom they work within a given industry. The word gets out.

Developing Talent

Every company needs to enhance the capabilities of its workforce over time. Companies change; employees must change and grow along with them. Thus, many companies provide formal and informal training for employees and are careful about how they deploy them within the company.

There is, however, quite a bit that employees have to do on their own. It takes exceptional striving and developmental efforts to achieve extraordinary corporate ends. People have to learn on their own. For many employees, this means caring sufficiently about the employer and their work to want to exert the extra effort and put in the additional time—although, admittedly, I have seen employees put themselves on a strenuous self-growth regimen solely for the purpose of becoming more marketable outside the company: getting themselves in shape to shop around.

Commitment toward one's profession/vocation and the organization is a helpful stimulus for personal growth. It helps in another way as well. Individual innovations and ideas have to be widely diffused throughout the organization to be of benefit. Personal work efforts also have to be integrated. Both of these require reliable social networks to be built. The strength of these networks depends upon their quality and durability over time. Employee commitment is the social glue that can help these social networks function well.

It is not only what people know (i.e., the quantity of information and where it resides) that matters, but how social goods such as information are structured, distributed, transformed, and combined by the corporate community. In this regard, social ties and connectedness are vital to the prosperity and economic well-being of the group. Productive group behavior implies various things about the group itself: about social intentions, norms and values, obligations, and so on—about the ability of the group to take advantage of individual pieces of intellect.

These social networks can't simply be plugged in or hardwired and expected to work without first being properly grounded. People have to feel a part of the group, to trust one another, to believe in the causes of the exchange, and so on. Many companies readily acknowledge the destructive qualities of "silos," intuitively understanding that the whole is not fully benefiting from the individual parts. The interpersonal dimensions needed to make this system work and develop lie in the ability of the organization to build a community, and commitment is one of the essential ingredients.

Increasingly, companies are assigning a senior executive to the role of Chief Learning, or Knowledge, Officer, whose duties include:[11]

- o Managing tangible intellectual capital such as copyrights, patents, and royalties

- o Gathering, organizing, and sharing the company's information and knowledge assets

- o Creating work environments for sharing and transferring knowledge among workers

- o Leveraging knowledge from all stakeholders to build innovative corporate strategies

Guess the largest barrier to effective knowledge management? It's those darn people again! Those who persist in their own endeavors, exclusive of what has been achieved elsewhere within the company.

Converting Talent

The object of corporations is to take raw materials (including intellectual parcels) and to transform them into something else of value: new products or profits, for example. How are the human capacities by which this is achieved harnessed? Public goods do not magically arise from the unbridled pursuit of private interests. Meaningful conversions require consistency of purpose and other-centeredness. That is, to produce something of value that is not specifically yours or mine, requires an investment in a relationship that is ours.

Let's look at two scenarios to see which is more likely to be advantageous to the company. First, consider a company that is populated by independent contractors, even the Chief Executive Officer. The Internal Revenue Service has specific criteria for independent contractors, but for our purposes, let's agree to the following general definition. An independent contractor is a person who:

- o Is self-employed, with business interests outside the current engagement
- o Provides his or her own tools
- o Is hired to perform a specific task with specific performance terms, for a set price, within a defined time frame
- o Exercises considerable discretion about how the work will be done

This work has a definite focus, time frame, scope, and price. As long as there is work that the contractor is willing to do and the money is right, the relationship continues through successive contracts. The relationship is built on a series of agreements.

Some contractors may eventually tire of the work and decide to move on. Others may find higher bidders in the marketplace for the same work and, not wanting to forego opportunity costs, move their talents elsewhere. Still others may remain content with the work and the money and stay put for a while; perhaps they don't actively market themselves to others. The relationship between independent contractor and the employer is loose, passive, and dispassionate. On the one hand, it is up to the independent contractor to grow and develop, to find satisfying work, and to promote his or her market worth. On the other hand, the company wants the performance for which it contracted and assumes minimalist obligations toward the contractors—a work space while on company premises and compensation for services rendered.

The astute observer will have noticed that I have described what many in corporations and academia believe to be the New Deal: the new psychological contract between employers and employees. These are transactional relationships typified by short-term time frames, highly specific performance requirements, weak ties to the organization, and monetary exchanges. There are little mutual commitment and low psychological barriers to exit.[12]

In my work on staffing, no company has ever told me what they would really like to have is a building full of independent contractors—no employees. Companies don't rely exclusively on independent contractors, because they don't want to risk losing firm-specific knowledge and delicate, proprietary information to the competition. Also, the company would worry that a collection of independent contractors would not develop the requisite cohesiveness and morale to deliver products and services of superior quality. How is the new psychological contract good for companies? Furthermore, if this is the philosophy we are asked to embrace, then why be upset if an "employee" leaves you when he or she was never really yours to lose to begin with? Feelings of personal injury may be in order only when one has actually invested something in the relationship.

Consider the alternative: employees, united and committed. I recently had the opportunity to sit with a group of senior human resource professionals to discuss organizational commitment. Most of them had despairing and resigned remarks about the new psychological contract and even seemed to accept it with a heroic fatalism. One manager from a regional supermarket chain then stunned the group with her description of a compassionate employer. She supplied examples of the personal attention, support, and economic investment that the company provided employees and the warm feelings that employees had toward the founding family. She sensed that employer and employees alike would go to great lengths to avoid letting each other down. Employees tried their hardest to do what was right for the company, and the company would not turn its back on giving employees. Many of the meeting's participants learned that day that there is another way to relate to employees.

Over the years, I have heard employees describe their relationships with their employers: Many describe themselves as renters or owners, and many describe themselves as dating around or marrieds. Both of these metaphors conjure vivid distinctions, neither perfect, but illustrative. Renters and daters have relationships that are transient, and legally and socially confining. For example, renters must abide by carefully crafted rental agreements, and daters must adhere to norms that define dating relationships (e.g., certain gifts, meeting parents, and so forth, are prohibitive acts unless one wants to alter the nature of the relationship). There are no substantive long-term obligations to speak of, nor is there joint participation in activities that would denote that the relationship had a more enduring character. On the other hand, ownership and marriage infer a strong expectation of permanence and a set of open-ended requirements or obligations designed to improve the value of the property or the quality of the relationship over time. Both imply work and uncertainty. Both can result in great disappointment or joy. Just about everyone thinks that it's worth a try.

Commitment in Context

Commitment is critical to organizational performance, but it is not a panacea. In achieving important organizational ends, there are other ingredients that need to be added to the mix. When blended in the right complements, motivation is the result.

Motivation is generally defined as behavior that is energetic and goal directed.[13] Motivational theorists differ on from where this energy springs and on the particular needs that a person is attempting to fulfill, but most would agree that motivation requires the following:

○   A desire to act (commitment)

○   An ability to act (requisite behavioral repertoires)

○   An objective (goal state)

Figure 1.3 illustrates the potential independence and interdependence of these components as applied to an organizational setting. To obtain action your company would view as worthwhile, an employee must be committed (properly energized), have the requisite capabilities to act, and understand what must be done. There are problems if any of these pieces are missing as is discussed in the following.

Great commitment and goals will be lost on an inferior workforce and/or on an obstructionist work environment. One of the great truisms of behavior is that you can lead a horse to a water trough, but she won't drink if water is not available or if she never learned how. No matter how great the desire or how rewarding the outcomes, behaviors that can't be enacted, won't. Indeed, if a company repeatedly erects barriers to goal completion (e.g., through such means as bureaucratic entangle-

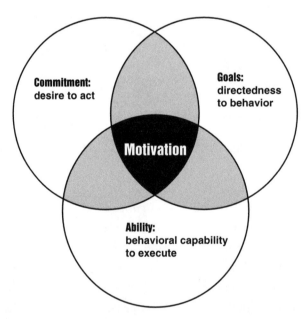

Figure 1.3 The contribution of commitment to motivation.

ments and insufficient allocations of resources) that cannot be over-come by the employee, motivation will not endure. The employee will either give up or look elsewhere for a more fertile environment. Whereas the committed employee will work diligently to improve upon his or her skills and doggedly try to remove obstacles that stand in the way of progress, in the short run, just how far he or she gets will greatly depend on what the employee knows and is capable of performing.

Generating great goals without the attendant commitment is futile. As Collins and Poras point out in their fine book, it isn't just the presence of a goal that stimulates progress, it is the level of commitment to the goal that matters as well.[14] Companies spend a lot of time and money on goal setting, believing that goals that are mutually set by boss and subordinate and, therefore, "owned" by the employee, are sufficient to elicit effortful behavior. Sometimes, the pledge of money adds luster to goal attainment but, more often than not, the tangible consequences are indiscriminate and insubstantial. In either case, as any manager will tell you, "There is meeting goals," and "There is meeting goals." Some employees approach the exercise as a technical formality and with the precision of a lapidary: working on the angles to produce the greatest sheen. Others pursue their goals with abandon, constantly reanalyzing and reconstructing, but never losing sight of the spirit of their endeavors. The real differences do not lie in who made up the goal or what the specific goal is, but on how deeply one cares about, and is committed to, the enterprise in which the goal is embedded.

Consider the differences between a mountain climber and a tourist, both of whom have the goal of reaching a mountain's summit. The mountain climber chooses a difficult route of ascent because the journey itself is filled with passion. In fact, standing at the peak wouldn't be as exhilarating otherwise. The tourist just wants to make it to the top alive; the tourist selects the easiest path and gingerly picks his or her way up. Differences in competence aside, the distinctions between the mountain climber and the tourist nicely illustrate the sterility of goals in the absence of any broader convictions.[15]

Instilling commitment without establishing direction squanders employees' ardor. Behavior is purposeful and goal oriented. Without any clear channels for action, organizational activity is like pouring water onto a mound of dirt: It runs down in many different directions, forming its own tributaries and outlets. Although committed employees will be much more inquisitive about what the company wants as opposed to uncommitted employees, who will pursue their own course, they still need help in finding their way.

In understanding the objectives that are most important to the company in both word and deed, committed employees are liberated to regulate their behavior in the way that is most advantageous to the company. Most of what employees do on a daily basis is outside the scope of direct observation and the control of external rewards that are too remote to be meaningful. Employees are on their own. It is up to each person to make the right choices with other employees, customers, suppliers, and so forth, when the moment of truth arrives. High commitment and a definitive goal state go a long way in securing the corporate future.

Myths and Misconceptions

Before moving on to the next chapter, where we will begin to take a closer look at the nature of commitment, there are a few myths and misconceptions about commitment, and related issues, to clear up. At various times within companies, I have seen these beliefs expressed as truths. However, they are either built on false premises, involve so many exceptions and caveats as to render them meaningless, or they are just plain incorrect.

Myth 1: Employees who stay with a company are committed. This is a common fallacy. There are types and degrees of commitment, and those who remain with a company may not be committed in the fullest sense. For example, people who stay simply may not have (or are the type of people who believe they do not have) very good options elsewhere. Employees can expect pretty much the same or worse at other places of employment. Therefore, as miserable as these employees may be, they remain where they are. Companies often mistake employee retention for commitment. Yet, it is always possible to get people to stay by instilling basic forms of commitment (e.g., *compliance* through money). However, these employees may not really care about their work or you, their employer.

Myth 2: When a company does something to increase commitment, it should see the results to the business right away. Many companies are impatient for results, and with very good reason, given the costs associated with absenteeism, turnover, reduced productivity, theft, and such — consequences of low commitment. Interventions aimed at improving commitment and/or any other aspect of the business have potential effects that are either immediate, gradual, or delayed, and that are either short lived or long lasting. When most companies speak about change, they want the immediate, long-lasting variety. This kind of change, however, really isn't possible. People's attitudes on matters of importance to them, like the quality of their work life, don't change easily or quickly. It takes time to get the changes in attitudes (i.e., commitment) that are needed to get the kinds of changes one wants—ones that will endure. It is all the harder if the starting place for attitude change is one of mutual distrust and animosity. Commitment takes time to create, and, fortunately, it takes time to destroy—although, as any child with Tinkertoys will tell you, you can dismantle more quickly than you can build.

The things that companies often end up doing are designed to yield immediate results. Again, this is understandable; however, these efforts mostly will yield short-term benefits—the effects dissipate with time. Providing more money is the perfect example. Companies pay out more money, employees temporarily work harder or stay longer, adjust to their new level of compensation, and subsequent "doses" of cash are soon required to sustain the effects.

Myth 3: Turnover and absenteeism are entirely different subjects. From a company's perspective, these involve different internal procedures, involve different policies, have their own cost structures, and affect companies in unique ways, but they are on the same escape-avoidance behavioral continuum; that is, they are similar responses to a lack of commitment. They are mechanisms of escaping or avoiding (to the extent possible) aversive conditions, accomplished either by changing companies or by reducing the time made available to the company. The goal is to minimize or eliminate unsatisfactory conditions. This is why punitive policies and approaches to absenteeism have little effect. They simply try to make absenteeism beyond a certain limit more painful than going to work, like a sign in the road that says, "Go no further, or else!"

To some extent, these policies invite people to the limits and, even so, clever employees on a mission can usually find a way past them. Punishments, such as warnings and threats, only convey what an employee should not do and not what they should do—they do not make the workplace more appealing or more desirable. Furthermore, punishment can instigate retaliatory behaviors (e.g., work slowdown, vandalism) against the punishing agent (i.e., the company), particularly if employees feel singled out by corrective actions or consider the punishment to be unfair.

Myth 4: Employees, by nature, aren't as committed as they used to be. We have already discussed this a little. Companies no longer afford the job security they once did. However, many employers believe that because they cannot provide assurances of permanent employment to employees, commitment is impossible. There is no use in trying.

Some employers go on to make the workplace as unappealing as possible to the degree that "Why would anyone stay?" becomes a legitimate question. As we'll see throughout this book, there is much more to commitment than promises about job security. Even so, it is possible for employees to feel secure in their jobs, even without explicit guarantees of job permanence, given the right organizational climate. For example, managerial stability (i.e., low internal or external churn in the management ranks) can enhance employees' confidence in the future and sense of permanence; on the other hand, frequent managerial moves can be unsettling to employees and can be a source of anxiety.

Myth 5: The people who are most likely to leave a company are new hires fresh out of school who have not yet developed a work ethic. Because commitment takes time to develop, new hires with equivalent prospects outside the company, whether they are fresh out of school, are at the greatest risk of leaving an organization. One of the truisms of turnover is that the longer employees stay, the longer they'll stay. With time, employees either have too great a personal investment in the relationship to forsake it, or they become increasingly committed to the relationship in other ways, or both. In either case, the time when employees are most susceptible to leaving the company is shortly after they've arrived—when they are still evaluating whether they've done good or made a colossal mistake.

Myth 6: Most employees leave because of money, not lack of commitment. It is generally true that most good employees who look for work elsewhere can find a job that pays from 10 to 30 percent more. Why, though, were they looking in the first place? One aspect of commitment is a reluctance to seek out and entertain alternatives. Most employees will say that they stay with a company for reasons unrelated to money and leave because of money. In exit interviews, money serves as the perfect, harmless rationale that leaves everybody smiling: Who wouldn't leave for more money?

Ask employees how they felt at the time they made their decision to leave, and a different story emerges. A more emotion-laden discussion emerges about squashed expectations, broken promises, abuses of power, and so on: Intense thoughts and emotions are neatly hidden by a discussion of money. Many employees leave *for* money, *because* they have not been enriched by the company in other ways.

Myth 7: Doing something to increase commitment is better than doing nothing. This assumes that the company knows what it is doing and why it is doing it. Different people within different areas of the company sometimes have unique theories of commitment and apply their own solutions. Without a uniform understanding of, or a consistent approach to, commitment, it is conceivable to make matters worse by implementing costly programs that have no effect because they address the wrong issues or are contradicted by other initiatives. For example, one part of the company may boast of its impressive set of worklife programs, while employees discover from local management that the use of these programs is frowned upon. Another example would be a company that imposes a 40-day-per-year training requirement for employees but discourages any training because it interferes with work; indeed, within one company in which I worked, training was relegated to the least busy. Being sent to training was perceived as something to be avoided—"You aren't busy, go to training." Problems with commitment may be magnified when one part of the organization creates employee expectations while another part undermines them.

Myth 8: There is really no use in trying to create commitment within certain industries (e.g., retail), because the jobs aren't that good and that reality can't be changed. Many companies believe that building commitment to retain employees is not worthwhile, because it can't be done—the nature of the work is not that good, and it can't be changed. I hear this most often with respect to positions such as salesclerks, customer service representatives, and cleaning and maintenance staff. However, when I ask people in these positions if they are happy, only a part of their answers focus on the duties that they actually perform. Most of their answers concern their relations with their boss, how they are treated by the company, and whether there are organizational barriers to performing their jobs to the best of their abilities. Their answers have more to do with feeling that they are valued, that they belong, and that they are involved in a meaningful activity, than with the actual work they do. It may not be possible to change the attributes of a job, but it is possible to ascribe value to it through the company's words and deeds.

Not everyone will suddenly choose to stay in a particular job, but many employees who are more committed will choose to stay longer. Even good associations come to an end when they are no longer functional: for example, when an employee wants more responsibility but there is no room to grow within the company, or when an employee's professional interests begin to diverge from the company's interests. This raises an underappreciated facet of commitment. Even when certain aspects of the relationship are no longer viable, and separation is inevitable, the relationship can remain cordial and inviting. In such instances, former employees will tell others about their positive experiences with your company.

Myth 9: Companies should address low commitment where it results in the biggest organizational returns. Big problems are usually diagnostic of deeper and more systemic trouble with commitment, and these should be addressed over time. Often, many aspects of the organization are askew, and many costly changes are needed. In these cases, a simple, single intervention will seldom counteract all of the messages that the organization is sending out about its commitment to its employees. Bringing flowers home to a spouse one day would be nice, but it won't have a lasting effect unless it's coupled with other behavioral changes that express similar attitudes. Building commitment isn't something that's done; rather, it's a way of life, a process, that takes time and effort to effect.

In staring at the intimidating size of some problems, companies are immobilized sometimes, or they lose sight of the fact that, in some quarters of the company that are less resistant to change, there are lesser things that can be done. That is, there may be lesser commitment problems affecting a small but significant cadre of people—that won't yield systemic results that are quite as large—but that can be handled more easily. The magnitude of potential results tend to be correlated with the scope and effort of change that is required. In summary, I have seen big problems act like a cognitive magnet, diverting attention away from minor changes that could be made, and exhausting would-be change agents before work has even begun.

Myth 10: Turnover is a binary event. True enough, turnover is a yes/no event, but that event is the culmination of a series of experiences that attach people to or disengage them from the organization. The misconception is that turnover is similarly precipitated by a discrete cause: something specific happens that produces turnover. Turnover is an evolutionary process by which employees gradually discover (some more quickly than others) what the organization is like and what kind of relationship they are in—and they make a choice accordingly to stay or leave. The decision is a product of numerous experiences, the final one of which may be the "last straw" or the one that "pushes employees over the edge." Causes can be insidious—the accumulation of experiences—with separations triggered by a single precipitating event.

In general, companies tend to think of the consequences of commitment in binary terms: people stay or leave, show up for work or don't, are or are not good citizens, are hard workers or slaggards, and so on. This sometimes leads to a logical fallacy that the causes, too, are simple and discrete. Employee commitment is the result of a complex of conditions stimulated by a myriad of corporate actions.

Myth 11: Very low turnover is bad. This is a way of thinking used by companies to cheer themselves up when their turnover is high. The implicit assumption is that if no one is leaving, the place must be too comfortable. Employees are complacent, not committed. I have seen employees fit snugly into an easy corporate lifestyle: no pressures or accountabilities. True enough, there are companies with low turnover that are reservoirs of nice people who aren't particularly ambitious or effective. This suggests that *involuntary turnover*—turnover attributable to the company's actions against the employee usually for performance-based reasons—should be higher. Low turnover, however, can also be a sign that a company is doing all the right things to gain the commitment of the employees—and companies don't suffer because of it. The Illinois Trade Association, Inc., hasn't lost an employee in five years. The employees are highly productive—the Association elicits this effort by showing that they respect their employees and by helping to enrich their lives in ways that go beyond money.[16]

Nevertheless, zero (or near-zero) *voluntary turnover*—turnover that is instigated by the employee—may reflect a state of perfection that is too good to be true. The work environment is structured so that no rational person would leave, regardless of the way he or she feels about the organization. For instance, many information technology departments gave their employees piles of stock options, and no one left; as soon as the options vested, however, the door to the gilded cage sprang open, and much wealthier employees stepped out. It is advisable to always leave room in the system for employees to opt out voluntarily if they so choose, because you don't want people to stay if they really don't want to work for you.

Myth 12: There is only one reason for high or low commitment. This is like presuming that all relationships succeed or fail for the same reason. Although this statement is self-evidently false, investigations on commitment and related issues such as turnover often proceed as if in search of the Holy Grail (e.g., all we have to do is offer more career opportunities). In general, the antecedents of commitment are "nested." There are corporatewide influences, group (e.g., departmental, workgroup, job class) influences, and individual differences. Thus, members of Information Technology, for example, will not have the exact same commitment-related issues as employees in Marketing. Furthermore, not everyone in Information Technology—even people with the exact same jobs—will be attitudinally identical on commitment. The same facts and circumstances can affect people in different ways. For example, certain people may make benign interpretations of unfavorable events, whereas others may interpret those same events as personal threats or slights. That is, there are people who are better prepared to be more committed than others. At the extremes, you can usually tell who these people are: the people who can't stay connected to anything or anyone and the people who can. Once, I was working with a company on a turnover/commitment problem that they were having, and I casually told them that I knew one of their new hires very well— as the son of a friend, he was someone I had watched grow up. They jokingly asked if he would stay. My reply was, "Of course." This was a kid who never quit anything. He held onto the same paper route longer than I'd ever known anyone to have a paper route. He was about to marry his high school sweetheart. He joined clubs and sports teams and stuck with them. Because he was satisfied with his decisions, and attachments just seemed easy for him—of course, he'd stay.

Myth 13: To understand commitment, we can just ask employees. It doesn't hurt to ask. Companies are usually interested in the answers for specific groups of employees—typically, those who have elected to leave the company. Assuming that employees can correctly reconstruct their rationales and that they are willing to divulge them, their answers should be contrasted with another (matched control) group to yield insights into causes. Companies aren't just interested in employees' perspectives on commitment; they really want to know how their commitment might differ from other employees who are more productive or who have greater intentions of remaining with the company. Thus, for example, if people who are leaving the company say the reason is they have a bad boss or a boring job, the company needs to know if those who stay think differently.

Myth 14: Happy employees are productive employees. Mood states such as happiness are relevant to performance, but they are not the same as commitment or motivation. Happiness doesn't imply a connectedness to the organization or a drive toward goal attainment. It is easy to imagine someone being immensely happy, personally, but an unremarkable performer. This myth is a simplistic remnant of the human relations movement, and it requires a host of limiting conditions or conceptual additions to make it workable. For example, a general state of happiness may be related to optimism and resilience, which, in turn, may be associated with particular types of performance, such as better service in tough customer contact positions. Someone who is happy also may be less sour about his or her pay and may be more positive about other aspects of the work environment, such as his or her job and, consequently, more productive.

Myth 15: Positive behavior change implies positive change in commitment. Organizations undertake many actions that are intended to thwart specific dysfunctional behaviors, such as lateness, by introducing incentives, punishers, and monitoring devices in an attempt to regulate those behaviors. Although these may lead to a notable decline in specific undesirable behaviors, the means used to achieve those ends may lower commitment to the organization by making the environment more aversive and/or by making people less trusting of one another. Without attendant attempts to change attitudes (e.g., commitment), new problem behaviors may emerge. Plug one hole and another develops someplace else. Thus, seeming solutions or treatments may make matters worse.

There are many other myths and misunderstandings about commitment and its antecedents and consequences that I will describe throughout the book. Now, let's look more closely at the five ways to create commitment and what, more specifically, commitment can do for your company.

2

LOVE AND COMMITMENT

Most of us have been blessed with an ability to form attachments. Constantly and selectively, we forge new connections in our lives: with spouses and children, our hometowns, the church, clubs and associations, the neighborhood video store, high schools and colleges, and yes, our companies. Naturally, the degree of our affections will vary from situation to situation, but every bond we make has a special allure that keeps us going back for more.

Employee-employer relationships break down, like any relationship, when there is no mutual commitment—when love is unrequited. When employees leave an organization, it is seldom the result of a passionless calculation based purely on the cold, hard facts. Most often, employees feel the telltale signs of disaffection—of being burned, used, neglected, unappreciated, offended, spurned, and so on. Employees terminate relationships when they are dissatisfied with the organization in some, or several, respects, or when they feel injured.

Not every organizational relationship ends for lack of commitment, of course. Sometimes, it has nothing to do with commitment at all, and there will be little the company can do in these circumstances. People need time off to spend with a sick family member; they feel obliged to follow a spouse to a new location; they go back to school; and so on. However, many people leave because they believe they have found a better, more satisfying deal elsewhere. You have been jilted, my friend, in favor of another company that has more to offer. Your only consolation is that you haven't necessarily lost out to the proverbial "younger" company—although many employees are flocking to start-ups these days—it could be an older company, too.

Defining Commitment

Because commitment is what this book is all about, an apt starting place would be to come to some early understanding of what commitment is and what it is not. The sustaining power of relationships comes from *commitment*. The word is derived from the Latin root meaning "to connect." *Webster's Dictionary* defines *commitment* as "the state or an instance of being obligated or emotionally impelled." Therefore, people who are committed feel connected, and they are motivated to maintain that connection.

Indeed, if you reflect upon a relationship that you are having, in which there is mutual commitment, you will probably find that such a relationship has several desirable properties.[1]

- ○ First, you are psychologically attached or emotionally bonded. Each of you feels understood, cared for, secure, and loved. The relationship is emotionally gratifying.

- ○ Second, the relationship has a long-term focus, which allows each of you to make sacrifices, to be altruistic, and to forgo short-term, self-interested acts for the good of the relationship—for there's always tomorrow.

- ○ Third, there is a high level of predictability and dependability to the relationship. Each of you has a pretty good idea what the other will do and can count on that person to be available when needed.

- ○ Fourth, to preserve the relationship, each of you is likely to make concessions or to make accommodating, constructive (versus retaliatory) responses when your expectations have been violated by the other. You avoid making destructive, injurious "low blows" in favor of more mature, conciliatory "maintenance acts," designed to preserve the relationship.

○ Fifth, neither of you probably pays much attention to or thinks much about other, similar possible relationships that you could have. You either think that others are, in some fashion, inadequate, or you simply don't care and drive your alternatives away—believing the current state of affairs is the best of all possible worlds. If the grass is greener on the other side of the fence, you'd never know it because, from your vantage, your yard is pretty nice, too.

○ Sixth, committed people tend to interpret one another's behaviors in innocent ways—as mostly right and performed with good intentions. A committed person holds the other in high esteem.

○ Seventh, you are probably willing to attest to your commitment in public. Commitments often are made in public and affirmed in public. That is, committed people openly acknowledge their relationship. If someone asks you if you're married, the answer shouldn't depend on who's asking.

○ Eighth, the relationship is viewed as *pluralistic*; that is, it is viewed as involving a *we*, versus two *I*'s. Robert Reich, the former Secretary of Labor, has referred to this as the "pronoun test" for commitment. The general perception is that you are in this thing together.

It is easy to see why companies like commitment. It's the word of the day in just about every company, because committed employees look forward to going to work. They are pleasant, conciliatory folks who are motivated to put in a good day's effort. They produce. They act in the interests of the company. They don't leave. Contrary to popular opinion, few employees desire to be organizational vagabonds; most employees would welcome reasons to be committed.

Contrast that with what uncommitted employees are like and what they do. Because they are emotionally unconnected, they are remote or aloof. They may pursue their own interests, regardless of what the company wants or needs. They may moonlight or have a business on the side. I've known employees who operated second businesses from their primary place of employment. Uncommitted employees may take full advantage of time off (e.g., sick or disability leave, workers' compensation, lunchtime, and breaks). They seem never to be around when they are most needed, and their work output barely meets minimum standards. They are frequently confrontational, defensive, oppositional, officious, and abrupt. If they are given the chance to take a better deal that comes along, they would gladly move on.

I have provided a short quiz in Table 2.1 that allows you to assess your own or others' commitment to the organization. It contains many of the concepts we just reviewed. Take it, and see how you do. In the following chapters, I'll describe in detail what companies can do to build employee commitment and what employees should look for from companies that are seriously interested in creating quality relationships with employees that last.

As worker mobility grows more prominent, the word *commitment* will continue to pop up more frequently in corporate hallways. The need to keep good people has become increasingly urgent as unemployment has shrunk and replacement employees become harder to find. Many employers, however, treat commitment as a kind of moral imperative: It is something that employees should have without the company providing any further justification of its own. Companies sound repetitive chants, as on Doctor Moreau's island: "What is the law? The law is to stay with your employer." Moral arguments only go so far before relationships begin to falter and fall apart. You recall what happened to Doctor Moreau.

To get at the heart of commitment, allow me to share a couple of love stories with you. We'll subsequently talk about their relevance to organizations.

Love story no. 1. You are desperate for companionship and walk into a bar. You see the person of your dreams, coyly smiling at you. After a brief conversation and a two-week courtship, you decide to marry. You drive to Las Vegas and wed before a justice of the peace and a ceremo-

Table 2.1 Are Your Employees Committed?

Instructions. Please read each of the following statements, and answer as you believe the majority of your employees would answer by circling the number that best applies. How would you respond?

	Mostly Disagree	Moderately Disagree	Slightly Disagree	Slightly Agree	Moderately Agree	Mostly Agree
1. Other companies just are not as good as this one.	1	2	3	4	5	6
2. I would like to spend the rest of my career at this company.	1	2	3	4	5	6
3. I like telling others about the company for which I work.	1	2	3	4	5	6
4. I often make sacrifices for the greater good of my company.	1	2	3	4	5	6
5. Disagreements between my company and me are handled constructively.	1	2	3	4	5	6
6. I try my very best at work— I give it my all.	1	2	3	4	5	6
7. Many of my professional/ vocational needs are fulfilled at this company.	1	2	3	4	5	6
8. I gladly do whatever my company asks me to do.	1	2	3	4	5	6
9. I consider the interests of the company as a whole when taking action.	1	2	3	4	5	6
10. It would be difficult for me, emotionally, to leave this company.	1	2	3	4	5	6
11. When I make a big mistake, I let my company know.	1	2	3	4	5	6
12. I like to wear clothing and use other items with my company's name (or logo) on it.	1	2	3	4	5	6
13. My company is the best in its industry.	1	2	3	4	5	6
14. I would not be as satisfied working some other place.	1	2	3	4	5	6
15. I think of my employment as a kind of membership in a club to which I belong.	1	2	3	4	5	6

Score

Key. Total your score, then refer to the following guidelines:

81–90 points = Extremely committed
72–80 points = Very committed

63–71 points = Moderately committed
54–62 points = Slightly committed
<54 points = Not committed at all

nial witness—each of you laughs at the line "until death do us part." At the request of your spouse, you spend your first married day cleaning the apartment and potting plants for the balcony. You are giving and thoughtful at first—you attend to your spouse's needs, but you never seem to get much in return. Time goes on. Special occasions like birthdays and anniversaries come and go without acknowledgment. There are no thank yous or other expressions of appreciation. Your spouse has become increasingly mysterious and noncommunicative. You begin to find telltale traces of trysts, which are met with vehement denials and far-fetched explanations. Your interests and attitudes have become more divergent; your spouse thinks you've stagnated. You do very little together, choosing to spend more of your time with your respective sets of friends. The things that once attracted you to one another—that night in the bar—no longer seem so appealing. You hire a private investigator to spy on your spouse. Disagreements increase dramatically. You begin to snipe at your spouse's personality, appearance, and habits; your spouse snipes back. Your spouse earns pretty good money but doesn't share much with you; you currently don't work. You feel trapped. One day, you are unsuspectingly hit with divorce papers. After an acrimonious struggle in which everything is said to one another through third parties, you legally and permanently split.

Beautiful story, isn't it? Now, let's look at a second story.

Love story no. 2. You are in the library of your college and begin chatting with the person next to you. You are attracted to the person. You talk about your mutual interests and see each other over the next few months, divulging more and more intimate details to one another— about your pasts and your futures. You continue to date and enjoy one another's company; after a year, you become engaged to be married. You set a date in eight months' time. You carefully and thoughtfully plan your wedding and swear your love to each other before a full church. After the reception, you are off on a romantic, two-week honeymoon. When you return, and before resuming work, you spend some time getting organized and settling into married life. With time, life together gets better and better. You always celebrate your anniversary and unfailingly remember special occasions such as birthdays. You enjoy each other's company and share in each other's interests, pleasures, and

pains. There are hardships and "bumps in the road," but you always per-
severe, and the relationship becomes stronger as a result. You have children whom you raise well together. You think about the future and plan
accordingly. As you approach and enter retirement, you are still as much
in love as the day you first met.

The interesting aspect of these stories is that they are not fabrications
from *Melrose Place* or real life, rather, they are built from what I have
seen companies actually do. I simply took what I have seen in the corporate world and made the translation into a more familiar and intuitive arena—close relationships. They are summary illustrations of
commitment in action.

Let's look briefly at our love stories. Love story no. 1 tells the tale of a
hasty employer and employee, both of whom are so desperate to fill and
find jobs that neither takes the time to explore their compatibility of
interests and values. Because the emphasis of the relationship is on fulfilling an immediate need (i.e., filling a vacancy), there is no discussion
of the future. There is no future, only *now*. These are companies in
which employees show up for work on their first day, and there is no one
there to meet them—employees who stand helplessly by the elevator
bank waiting for someone with a card key to let them in. These are companies whose employees show up the first day and who don't have offices
or a few of the gadgets of productivity, like paper and pencil, computer,
and such. In developing our first love story, I was reminded of companies
that put their new people to work the moment they walk in the door or
send them out on assignment on their first day. This is the equivalent of
"cleaning the apartment": confused and bewildered employees trying to
find their way through the ambiguous instruction, "Well, get to work."

I'm not making this up. It gets worse. Working in some companies is
like the man in Germany who, *after four years*, was discovered dead in
his apartment in front of the television. In all that time, no one knew or
checked whether he was dead or alive. What's more, no one cared.
Employees, too, often feel the neglect of employers. There is no recognition for a job well done and no remembrances or celebrations of
their years of service. They may as well be dead.

You get the picture. Over time, employees and employers don't have much to do with each other. The company doesn't give much direction, and employees don't say much about what they are doing. It is the perfect, loveless relationship with each, at a distance, suspicious of what the other is doing. Maybe the employee is working two jobs (e.g., running a mail-order company from his or her current company), stealing customers, or sabotaging equipment. Perhaps the employer is putting the employee into impossible situations in which failure is certain, plotting a demotion or undesirable transfer, or thinking of wiping out the employee's department. Maybe the company is sneaking peeks at the employee's electronic correspondence or tracking his or her telephone calls. There are periodic flare-ups from frustration. The company shouts, "You're not doing enough. Work harder." The employee fires back that he or she is an excellent employee who is doing everything within his or her power—and if they have a problem with that, the company can talk to his or her lawyer.

Employee-employer relationships don't have to be bad. Consider Love story no. 2. The company knows who it is looking for and knows where to look. To be sure that the employer and employee are right for each other, they spend time together exploring one another's interests. From early on in the relationship, the focus is on the long term, so when they "wed," there is the assumption that the relationship will work out over the long haul.

When the employee shows up for work the first day, he or she is greeted by someone who actually knows him or her. The employee is given a "family album" in which to record and store memories of the company. The new person is introduced to people throughout the company, including his or her new mothers- and fathers-in-law—that is, the corporate executives who he or she will see again and again throughout the year. The new employee is provided with an extensive weeklong orientation that explains everything about the company and its operations as well as basic policies and procedures. The new employee knows what to do and what to expect; he or she receives more instruction periodically throughout the first two years.

The new employee is given general instructions and, during the first couple of weeks, is rapidly integrated into the business as a valuable associate and colleague. The employee makes a few quirky mistakes during this time period (for example, asking for a *Coke* while working at *Pepsico*, or saying that he or she will *Xerox* instead of *copy* while working at Canon). Also, the employee inadvertently "goes over someone's head" for an approval, argues for initiatives that the company doesn't sanction, fills out the expense report incorrectly, and makes one or two policy snafus. The company patiently and constructively helps the new associate make the corrections and figuratively points him or her in the right direction. The company doesn't overpower or punish, but gently corrects.

The company is honest in its dealings with employees (in terms of pay, performance, and promotability); over the years, it gives employees many great opportunities they had never imagined they would get. They support employees' development, and the employees take full advantage, growing and maturing in their respective professions. They voluntarily take on new challenges. They give their all.

In many ways, the company treats each employee as an individual with unique needs and interests, rather than as a body or a part of an undifferentiated mass. The company shows its special appreciation for contributions made, recognizes employees' service to the company, and gives them special considerations when needed. For example, a company with which I recently consulted bought a running machine for an employee's office to help with his rehabilitation following heart surgery. Another example is the company that helped an employee who was experiencing difficulty during pregnancy set up a home office—and then informed other employees that they could attend meetings at her house if she wished.

There are disagreements over the years, but they are settled in an atmosphere of trust, and given the long-run view of the relationship, it is easy for each party to make short-term compromises. The pervasiveness of trust enriches the entire social milieu, creating kinder, gentler relationships with peers. It's a good place to be. Even after retirement, employees continue to see one another and their old friends back at the company—they never really leave.

The metaphor of close relationships helps to illustrate the meaning of commitment. Indeed, people generally view commitment in friendships and marriages as the essence of commitment—commitment in its purest form.[2] As such, these relationships serve as excellent prototypes in which to ground discussions of commitment. Our lay understandings permit a glimpse of the truth. You certainly know commitment when you see it. Employees certainly know it when they have it, and they feel the consequences when they don't.

The Antecedents of Commitment

Companies might say that they are no longer concerned about employee commitment, but serving employees breakfast in bed is about the only thing that they haven't tried in order to get it. Companies have devised an assortment of programs and services in an earnest attempt to make life easier and of higher quality for employees. However well intentioned these conveniences and services might be, they may have little to do with building commitment. Indeed, in many respects, employers are acting as hoteliers: "I hope everything was to your liking, Sir/Madam, that you were comfortable, and that you enjoyed your stay; do come again." Attending to creature comforts is a daily chore and is unlikely to produce any lasting sense of permanence.

Much of what companies do is the equivalent of putting mints on the pillow. In fact, companies seem to assume that the more service-oriented novelties they introduce, the better. Many employees welcome the attention, but they also say that it doesn't make much of a difference to their general attitudes toward, and attachment to, the organization.

I have found that there are five general conditions related to the development of commitment.[3]

1. *Fit and belonging.* The extent to which employees' interests and values are congruent with the company's (and with other employees'), and the degree to which a social milieu is created in which employees feel wanted and incorporated by the company, and enjoy the friendship and camaraderie of peers.

2. *Status and identity.* The extent to which employees think of themselves as belonging to the organization (as part of a group) and derive value through their membership in the organization—their self-concepts are partially shaped by their corporate affiliation.

3. *Trust and reciprocity.* The extent to which the company is believed to act in the employees' behalf and to which it engenders a sense of mutual obligation in which both the employer and employee feel an ongoing sense of indebtedness toward one another.

4. *Emotional reward.* The extent to which employees find the work to be satisfying and the work environment to be free of obstacles to and/or supportive of that satisfaction.

5. *Economic interdependence.* The extent to which employees believe they are engaged in a fair economic exchange in which they are benefiting from the relationship in tangible ways—compared with the alternatives; there are inducements to enter and remain in the company, and there are barriers to exit.

Each of these dimensions forms the basis of ensuing chapters. Thus, much more will be said about each—about their essence and what companies can do to establish them. Collectively, they give relationships their necessity and passion and are based on needs that we all have.

Need Fulfillment

Each of the components of commitment is concerned with the fulfillment of basic human needs or desires. Creating commitment involves a complex of emotions that may or may not be sufficiently engaged in the relationship. As illustrated in Figure 2.1, the formation of commitment deals with basic interpersonal questions: Do I feel wanted? Am I proud to be associated with . . . ? Will my interests be taken to heart? Is the relationship gratifying? Do I feel like a full participant in the relationship? Am I uniquely benefiting from this relationship?

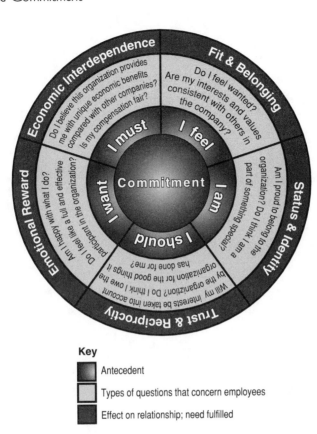

Key

■ Antecedent

□ Types of questions that concern employees

■ Effect on relationship; need fulfilled

Figure 2.1 The antecedents of commitment.

Figure 2.1 highlights the types of connections that can be established between employees and employers. Employees can experience their attachments as attending to one or more of the following needs:

○ *Acceptance (fit and belonging)*. The relationship fulfills employees' basic needs for acceptance and inclusion—to be wanted, to fit in, and to belong—through the bonds of shared values, interests, meanings and expectations, common experiences, and sense of team.

○ *Esteem (status and identity)*. Employees' self-concepts are cognitively expanded to incorporate membership in a given organization—employees' status and sense of self are intertwined with, and enhanced by, their association with the company.

○ *Security (trust and reciprocity)*. Employees feel safe and protected by an employer's benevolence and acts of goodwill—the surety of the relationship is substantiated by ongoing give and take in which each party considers the interests of the other.

○ *Growth (emotional reward)*. The relationship is felt to have many desirable, satisfying features: It's exciting, it's personally rewarding and fun, and it's perceived to be moving in the right direction—it is getting better and better.

○ *Sustenance (economic interdependence)*. The organization provides for the support and subsistence of employees by distributing benefits in a manner that employees regard as fair and nontyrannical.

Thus, ultimately, commitment is grounded in the personal—in those things that people find important. Commitment is tied to needs that have universal appeal: to belong, to feel safe, to be fulfilled, to feel good about oneself, and to have enough. Companies that simply offer employees contentment and comfort are just scratching the surface. The offer must go much deeper to nurture relationships that are strong and enduring.

Conceptualizations of Commitment

The five components of commitment are related but not identical. This suggests that commitment can be decomposed and understood as the combination of overlapping elements.[4]

This is different than the way most companies think of commitment. Commitment tends to be conceptualized in one of two ways, which are depicted in Figure 2.2, *a* and *b*. Figure 2.2*a* is a unidimensional, nondecomposable glob of affect, such as felt connectedness to the organization. Thus, commitment is the sum total of an employee's emotional attachment to the organization. With this model, it is possible to be more or less committed, but not committed in different ways—there is one general form of commitment.

Figure 2.2*b* is similar to Figure 2.2*a*, except in this instance, commitment is conceived as a composite of feelings: toward the job, the

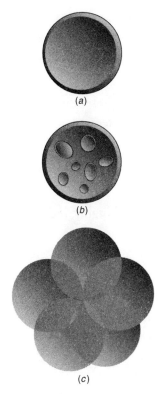

Figure 2.2 Concepts of commitment.
(*a*) Commitment as a unidimensional whole.
(*b*) Commitment as a composite of feelings.
(*c*) Commitment as a set of overlapping,
          decomposable components.

boss, policies and procedures, the company, and so on. Thus, rather than viewing commitment as a gestalt, Figure 2.2*b* shows that commitment is a general attitude formed by the synthesis of many perceptions—the sum total of which is commitment. The particles of commitment themselves, however, are conceptually inseparable. They may be measured independently, but they are ultimately added together to obtain an employee's overall degree of attachment to the organization. Once again, commitment is seen as a summary feeling of which employees have more or less.

The position I maintain is that commitment is made up of five correlated but distinct components that converge to form different species of commitment. Thus, it not only makes sense to ask about how much commitment there is in an organization, but what kind of commitment is present as well. Figure 2.2*c* depicts this model.

A company may offer more or less of each of the components of commitment (each of the circles in the diagram can be bigger or smaller), creating a particular organizational character. Specifically, commitment has the following attributes:

○ *Intensity.* How much of each component is present within the organization, indicating the degree of connectedness.

○ *Density.* The number of components rated highly (i.e., the number of components with relatively high intensities), indicating the scope of connectedness.

○ *Form.* The specific components that are rated highly, indicating the nature of connectedness.

Whoever said relationships were simple? What this suggests is that our attachments can assume many forms: It is possible to be committed in many different ways because one component may be present and another may not. This model helps to explain why relationships may persist without having emotional tone or why relationship partners who appear to have so much in common never form deeper bonds. Relationships can be positive *and* negative, good *and* bad.

The basic forms of organizational commitment in which either one, all, or none of the commitment components is present are described hereafter.

○ *Noncommitment (low on all commitment components).* This is where none of the commitment components registers very high marks, typical of casual and/or temporary relationships. An employee may be working for you as a matter of convenience or immediate circumstance. There are extrarelationship factors involved, such as wanting to stay busy while a spouse is on an extended trip or learning the combination to the vault. Because the relationship has no redeeming virtues to the employee, including pay, as soon as the personal utility of the association wanes, the relationship will dissolve forthwith.

○ *Consummate commitment (high on all commitment components).* This is complete commitment as portrayed by uniformly deep connections on all of the commitment components. The employees' range of needs is satisfied by the relationship. Please keep in mind, however, that all relationships have a temporal dimension: Thus, even excellent relationships have to be maintained over time.

○ *Affiliative commitment (high fit and belonging).* The social and affiliative aspects of the workplace are dominant. Through mutual convictions, common purposes, and/or happenstance, people who enjoy one another's company have come together. As in a pickup baseball game, the activities are tangential to the social engagement. As long as there is a field of play, favorable conditions for interaction, and a group of people who share interests, the game has a chance to go on.

○ *Associative commitment (high status and identity).* The institutional connection is paramount, providing a derivative source of esteem to the organization's members. Employees feel privileged to be associated with the organization and boast of their institutional ties. Provided that the institution's ideals are upheld and reinforced, as well as remain in vogue, the organization's allure and adhesiveness may endure. The star quality of the institution, however, may fade if the relationship fails to nourish employees' other needs—just as, eventually, the husband or wife of a famous spouse may find notoriety to be secondary to the suffering of neglect.

○ *Moral commitment (high trust and reciprocity).* The relationship is held together by moral imperatives. Employees think they should stay in the relationship because the company has always been good to them and has treated them well. Thus, employees feel a sense of obligation to the company, a duty to stick with it through thick and thin. The employer-employee connection is forged through mutual feelings of reciprocity: as one sometimes feels compelled to give something back to their church, school, or community. Duty, however, can become onerous or burdensome if it repeatedly is exercised in an otherwise vacant relationship, or if one is always being called on "to live up to one's obligations"—duty is invoked far too often.

○ *Affective commitment (high emotional reward)*. The relationship exists because it is pleasurable. Employees are involved in occupational activities that they enjoy and that they are able to effectively pursue, unfettered by unnecessary organizational constraints or the weight of stressors. The relationship is stimulating and is seen to be growing and flourishing. One's gratifications can either be attached to lifelong pursuits or passions, or they can arise from novelty and change in the workplace; if it's the latter, the excitement can quickly dissipate, just as an infatuated lover may lose interest abruptly. This component of commitment is likely the most critical because it embodies a person's wanting to be in the relationship: It is a primary motive for entering and remaining together. My own research with companies suggests that its absence greatly compromises the degree to which employees are able to feel attached to the organization.

○ *Structural commitment (high economic interdependence)*. The relationship endures because there are external factors holding it together. There are pressures that maintain the relationship, either by imposing costs on its dissolution or by creating incentives for its continuance. The employees' connection to the company, for example, may be purely financial. One is hooked in because the organization provides the best opportunity for income and/or wealth accumulation. Without emotional involvement or other attractions, these relationships can be loveless and stagnant. The attachment is under the conscious control of the employee, who rationally trolls for feasible alternatives.

It is naturally advantageous to have greater, rather than fewer, interrelational connections in an organization. Stronger forms of commitment are more likely to yield positive organizational results and will be more resistant to events that can potentially disrupt the employer-employee bond.

The Consequences of Commitment

There are socially responsible companies that would go to great lengths to heighten employee commitment simply because it is the right thing to do. Other companies promote commitment because it is the right business thing to do. Regardless of intentions, the effects are the same. Commitment is good for business in three general ways:

1. Enhances employee persistence
2. Promotes citizenship behavior
3. Increases organizational performance

Each of these benefits is described in greater detail in the following text.

Persistence[5]

People who are not committed to a relationship are aloof and easily distracted—and display various degrees of separation. Figure 2.3 shows the methods that employees use to avoid or escape an unpleasant work situation, as well as other consequences of commitment. The most common varieties are to show up late, to miss an inordinate amount of days of work, to be first in line to volunteer for early retirement, to be slow to return to work following disability, and to leave the company. In all of these cases, alternative behaviors are preferable to showing up or to remaining with the company. Employees are either "too tired" or "too sick" to be at work, or an alternative offer is just "too sweet" to pass up. The interesting issue is how commitment is instrumental in setting where the employees' threshold for absenteeism or separation lies.

It is possible to have two employees at two different companies who have similar job duties and extrawork circumstances who are each presented with the same opportunity to work elsewhere. One might take it and one might not because it is not just the opportunity that matters. It is the opportunity relative to one's current circumstances. It will be harder to lure a committed employee away because they are more pleased with their present conditions. A suitor can't just be attractive. The company vying for attention has to be more attractive.

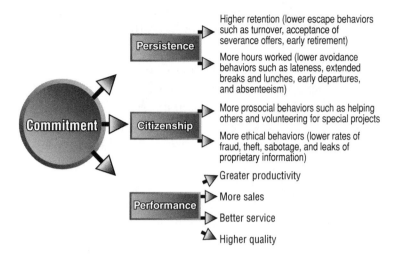

Figure 2.3 The positive consequences of commitment.

People's judgments are relative, based on the tangible and intangible costs and benefits that are associated with the choices presented. Absenteeism, for instance, can be explained using the pushes and pulls of these relative costs and benefits. Again, assume there are two people who have similar jobs and family circumstances, but one is committed to his or her organization and the other is not. One day they both wake up with mildly sore throats. One stays home and the other doesn't. For the person who calls in sick, it may be a tough choice and a legitimate action, but it is not the same choice that someone else who is more attached to the organization would necessarily make.

Companies are well aware of the costs associated with lack of persistence in their workplace. In addition to the vacancy times of the position and the lost productivity, there are the direct costs associated with search and replacement (e.g., recruitment and advertising expense) or coverage for the lost time (e.g., overtime, use of contingent workers). The avoidable portions of these costs can be so pronounced, that they clearly intrude on a company's profit margins. For example, turnover is estimated to cost employers the following amounts by employee level:

○ *Nonexempt employee.* 50 percent of base salary per person.

○ *Middle management/professional.* 100 percent of base salary per person.

○ *Senior management.* 150 percent of base salary per person.

○ *Executive.* 200 percent, or greater, of base salary.

Similarly, a recent survey from the Commerce Clearing House shows that the average annual cost of unscheduled absences is $600 per employee, not including indirect expenses such as lost productivity (the average costs are based on an average rate of absenteeism of 2.7 days per person per year—the costs would be higher for higher rates).

Citizenship Behaviors[6]

We are all citizens of one community or another, including organizations. As citizens, we can be passive or active. *Passive citizens* simply act within the broad boundaries of the roles and responsibilities defined for members. Essentially, passive citizens act in ways that maintain their membership in the community—or, more correctly, they refrain from acting in ways that would lead to the suspension or loss of membership. Passive members, then, go about their business fulfilling their basic obligations under the terms of membership. In organizations, this usually means showing up a minimum number of days per year and doing a modicum of work.

Active citizenship implies that employees engage in three behaviors:

1. *Discretionary.* Behaviors for which there are no performance requirements.

2. *Extrarole.* Behaviors that do not conform to a particular role or function.

3. *Prosocial.* Behaviors that are performed for the community's good at large, but for which there is no obvious recompense and, indeed, that may be performed outside of public observation (i.e., private acts).

There are various types of behaviors that are indicative of active citizenship. They go outside of the scope of the job and, in individual instances, may appear trivial, but they are collectively potent and facilitate attainment of organizational goals.[7]

Behaving ethically. Employees adhere to moral norms (e.g., tell the truth, don't steal) and refrain from acting spitefully (e.g., retaliate, sabotage) if disappointed by a corporate action. They serve as role models for personal integrity.

Developing oneself. Employees actively work at bettering themselves, sometimes on their own time and at their own expense; employees conscientiously acquire new knowledge and skills needed to function more effectively.

Helping coworkers. Going to the aid of another who is behind on work or who requires special instruction on how to perform an activity, complete administrative tasks (e.g., fill out an expense report, etc.); helping also may involve using one's own time productively — rather than read a novel, an employee looks for ways in which he or she may assist others.

Making constructive suggestions. It takes effort to conceive of alternative ways to improve a work process, reduce the costs of doing business, make money, and so on. An employee not only has to be aware that such opportunities exist and consciously look for them, but to care enough about the idea and its benefits to develop and act upon it.

Protecting the organization. Companies spend many millions of dollars insuring themselves against potential risks of all sorts. One of the best defensive measures against loss, however, is having employees who alert the company to potential hazards (e.g., pointing out a potential fire hazard or holes in security) or who coach others on proper safety protocol.

Spreading goodwill. Employees inform others outside the company about its products and services and about the work environment. Essentially, everyone in the organization becomes an advocate and salesperson for the organization.

There are many things employees don't have to do, but acting as a good citizen enriches the workplace—often in nonobvious ways. A good index of commitment, then, is the degree to which an employee cares for his or her work environment. If you don't care about the broader community and don't feel attached to it, acts on behalf of the community seem effortful and burdensome rather than rewarding. The organization only gets those behaviors that are required or heavily prescribed by norms and expectations. Volunteerism and prosocial acts go begging.

Sometimes citizens turn bad—indifferent to the basic tenets of social organization. Employees may stretch citizenry to its limits and elicit a reprimand, such as when an employee airs dirty laundry about the company to the press. Employees may so severely violate ethical and normative standards that expulsion would be the only recourse. Sabotage, leaking proprietary information to competitors, double-dealing, fraud, and theft would all qualify as dismissable offenses, and all occur in organizations as acts of commission. Acts of omission are far more subtle. The latter occurs, for example, when employees innocently watch faulty parts being produced in mass quantities without immediately intervening—and there are countless other instrumental or preventative acts that employees can take, but through aggressive acts of omission, they refrain from making them. The intriguing aspect of unethical behaviors is that the actor may not see them as unethical at all within the context of a ruinous, low-commitment relationship— he or she may see such behaviors simply as evening the score.

Organizational Performance[8]

Imagine that you are at a party with your spouse who introduces you to colleagues with whom you either have never met or have not met for some time (i.e., they are not your friends). Assume that you feel emotionally distant from your spouse and, if it weren't for the extramarital bonds of children, are quite certain that the relationship would disintegrate. You appear to be equally disinterested in your spouse's friends as you are in your spouse, not straying too far from basic norms of politeness or offering conversation beyond marginal cordialities. It is a chore to interact with the people who, by association, mean so little. You are uninterested in the people and things your significant other cares about.

Similarly, employees who dislike their employer may feel an obligation to handle the customer "professionally," but that is about the extent of it. They fail to personalize the service, to ask questions that can illuminate needs or resolve problems, or to follow through. Others get the base version of sales and service, whether the customer is outside the organization or another employee.

Sales and service are just two of the performance dimensions that suffer from the lack of commitment. There are others, namely, productivity (e.g., units produced; waste) and quality. High commitment as opposed to low commitment entails a caring attentiveness, stewardship, and conscientiousness toward the relationship. Committed employees try harder.

I don't think it would take a hard sell to convince you that employee attitudes (i.e., commitment) have performance consequences. There is a surface logic to the connection reinforced by observations of what people with positive and negative attitudes actually do, or don't do, respectively. We know those who give it their all and those who simply try to get by. The distinction is duly noted by customers with predictable results on sales. There appears to be a direct link between commitment, effortful behavior, and results. Again, the degree to which a company realizes a benefit from this effort will naturally depend, in part, on the knowledge and abilities of employees.

Sometimes, the performance in which a company is interested can only be measured at the group, or aggregate, level—such as customer retention or net profits. Under these conditions, the simple equation that relates commitment and performance no longer seems entirely satisfying, or convincing. First, it is obviously incomplete. (Some would say the model is *underspecified*—this is a statistician's polite way of saying that there are obvious shortcomings to your conceptualization of the problem.) Indeed, even though commitment matters, group results are clearly dependent on factors outside of immediate human effort such as the nature of the product, operational efficiency, marketing prowess, and such.

Second, when one moves from individuals to groups, the model (i.e., the relationships among variables) may change even if the important variables do not. Frequently, what is known and applied at the individual level just doesn't hold in the same manner at the group level. Our inclination to use the same assumptions that we make for individuals to describe group measures is so powerful, however, that there is a term for this error, known as the *ecological fallacy*.[9] The classic case that illustrates the flaw in our thinking examines the relationship among income, place of residence, and education. For individuals, it can be argued that education affects income, which affects place of residence. At the group level, however, the model that best describes the relationship among these variables may be the following: Place of residence determines education, which determines income.

The same types of transpositions may be obtained with our variables of interest: commitment, effort, and performance. Although it is tempting to think that aggregate commitment leads to aggregate effort, which yields aggregate performance, a convincing case can be made for the primacy of performance at the group level: The more customers retained, for instance, the greater the employee effort (because of familiarity and liking, perhaps) and the more committed the employees (because they may like their jobs more). This is all speculation, of course. The central tenet to keep in mind, however, is that the way commitment and performance relate to one another may change with the complexion of the problem.

Third, the way commitment affects performance may change at the group level. At the individual level, we may surmise that the relationship is mediated by effort. At the group level, we may maintain that commitment affects performance partially through systemic influences on behavior, such as absenteeism and turnover. Any one person's absence, for example, doesn't make a difference. However, a host of absences on a given day (due to low commitment) has a definite effect on the group's performance—such as its ability to deliver superior service.

In summary, then, the relationship between commitment and performance is complicated by such factors as the particular measures of performance and the level or unit of analysis. The relationship is there, but you have to give some thought to its nature and then do some digging to find it.

Commitment Processes[10]

Imagine yourself coming upon a wooden suspension bridge that traverses a cavernous valley. You start out cautiously, testing the strength of the bridge, not knowing what to expect. Suddenly, your foot breaks through a board; you gasp, stiffen, and hold on.

From here, it is easy to imagine several endings describable by three attributes:

1.   *Duration.* The length of the adventure (short or long).

2.   *Stability.* The volatility of the adventure (few or many ups and downs).

3.   *Quality.* The emotional content of the adventure (exhilarating or frightful).

The remainder of the journey can be durable, steady, and fun, or the adventure can come to an abrupt and unfulfilling conclusion. All relationships have a time course. Because of the multifaceted nature of commitment, these longitudinal sequences are rich and complex. It cannot be assumed, for example, that long relationships are necessarily happy ones or that happy relationships are immune from troublesome episodes of conflict and discontent.

For our purposes, the central question is: How can companies, metaphorically speaking, keep employees moving across the bridge such that employees enjoy the enterprise (and would do it all over again if given the chance)—knowing that there occasionally will be chilling disruptions to employees' footing en route? In addition to building strong employee commitment as described in detail in ensuing chapters, a few personal and contextual ingredients are helpful to a long, successful journey as well.

Resilience

People approach and enter relationships with different beliefs and expectations and for different reasons, making them more or less vulnerable to what is to follow. For example, some employees have romantic, idealized notions about their relations with their employer. Any turmoil is a violation of their standard and evidence of relationship failure. Many employees have high expectations about their employment that border on perfection—sometimes derived from nothing more than primitive fantasies of what any good relationship should be like. These employees will be particularly disillusioned by negative events, in contrast to employees who anticipate the relationship to mature over time—and inevitably to encounter problems. Thus, the latter employee may be less devastated when one's foot punctures a floorboard on the bridge and will be more inclined to move on.

Employees also enter relationships for many different reasons, which broadly may be classified as either event-driven reasons or relationship-driven reasons. To continue our metaphor, one may want to cross the bridge simply because it is a convenient means to get to the other side where one wants to be [the decision to cross is guided by reasons that are external to the journey itself (i.e., event-driven)]. Alternatively, one may start across because one relishes the excitement of high places (the decision to cross is intrinsic to the activity, or relationship, itself).

Employees can join organizations for a myriad of instrumental reasons entirely unrelated to what they will be asked to do: They need a job, any job, to pay the bills. A job can be unpleasant but necessary preparation for another job that a person prizes. In either case, the job is a means to an end. In contrast, many people look for work that will be stimulating because of its challenge, purposes, and so on.

When confronted with obstacles or personal trial, it is far easier for an employee who derives little satisfaction from his or her work to seek out alternatives. Surely, they think, there must be easier and more lucrative ways to make a living. Most employers understand that hiring employees who have no investment in their work will succumb to superior offers made by other employers—it's just a matter of time. Employees, too, feign interest in a job when, in fact, they have ulterior motives. Each party recognizes that relationships entered because of the potential fruits of the relationship itself engender greater long-term prospects.

Maintenance

Every relationship encounters rough spots or turning points, but not every relationship succumbs. The people involved may have hardier constitutions and be more resilient for reasons we have just discussed. However, external supports are needed as well to help relationships along.

Social supports are the most notable props. These include people both inside, as well as outside, the organization who offer understanding, encouragement, reassurance, and advice. They are the sturdy railings on the bridge. These are the people who say, "You will be all right, we are not going to let you fall; if you do fall, don't worry, there's a net." They take relationship strains and disappointments and positively transform them through gestures that connote the indispensability of the relationship. A company or individual can easily convey bad news and the need for change without savaging the viability of the relationship itself. Thus, one reason employees may view their employment journey as less treacherous—or exciting even—is because they know they will be helped along and, ultimately, will be all right.

It works the other way as well—countersupports. This may be the old, haggard employee who whispers to newcomers, "Turn back while you can," or friends or family members who warn of imminent doom if one continues—remembering what once happened to them. Relationships are more likely to flourish when surrounded by positive people who want the relationship to succeed.

Time also plays a role in stabilizing relationships because time is related to the personal investments one makes in and the experiences one has with a relationship. Let's take a hypothetical scenario, again drawing upon our bridge metaphor. Person A takes just two steps before having a foot break through one of the bridge's planks. Person B has just two steps to go before breaking through. The same physical event will be interpreted differently and result in different behaviors, all else being equal. Person B won't turn around, but Person A might. In the latter instance, the uncertainty coupled with the distance makes for a daunting journey—which many would refuse to make.

A large part of what companies have to do is reduce the uncertainty that many employees experience early in their tenure. Attempts at persuasion may provide temporary solace but grow tiresome to employees if unaccompanied by action. It is not until the employee can take repeated steps with positive results that he or she is able to gain confidence in the employer-employee relationship. The only thing worse than uncertainty is the surety of a future fall: the psychological equivalent of sending an employee out alone across the suspension bridge while the employer jiggles it.

Adjustment

To be successful in one's environment, a person needs to learn from the past and experiment with new modes of behavior: to adjust to changing conditions. Circumstances change, people change, and employers and employees must modify their behaviors accordingly. Adjustment is an ongoing, reflexive process of acting, receiving feedback, adapting, and such. If something doesn't work, try something else. You learn to get across the bridge, for example, by seeking out and by avoiding boards of a certain pedigree (firm versus rotted boards).

Optimally, employers and employees seek out ground that is mutually rewarding, and they avoid territory that is interpersonally dangerous—that is, out of bounds because it is underhanded or indecent. Couples, for example, learn to stay off of certain topics of discussion. Employers and employees learn that resurfacing ancient wrongs and injuries serve no useful purpose. They learn what works and what doesn't, what's best and what isn't—and through ongoing dialogue, they recurrently fine-tune their collective course.

To be adaptive, however, in a way that benefits the company requires hospitable terrain. Hostile environments have a way of inviting adaptations that favor personal survival. People retreat (flee), limit their visibility (camouflage), or stick to the tried and true (freeze). People give up when attempts to succeed repeatedly fall short. No matter how great the potential prize, one's enthusiasm for work quickly fades when every step (day) is preceded by feelings of dread and when daily regimens are attempts to find peace 100 feet above the ground.

Companies cannot succeed when the only adaptations employees make are idiosyncratic and personal. Employees decide all of the time whether they should try out new behaviors in the service of their company or whether they should concentrate on the inconspicuous and self-serving. It all depends on whether they find solid ground when they put one foot forward and whether they are given what our metaphorical bridge cannot give—the encouragement of commitment.

COURT AND SPARK

The Need for Fit and Belonging

One of the most fundamental needs that people have is to belong: to feel a natural affinity with others and to know that one is in the proper place. This is true wherever we are—inside or outside the corporation. We never outgrow our teen years' preoccupation with fitting in—we just become less conspicuous.

Think of this: You just moved to another part of the country and a new acquaintance invites you to a party. Later, you arrive and are greeted by a stranger with an unknowing look. You nearly have to talk your way in. You spot your acquaintance across the room who offers a partial wave and returns to a private conversation. You make a couple of attempts to nudge your way into social circles by inserting comments into ongoing conversations. However, you are disregarded and edged out of cliques by shoulders and backs. You make a few trips to the punch bowl, pretend you are enjoying the music, and meander coolly around a bit before making an early departure—naturally, thanking the host for the wonderful evening.

Everyone has been in the situation where no room has been made. It is hard to stay and easy to leave. You come with high expectations and leave unfulfilled. It's hard to throw a good party. It is easy to imagine more inviting and inclusive ones, however. You can be expected, for example. You can be welcomed, debriefed on who certain people are, and introduced to others. People can incorporate you into discussions and take an interest in what you have to say. Guests can share your interests and attitudes. You can be asked to join others on excursions outdoors, on the dance floor, and so on.

These stories have clear parallels to corporate initiations and, without much of a stretch, you can determine the kind of "party" you throw for employees. Some employers would argue that the party metaphor is irrelevant because the purpose of organizations is singularly to work as opposed to having fun. It's true, we don't call it the fun place, but work and play greatly rely on people, and it is hard to tease apart the social and functional aspects from either. When I conduct surveys and focus groups in organizations, one of the pluses and minuses of a company cited most often are the people with whom one works. It is possible for people who hate their jobs to look forward to seeing their friends at work. It also is possible for people who enjoy what they do to be deeply distressed by conflict and difficult personalities in the workplace.

Let's go on for the time being with the party analogy and back up to the time when you first arrived. You hadn't thought to ask about the nature of the celebration, but you quickly discover that the party is a benefit for "Otter Slaughter"—a fundraiser for surprisingly normal-looking people who like clubbing helpless otters in the wild. You feel disgusted and estranged. You lose your enthusiasm for the party and for the people who surround you. You feel miscast and out of place. You exit hurriedly.

You have two responses as the nature of the benefit is revealed. One is that this is not a good place to be, because you don't agree with such things. The second is that you cannot feel close to people who harbor these beliefs. Similarly, organizations have goals and values to which you may or may not subscribe, and those goals and values will tend to attract people with whom you may or may not care to affiliate. The people make the place, and the place makes the people.[1] Employees want to be in environments that make them feel comfortable, not like social pariahs.

One company that knows how to throw a good party is Trilogy, a fast-growing, Texas-based technology company specializing in order-processing/configuration software.[2] They specifically look for good technical and cultural fit in new candidates—and they look very carefully. In 1998, the company reviewed 15,000 resumes, conducted 4,000 on-campus interviews, and flew 850 prospects (along with girl-friends, boyfriends, or spouses) to its headquarters for a three-day visit—at a recruitment cost of $13,000 per hire. The visits incorporate both business (company interviews) and pleasure (e.g., dancing and mountain biking).

New employees go through an intensive three-month crash course on the business, software, and Trilogy culture. During this period, new employees work in teams on applied business problems that Trilogy is currently trying to solve or are asked to pursue new products. New employees, then, are immersed immediately in business issues of consequence. The hard work is punctuated by social events such as picnics, softball, and the weekly Friday afternoon "party on the patio."

The underlying recruitment and assimilation philosophy is straightforward. Trilogy conveys a fast-paced, results-oriented culture that is enticing to bright people. Through a rigorous selection process, they invite smart, interesting people who will fit in with the cultural values of the organization to join. They expend a great amount of time and money building cohesiveness among employees, and provide them with the high-energy environment that was promised. The company practically insists that people have fun (together). Trilogy, for certain people, is a very compelling place to work because of the quality of people with whom each employee is able to associate. The common work ethic and camaraderie provide Trilogy with a distinct competitive advantage, and employees with a sense of belonging that will be difficult to replace elsewhere.

Feelings of fit and belonging start to develop well before employees show up for work on their first day and are influenced by many little things thereafter. Everyone who has ever joined an organization has gone through a series of familiar steps, each of which is instrumental in shaping employees' attitudes toward the company. Briefly, these include:

○ *Dating (attraction).* Mutual attention and attraction—company promotes itself, advertises for a position, and so on, and the employee makes contact (e.g., submits a resume).

○ *Going steady (selection).* The employer and the employee get to know each other better through interviews, testing, wining and dining; they exchange information about the past, present, and future, and they try to size up their own, as well as the other's, interests.

○ *Engagement (hire).* The employer and the employee make a pact—a formal offer is extended and accepted to begin work on a specified date.

○ *Marriage (organizational entry).* A publicly recognized union that generally commences with a brief period of adjustment, or honeymoon, and may last a lifetime.

There is no secret to the goal of the process. It's to unite or pair people (or employers with employees) who believe that a longer-term association is mutually desirable and that the prospects of success are good. This, however, is much easier said than done, because both the employer and the employee must survive each of the preceding prehire stages, as well as the critical first three posthire years. At a minimum, the process requires ongoing employer sociability and attentiveness. The relationship also has to grow closer progressively and quickly with additional interactions; it has to be perceived by employees as going somewhere. There are certain things an employer can do to make employees feel increasingly welcomed and valued by the company as the process unfolds.[3]

○ *Self-disclosure.* Companies can share more intimate details about themselves and become more open in their communications, telling employees more about their strategies, markets, products, operations, and such.

○ *Responsivity.* Companies can provide instrumental and emotional support to employees when needed—they can be perceived as helpful and accommodating throughout the process.

o *Mutual interests.* Companies can convey the interests and values they share with employees (i.e., that they have much in common).

o *Relational expression.* Companies can make explicit or implicit references to the closeness and value of the relationship—without making promises, the company can let the employee know about its interest. For example, asking a top prospect to meet the top executives of an area of the company is one such form of expression.

Even with the best of intentions, however, relationships are easily derailed. Although many are called, few are chosen. Simple violations of social scripts are frequently sufficient to terminate would-be relationships.[4] Scripts are conventions that guide social behavior. They routinize recurring behavioral transactions so we don't have to keep reinventing social protocols over and over; also, they are used as templates for appropriate behavior. Thus, for example, during the recruitment process, it is important for the employer and the employee to abide by the script; otherwise, they risk losing the interest of the other party. An employee can make big social snafus, such as the recruit who was told to dress her best and showed up for an interview in her prom dress, or the recruit who was asked to bring references and appeared at the interview with two friends.[5] These are monumental breaches that suggest that something is profoundly wrong with the person sitting across from you. There are, however, more subtle ways for an employee to break protocol. For example, the standard resume is organized chronologically. A minority of companies accept functional formats in which a candidate summarizes career objectives and expertise. Resumes that are arranged functionally often are perceived as deviations from accepted practice and as a tactic to disguise frequent job moves or interruptions in employment—and are consequently discarded.

Similarly, employers can botch things up in many ways. Asking illegal or objectionable questions, forgetting the recruit's name, not acknowledging receipt of a resume or returning recruits' phone calls,

and showing up late for an appointment without good reason can compromise the relationship. Intrusive or inappropriate questions such as,
"If you were at a dinner party meeting and the man next to you put his
hand on your thigh, what would you do?" or "Is your boyfriend white?"
can drive qualified candidates away; indeed, about 20 percent of job
seekers say they have been insulted in interviews.[6] Some types of inter-
viewing/testing can drive candidates away and into the judicial system:
specifically, testing that violates the Age Discrimination in Employment Act, the Americans with Disabilities Act, or Title VII of the Civil
Rights Act. The combined intent of these laws is to prevent discrimination on the basis of race, color, religion, gender, national origin, age,
and disability.

Employers and employees also have to effectively manage silence
during the courtship to keep potentially gratifying relationships alive.
That is, they have to create the semblance of continuity while they are
apart from one another.[7] Otherwise, the separation may be construed
as disinterest and the relationship may become overly inconspicuous
(out of sight, out of mind; "absence extinguishes small passions and
increases great ones").[8] Employers who want top prospects don't give
them the chance to cognitively uncouple or disengage from the
process. Capitol One, known for its innovation and efficiency in
recruiting, admits that one of the biggest challenges in recruitment is
building a system that moves people from one part of the hiring process
to another without losing them.[9] There are four things a company can
do to maintain relationship continuity:

1. *Framing.* Describing the meaning and length of separation and
   specifying a future time and place to talk or meet. *Farewells* also
   hint that the relationship will endure; failing to say *good-bye*, or
   saying it in a manner that does not express sufficient concern
   about the impending separation, is unsettling. Consider the
   times when someone you knew tried to leave without saying
   good-bye—you probably stopped them and forced an *adieu*.

2. *Providing tokens and spoors.* Providing salient representations
   of physical presence (e.g., business cards, promotional videos,

information packet, company products and trinkets, web site location, etc.). Similarly, couples exchange photos (or audio-tapes) or leave something of value behind as traces of the relationship and its likely resumption at a later time.

3. *Making intermittent contact.* Engaging in mediated (e.g., through a recruiter) or direct contact (e.g., note of thanks, question-and-answer sessions). This is the obvious mechanism of relationship continuity and the one in which employers and employees refrain when there really is no interest: a fact not lost on the recipients of the silence. Employers can seriously damage their reputations by failing to treat people, who have given time and energy to the discovery process, well.

4. *Debriefing.* Filling in relationship gaps by getting caught up on what has transpired since the last meeting. This may seem like idle conversation, but the purpose of debriefing is to remove conceptual holes in the relationship—it doesn't feel complete and can't successfully move ahead without first filling in the missing details in the relationship's history. Getting caught up is important.

Attraction

Companies need to be alluring to attract employees in sufficient supply. It is a competitive marketplace in which many candidates make choices among a set of possible employers. No company wants to be in the unenviable position of having to take whoever is left over. There is a reason why the last to find jobs are the last to find jobs. Thus, it is self-evident that employers need to be adept at attracting viable candidates and carefully selecting from among them.

Companies try to hire a sufficient number of quality candidates as efficiently as possible. To evaluate their success, they track such measures as the number of unsolicited resumes received, the percent of vacancies filled within a given stretch of time (and the average time to fill them), the ratio of acceptances to offers, the cost per hire, the ratio of candidates hired to the total tested, the impact on Equal Employment Opportunities/diversity, the average time to proficiency in the job, and the retention rate of new hires during the first year.

Collectively, these are measures of quantity, quality, and efficiency. Also, there is a dynamic among these indices.[10] A company might try to maximize the quantity of resumes it receives through media extravaganzas and other ubiquitous recruitment measures (e.g., a broad-based college recruiting drive, de-skilling jobs to make them more accessible to more people). The direct costs of these initiatives, accompanied by the time it takes to sift through resumes, may lower efficiency. A company that insists on quality and is highly selective needs a steady stream of high-caliber candidates (quantity) if a position is to be filled within a reasonable period of time. Finally, a company that is trying to contain costs may not promote itself widely or screen and select employees rigorously: The emphasis is on keeping the cost-per-hire efficiency measure as low as possible. Such an employer may see quality slip because of an increased tolerance of Type II versus Type I errors. (A Type II error is the probability of accepting an employee who will not succeed; a Type I error is the probability of rejecting an employee who will succeed.)

Figure 3.1 is a simple graphic that depicts the potential trade-offs involving attraction and selection. Companies that are thoughtful

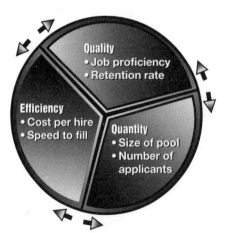

Figure 3.1 Trade-offs in recruitment quality, quantity, and efficiency.

about this dynamic may be able to optimize on all three if they are able to:

- ○ Target effectively the populations who will find the company appealing (to avoid spending money to attract "customers" who will never buy)
- ○ Enlist a healthy share of these recruits
- ○ Retain these employees at least to the break-even point (i.e., the point at which the total hiring expenses have been recovered through the employee's cumulative productivity/output)

This final point is critical because it moves us firmly back into the domain of commitment. Employee defections early in their tenure suggest that, despite your best intentions and efforts, these employees never really connected with you. Indeed, a good index of how well a company attracts and selects employees is the difference between the company's retention rates for employees with one year or less of experience compared with five years or more of experience: No difference is evidence of people *wanting* to stay and of the company doing a good job of selecting the right people and effectively enculturating them into the organization.

Too many early departures are the beginning of a cycle that is hard to break: Many jobs need to be filled; the company tries to accommodate the need by accepting people it normally would not accept under better circumstances; many of these people leave shortly after hire because the job and work environments aren't viewed favorably, and so on—and so we sometimes think we are digging out of a hole by digging deeper.

At any rate, it certainly helps an employer's cause if a good number of prospects find it attractive. Like in any relationship, the desire for future interaction hinges on surface characteristics and first impressions. Only when there is initial, mutual interest does the relationship move forward with the exchange of more intimate details. Like in a relationship, impressions begin to form on the basis of observable characteristics: outwardly physical attributes or readily available information.

Information about companies initially comes from three sources. First, there are the apparent natural endowments of the company, including industry, geography (location), size, physical plant, and products/services. Second, there are the opinions and observations of third parties, such as the media, the government, analysts, and so on. Many of the reports produced through these venues critically examine the financial outlook of the company, its overall strengths and weaknesses, quality of management, social responsiveness, and so forth. Third, there are the first contacts that candidates have with an agent of the company (e.g., a recruiter).

The initial contact between employees and a representative of the company is crucial because, from the employees' perspective, the recruiter *is* the company. The attributes and demeanor of the recruiter are generalized to the company. A rude, obnoxious jerk will either cause candidates to remove themselves from consideration or to look much more cautiously at an organization. Indeed, I have heard numerous stories from candidates who lost interest in companies because the recruiter was unpleasant and unprepared. On the other hand, recruiters (or other employees who make the first contact with prospects) who are friendly, respectful (e.g., are on time), and are perceived as competent (i.e., able to answer questions about the company, the functional area of interest, and the job) are instrumental in elevating the attractiveness of the company.[11]

In today's environment of worker scarcity, some companies have added a personal touch to recruitment by assigning *shepherds* to potential employees. These are employees with the same educational backgrounds and/or interests as high-potential candidates whose primary mission is to advise and coach recruits through the hiring process. Employees confirm that the attention and candor of shepherds positively influence their decisions to join. Some companies add an interesting twist to this process. Shepherds are held accountable for the success of the employees they recruit. Thus, if someone believes enough in a person to bring them into an organization, they are also accepting responsibility for that person's performance.

Companies actively court recruits using a variety of search-and-solicit methods. These include ads in newspapers and trade journals, college placement offices, job listings in association publications, chambers of commerce, career fairs, professional recruiters and executive search organizations, staffing agencies, employee referrals, signage, and the increasing use of the Internet. Companies also try to affect prospects' attitudes indirectly by controlling what appears in the media through such means as press releases, concerted efforts to appear on one of a variety of "best" lists (e.g., best places for mothers), or through image advertising.

Increasingly, companies are working to "touch" the public in a coherent way by developing an employee brand to rally around.[12] The brand is intended to capture the essence of the company: what it stands for and what it would be like to work within it. This is an interesting trend that applies the way products (e.g., detergents, soft drinks, cars) are generally sold to how companies may be "sold."

The primary purpose of a brand is to efficiently bring buyers (employers) and sellers (employees) together to establish an enduring relationship. People with certain preferences can easily locate a company that uniquely claims to cater to these preferences. Thus, the company espouses having something that is *distinct* and *relevant*. It is a portrayal that distinguishes the organization from its competitors in the marketplace and is sufficiently appealing to attract a significant (relevant) number of people.

Most brands do not have universal appeal; nor should they try. Doing so would compromise the message by making it too amorphous—of the mom-and-apple-pie variety. For example, there are quite a few companies that want "team players" to work in a "diverse" and "challenging" setting. The brand is watered down and the company (or product) ends up attracting people it doesn't want and missing people it does want. More typically, brand awareness is tailored to a particular audience.

There are several advantages to broadcasting a strong, favorable message that attracts the right candidates to the company. It helps companies obtain the quality of talent it needs to grow and prosper. In addition, because brands are associated with corporate characteristics that employees covet, brands have inherent value. Consequently, an employer should not have to pay top dollar to get the best candidates, because the company ostensibly is supplying value in other ways.

For employees, a distinguishing brand reduces risk. Through the brand, a company is entering a compact with employees. It describes, in broad terms, what working for the company will be like. Employees, then, are in a better position to decide if the corporate offering is commensurate with their personalities, interests, and preferences.

The beginning of a brand is critical self-examination of your company's positives and negatives: What is so special about you? This is not the time to be overly wishful or delusional. Whatever you communicate will create expectations that either will be confirmed or disconfirmed by experience.

You also have to understand what employees see in you: Who joins your company and who doesn't? Who stays and who leaves—and why and why not? Which employers are competing for your talent? How successful are they at hiring and holding onto choice employees? This requires extensive research. However, if you understand your unique value as well as employees' (and prospective employees') current choice behaviors, you will have a good sense of what you are and are not doing well—particularly with regard to the employees you are missing out on, but who you want—or losing, but who you would like to keep.

A good employee brand should convey two messages:

1. The unique benefit of the corporate environment

2. The type of person who is likely to thrive in that environment

One message without the other is incomplete. An employee wants to know how pleasant or grueling it would be to be locked inside the company with fellow employees forever.

These messages together, and in association with other overt corporate traits, are decision aids that employees use to make choices among alternative employers. For the brand image to be effective, it must have personal and emotional import to employees. It allows them to link who they are and what they want to the personality and values of the corporation. It helps employees answer: What will I get out of the relationship? Is this the right company for me?

Invariably, the brand will draw its appeal by tapping into some element of commitment, one of which necessarily will be fit and belonging. Let's take two well-known examples to make the point. The tag line for the Marines is "The few, the proud, the Marines." The emphasis is on selectivity, membership, and status—the subject of the next chapter. In addition, it denotes consistency and uniformity, and the attendant visual of a Marine is highly suggestive of orderliness and discipline. These are traits that not everyone has or desires, nor is status necessarily the most important value or need for the population at large. It offers, however, what many 18- to 25-year-olds seek.

In the Army, you can "Be all that you can be." This conjures a sense of action and adventure. The values it underscores are growth and striving to fulfill one's potential—of making something out of yourself. You will be engaging in activities that will make you a better person, and the upbeat theme that accompanies this slogan indicates that the soldiers will be rewardingly challenged along the way. Again, this is a positive message for a young person.

Both of these, which are excellent examples of branding, illustrate additional points:

o   The organizations do not feel compelled to restate the obvious, which would not be a differentiating factor. They don't say, for example, "We're defending America"—all of our armed forces do that. They give us a little credit for knowing something about them.

o   The organizations keep it personal. The Marines, for instance, don't say "Making the U.S. proud"; they infer that you will be proud. More people take action based on personal relevance than on theory or abstractions.

o   The organizations combine media that enable recruits to form a clear mental picture of what life on the inside is like. They don't rely exclusively on the written word but create a central message by merging images and symbols, including jingles.

o   They keep the message simple. The purpose is to get people's attention and to stimulate action: You want those people to whom adventure and job challenge are appealing, for example, to look more closely at a career with the Army. When they do look, they should see that many of the programs and activities are shaped around striving and personal excellence and that assignments indulge one's tastes for daring.

○ They don't try to win over everyone who could potentially work for the Marines or Army. Each service employs many nonsoldiers, but it's soldiers they want. Thus, they focus their message on the core positions that are most valuable to them. Admittedly, however, it would be feasible to engage in more encompassing brand strategies—a company, for example, may create a core employee brand but adjust it slightly to fit specific subpopulations.

○ They don't pretend to be something they are not. A brand can't tell the whole story, but it also shouldn't mislead others by creating expectations that an organization is unable or unwilling to fulfill. Thus, in our examples, the brands never exclude the possibility of war.

○ They generate believable messages. Potential recruits, based on their knowledge of these branches of the military and the credibility of the source of information (i.e., the government), strongly believe that the Army and Marines will keep their promises.

○ The organizations relate consistent messages. They have their story and they are sticking to it. Each military branch has made a decision about what it is and who it wants to attract, and it repeats messages that reinforce those ideas. Furthermore, there is someone who is responsible for protecting the brand image and conveying a unified message.

○ The messages mostly are culture-specific. They will have the intended meaning and appeal only for those to whom they specifically pertain.

For potential employees to develop a sense of whether they will fit into your organization, they make evaluations of the corporate character based on information to which they are initially exposed and to which they are subsequently privy through their ongoing investigations. Their evaluations begin as hunches and become more refined as the hiring process advances.

People tend to organize descriptions of the company's personality in five general areas of traits. I summarize these in Figure 3.2. These substantially overlap with measures of corporate culture that are found in

Figure 3.2 Personality types. *Note:* The chart contains sample traits that align with each personality type. Companies can be higher or lower on each of the trait dimensions. For information on the "Big Five" personality types, see the following: R. D. Bretz, R. A. Ash, G. F. Dreher, "Do people make the place? An examination of the attraction-selection-attrition hypothesis, *Personnel Psychology*, 42 (1989): 561–581; J. M. Digman, "Higher-order factors of the Big Five," *Journal of Personality and Social Psychology*, 73 (1997): 1246–1256; S. V. Paunonen, "Hierarchical organization of personality and prediction of behavior," *Journal of Personality and Social Psychology*, 74 (1997): 538–556; G. Saucier, "Effects of variable selection on the factor structure of person descriptors," *Journal of Personality and Social Psychology*, 73 (1997): 1296–1312; G. Saucier and F. Ostendorf, "Hierarchical subcompenents of the Big Five personality factors: A cross-language replication," *Journal of Personality and Social Psychology*, 76 (1999): 613–627.

the management literature and reflect the collective behavior of the organization.[13] To return to our military examples, the messages sent out to prospective recruits are that to succeed in the Army, one should be extraverted (as defined in the chart). To succeed in the Marines, it helps to be conscientious. Without these trait sets, there is a good chance that a soldier will not fit in with peers or enjoy his or her experiences.

Think about companies to which you have belonged. How would you describe the people? Did the company have a distinct personality? Chances are it did and that you can use one or two of the categories in Figure 3.3 to describe it.

Selection

Selection is a samba in which employers and employees try to decide if they are right for each other by stepping close, stepping away, stepping close, stepping away. It is not an easy dance. If you think about all of the potential employers and potential employees that can come together, the odds of a happy, long-lasting union materializing by chance are not good. Thus, each party tries to take chance out of the equation by getting to know each other better.

Employers, for example, use a variety of tests to inform their decisions: tests of general mental abilities, work samples and job tryouts, assessment centers, structured and unstructured interviews, tests of job skills and job knowledge, reference checks, biographical data, and so on. There also has been a resurgence in the use of personality tests, particularly those that assess character traits such as integrity and conscientiousness. The reliability (i.e., the accuracy of the tests) and validity (i.e., the degree to which the test measures what it is supposed to measure versus something else) of these tests vary depending on the nature of the test and its construction and whether the test is administered singly or in combination with others as batteries. There is extensive literature on the statistical quality and utility of various selection methods that need not concern us here.[14]

Employees, too, are evaluating employers. One of the things they notice is how they are treated during the selection process. Is the tester warm and personable? Does the tester invite employees to voice their observations, concerns, or questions, or is conversation one-sided? Is the tester professional and respectful throughout, or does the session feel like a hazing in which employees are asked to perform nonsensical activities at the persecutorial whim of another?

Employees expect to be treated graciously and politely, and they expect the employment tests to be fair. With regard to the latter, this means that employees should see the tests as job related: There is an obvious connection between what you are asking employees to do and the job for which they are being considered. If the connection isn't clear, the rationale should be prospectively or retrospectively provided. The testing environment also should give employees the chance to perform at their best. Thus, anything that employees may perceive as handicapping them (e.g., distractions, incomplete and half-hearted instructions, and a schedule that is unduly fatiguing) should be eliminated. The perception of unfair tests unfairly administered by arrogant examiners will pose a severe threat to job acceptance by the most talented of employees—by candidates who do well on the employment tests.[15] People with choice will not want to be associated with a company that puts them through a disagreeable process.

Much of the dialogue between employers and employees who are evaluating one another stays pretty "safe." Employers focus on employees' job-related course work and experiences, and on evident characteristics such as physical appearance and general communication skills. Similarly, employees ask questions about what they will be doing on a daily basis and about broad corporate policies and procedures. In terms of interpersonal dynamics, this is about as penetrating a discussion as one on the weather. It may be worthwhile, but it's terribly inadequate if that's all there is.

Work is performed in a social context, and where and with whom it is done is equally important as the nature of the work itself. Most of us know of people who had perfectly good jobs with fine employers who left the company anyway. I know of employees who, on their first day at work, realized that they had made a mistake; there was no question that they could do the work. I have seen companies, too, quickly determine that a very capable new employee simply did not fit in.

In addition to hiring an employee to fit the job, it is just as critical for an employee to fit the organization—and employers and employees need to rigorously investigate this dimension of the relationship. Employees can ask questions about the founders, key incidents in the corporate history, and for explicit evidence of values. Employers can devote a portion of the selection regimen to discerning cultural fit— being sure that "fit" doesn't exclude protected classes of employees. Amazon.com has grown from an idea to about 3,000 employees. Chief Executive Jeff Bezos maintains he only wants stars on his staff, and this entails hiring employees who are talented in their field, fit the cultural values of the organization, and excel in some area of their lives outside of the workplace. The concept is straightforward: If employees are going to work lengthy hours, they should be with people who are interesting and fun.[16] A fundamental property of the binding power of organizations is their ability to bring people together who enjoy being with one another while collectively fulfilling the company's purposes.

A criticism I have heard on hiring for cultural fit is that it creates a homogenous group and organizational stasis: Similarity somehow interferes with performance. In fact, similarity promotes interpersonal liking and forthright exchanges—these relationships are safer than having to deal with people on a regular basis who are not liked as highly. In a quasi-competitive environment in which there are clear organizational and individual goals, similarity has facilitating effects—people compare themselves and try to outdo one another.

One cost-efficient way to attract people who fit the culture is to rely on the referrals of current employees. They will know others who share their enthusiasm for the company's values and aims, and one another's interests and attitudes. Some companies have resorted almost exclusively to referral recruiting. Offroad Capital, an Internet-based company that arranges investments in businesses, hired 33 of its 40 employees in two months through the referrals of founders and staff. PostX Corp., a company that provides bill-paying services via e-mail, doubled in size in less than one-half year through the zealous recruiting of current employees.[17] In addition to the speed and cost-effectiveness of talent acquisition, these companies will find that their staffs will perform better and stay longer than if they had hired employees using more traditional means. This assumes that these and other companies do not get carried away with referral bonuses. Extravagant referral bonuses (bonuses paid to employees for finding recruits who the company hires and retains for a specified period of time; I have seen these as high as $10,000) could encourage employees to bring in candidates with whom they have little affinity in the hope they will pass muster.

There are organizations within closely knit industries that view referral programs as company-sanctioned poaching, because the logical place to look for new recruits is within companies in the same industry. Companies that tend to dislike these programs are those that experience a net loss of employees to the competition—and that are less effective at instilling commitment. Thus, outside organizations that get in the way of the company and *their* employees are vilified as poachers (something like home-wreckers). Understand, though, that the use of this emotionally charged language is designed to keep suitors away and to preserve the existing relationship. Think about what poaching is: illegal. Also, think about who poachers are: despicable low-lifes. There is nothing illegal or verminous in presenting employees with options; people who are committed will reject the advances.

There is a saying that the best divorce is the one you get before you get married. In the perfect world, mismatched mates would be filtered out, leaving only couples who are ideally suited for one another. This isn't the perfect world for couples or corporations. Where only two-decision outcomes exist in selection, right ones and wrong ones, the wrong ones often are made.

There are a number of reasons why employers and employees who are ill-suited for one another end up together. I'll begin by summarizing the common mistakes that corporations make, but clearly this is an area where it takes two. Thus, I'll subsequently look at the employee's role in entering relationships that, from the onset, are doomed.

○ *Desperation.* Employers feel under severe time pressure to fill a vacancy and believe they have no recourse but to take whoever is available. It is unfortunate that employers find themselves in this position either because they are not attracting a sufficient number of candidates to the organization and/or because they are not adequately developing replacements. Even so, often I have found corporate reactions to scarcity to be lacking the requisite patience. The attractiveness of candidates becomes distorted when companies believe they have to act within a self-imposed deadline. As Mickey Gilley once sang, all the women (or men) start to look pretty good as the end of the night approaches.[18] Even marginal employees begin to look pretty good if you think time is running out.

○ *Erroneous criteria.* The wrong criteria are used when making selection decisions. There is little excuse for this. A great deal is known about selection and how to do it well. Companies uniformly agree that selecting quality employees is imperative to corporate growth and profitability. Yet, selection remains one of the most haphazard procedures within companies. The bases for selection are frequently ill defined or undefined. Managers are poorly trained on selection-interviewing techniques. Interviewees often are rounded up at the last minute with little forethought on how information collected will be combined. Without preconception of who would make a good employee and how to proceed with a deliberate discovery process, there is a slim chance of finding the right person. Indeed, in the absence of agreed-upon criteria for candidates, managers use their own criteria—and these can be quite biased and irrelevant. Here is something scarier: They don't realize how ridiculous their own criteria are. Over the years, managers have proudly divulged their selection secrets to me: There was the manager who refused to hire short people because "there is something psychologically wrong with them"; there was the manager who would sneak into restrooms to see if the candidates (mostly males) were urinating in the center of the toilet—apparently a sign of self-confidence; and, I've met managers who liked gabby people, funny people, artistic people, and so on.

o *Misrepresentation.* Companies sometimes falsely portray what they are to others, confusing aspirations for reality. For instance, I recall a director of human resources telling me how quick and nimble his organization had become—while we waited 45 minutes for a van to take us to another part of their corporate campus. To be accepted, we sometimes stretch the truth, right? Some companies are adept at describing the future and the exciting journey that it has begun—failing to fully articulate the way things presently are. Because companies are motivated to hire people, they are motivated to sell the finer features of the organization. It is natural for agents of companies to view their company positively and to focus on its better qualities; employees can contain little biases with probing questions and due diligence. The bigger exaggerations sometimes occur when agents are strongly incented for bringing people into the organization with little consequence if new employees leave prematurely. For example, sales managers may have bonuses tied to the number of new salespersons they hire, but they have no disincentives for quick departures. The recruiting arm of a human resources department may be measured on the number of position vacancies filled, but it may have no accountability for the quality of recruits—their productivity and longevity.

o *Compromised decision criteria.* Employers make decisions about who to select and reject. There are different decision criteria that employers can adopt, making it easier or more difficult for employees to get in. Generally, the decision criteria have not been formalized; in these circumstances, companies usually default to a decision strategy known as *satisficing.* Employers choose the first employee who exceeds the minimum requirements on most or on all of the implicit or explicit selection criteria. This doesn't ensure selection of the best employee among alternatives, just one that is acceptable. Companies engage in this practice when they value expedience over precision and when they are unconvinced that people have a significant impact on the business. In instances in which the selection criteria are either lowered or waived, selection decisions become even more suspect. I see this happen when employers know the candidates; usually friends or temporary workers who are seeking regular employment. These are not necessarily the best people to fill available slots nor are they necessarily the safest options in terms of commitment and productivity.

You can undoubtedly think of many other reasons why the selection process yields suboptimal results. Undoubtedly, you will realize also that employees may contribute to the problem. You are a motivated buyer, they are motivated sellers. Here are a few attitudinal/motivational traps that can ensnare employees:

○ Making getting the job the preeminent concern versus finding the right job—they don't care about fit.

○ Being seduced by superficial corporate characteristics, such as an on-site health club, while failing to attend to characteristics that are more relevant to daily experiences. One of the reasons for "fatal attractions" is that people sometimes become infatuated with others (e.g., employers) based on salient characteristics that are rewarding in the short run but that are not necessarily conducive to extended, committed relationships.[19]

○ Believing that any job with any company would be an improvement over one's current circumstances.

○ Accepting a first job on the rebound (e.g., following a reduction in force) to combat feelings of self-doubt and to preserve self-esteem.

○ Feeling that one is unremarkable and should settle for any opportunity that presents itself.

One or more of each of these may lead to cursory or hasty decisions, inflated self-representations, and mistakes.

Hiring

By now, employers and employees have become better acquainted. You are confident to whom you wish to extend job offers. Employees have had the chance to learn more about the company: compensation, benefits, career path, policies and procedures, job objectives and duties, the people, and so forth. The worst thing that can happen at this juncture is for an employee, who you really want, to join another company—perhaps a competitor. It is possible that money may pose a final obstacle, but by this stage it shouldn't—unless an employee is belligerent and demanding about pay, which would give you pause. Discussions, by now, will have turned to compensation, and both sides will know that it no longer presents an impenetrable barrier. Meanwhile, employees are weighing their options, which may include continuing to work for a current employer or starting a business for oneself. You may have to woo an employee from the arms of another or, in the case of freshly minted graduates, simply win their hearts.

One of the workhorses of psychology, expectancy theory, is useful in describing the basic components of employees' choice behavior.[20] Put simply, employees choose the alternative that is expected to yield the highest utility. Utility is defined as the probability of obtaining something of value.

There are two critical pieces to utility, then, in the context of employment choice:

1. *Value.* This is the employees' determination of the overall attractiveness of each of their options, given what each has to offer and the aggregate desirability of these offerings. This is why it is essential for a company to distill a plethora of offerings into those that are most important to employees within a particular function, of a particular age, marital status, and so on: to emphasize attributes that are most meaningful and appealing to employees.

2. *Probability.* This is the employees' assessment of the likelihood that they will obtain what is valued; it's an evaluation of their

chance of employment with the organization or of the likelihood that they will have access to the most desirable aspects of the company once they are employed (e.g., eligibility for certain benefits, specific types of assignments).

Expectancies address why a bird in the hand is worth more than two in the bush: the certainty of having a bird raises the utility of that option, even though two birds have greater value. Thus, the speed with which an offer is made can make a difference. Sometimes, the man at the altar is the person who asked first.

Expectancies also help explain why it is a mistake for a company to believe that its work is done following a successful courtship—that nothing more needs to be done after a formal offer is extended, whether the employee has accepted or declined. The attractiveness, or value, of a company is subject to change with new bits of information that prospective employees might encounter from friends, the press, and your competition, for instance. It's like having an opinion about something of which you know very little—additional facts can sway you because your attitudes haven't been solidified. The marriage isn't consummated until the employee is at work on the appointed day of employment.

Believe it or not, even after employees say, "I do," they change their minds. A few recent, high-profile cases are illustrative. After publicly announcing the hiring of a new executive, E*Trade was informed that the executive had reversed his decision and would return to his former employer for personal and family reasons. Recently, a former executive of Black & Decker accepted a job with PepsiCo but ended up at Amazon.com.[21]

Also, it is interesting to note that a surprising number of employees never show up for work on their first day—they are no-shows on their wedding day. This is a good reason for you to start building a quality relationship with employees before they formally begin work. I see the no-show phenomena when I conduct research on employee turnover and find that there are employees who technically had been hired but who never checked in. Is that turnover?

At any rate, to prevent losing good candidates or from being jilted at the altar, it is imperative to put in the extra effort to maintain the perceived attractiveness of the company until the hire date—and thereafter. This might entail sending out updates on the company (e.g., information on new patents, a new employee benefit, new country of operation), letting an employee know about a program that is of special interest, or informing the employee of upcoming corporate events. Displays of continuing interest are essential.

I'd like to tell you that managing expectancies is really quite simple, but there are complications of which you should be aware. Following are two extreme scenarios that illustrate potential problems that you might encounter.

○ Consider a company that develops a reputation for hiring any warm body it meets and, consistent with that reputation, tends to make quick job offers—on the spot even. Much of the estimated utility of this company will derive from the ease with which this alternative can be obtained. It doesn't mean that the employee is necessarily enamored with this company; he or she may be marginally attracted to it at best (i.e., there is a nonzero valance on attractiveness). Once inside, however, the perceived value of the organization may change, plunging to a negative number where the minuses of the organization outweigh the pluses. The employee quickly separates.

Thus, one of the reasons companies may experience large quantities of early exits is because a company's total utility may be enhanced through easy entry, not the substance of what it has to offer employees. The people who will think this is a really good deal are people who are unemployed or who hate their current jobs but who have no alternative offers. Although it is efficient in getting people in the door, easy entry presents no barriers to exit. Early organizational experiences can quickly erode perceived utility because there may not have been any special attraction to begin with other than a paying job—perhaps to the point at which no job becomes better than the one they took. Additionally, because the personal costs of time and effort associated with entry were negligible, there is not much lost through an early separation. Thus, the easier it is to get in (to a limit), the easier it is to get out (before too much time elapses).

○   Next, consider a company that is judicious about selection but that offers magnanimous sign-on bonuses and stock options. This increases the comparative attractiveness of a company (i.e., value) for most candidates. The money is measurable, salient, and desirable. Proportionately few people who are offered jobs turn them down under these circumstances. Again, the utility is quite high, mainly due to the financial aspects of the arrangement. However, new employees discover many other aspects of the work environment that they may have previously overlooked and that are less enticing. The attractiveness of the organization and its utility as an option decline. Employees suddenly want out.

I am a believer in the *pressure-valve theory* of attraction and retention. You never want to turn a valve so tightly that no steam (people) escapes; pipes crack and break that way. You want to adjust the valve so that some people can self-select out of the system (either before or after they are in it) for the right reasons at the right time. Making offers that can't be refused is counterproductive, because the goal isn't just to bring people in and keep them for as long as possible. The goal is to build commitment: to have productive and ethical people who choose to be with you.

Some employees tend to idealize future employers and have inordinately high expectations when they begin work—the perceived utility of the company is inflated. Consequently, they may be disappointed once they start work. To combat slippage in employees' enthusiasm for the job shortly after hire, some companies have instituted either realistic job previews or expectation-lowering procedures as a way to moderate employees' expectations.[22] Realistic job previews portray the positives and negatives of an employment situation to recruits so that there are no surprises upon entry. Typically, an employer will extract a few aspects of the work that past and current employees find to be most and least appealing and share those with recruits in a structured, consistent way. Expectation-lowering techniques are general reminders to prospects that expectations toward the company tend to be elevated and that employees should make sure that their viewpoints about what the company is and isn't and can and cannot do are realistic so that they are satisfied after they join. Some managers engage in expectation-moderating tactics when they send out letters to employees to confirm employment and the employment terms: they reiterate departmental goals and the objectives pertaining to the employees' role. Managers have told me that, on occasion, these letters generate follow-up phone calls from new hires seeking further clarification, leading to healthy dialogue on what the employee can expect during the first few months (e.g., training) of employment and what the company expects with regard to performance. Please keep in mind that the goal of expectation-moderating techniques is not to minimize the positive qualities of the workplace, but to ensure that prospective employees have a balanced view of the company.

Choosing a company is a complex social choice.[23] Think about employees' daunting task. An employee is presented with a wealth of different information, in different formats, in different orders, by different people, from different companies. He or she also selectively seeks out other information. Somehow, the employee has to put all of this data together and appraise the relative attractiveness (value) of the company.

It's speculation, but I have some general ideas on how employees go about this. Basically, employees who like your company will answer in the affirmative to the following questions:

o   Is it good?

o   Is it strong?

o   Is it fast?

For the record, psychometricians have labeled these *evaluation*, *potency*, and *activity*, respectively. Following is a brief review each of these.[24]

Evaluation. This dimension concerns attitudes about value and worth—the overall perception of the company as desirable and useful.

Potency. This dimension concerns attitudes about strength, control, influence, cogency, and authority—the ability of a company to sway others and effect change.

Activity. This dimension concerns attitudes about action, move-ment, liveliness, and energy—the perceived vigor and dynamism of the company and its capacity to act.

If an employee doesn't see your company as an evaluatively pleasing choice, chances are you will not be a serious contender. Employees have to see you as fulfilling their purposes (e.g., offering a convenient location) or interests (e.g., providing unique job opportunities) and as a desirable place to work, given the alternatives. The more that employ-ees believe that there is a seeming inevitability to the relationship— that they fit and belong, for example—the higher will be their evaluation of your company.

There are other considerations, however. Some display of corporate muscle and motion would be advantageous as well. For instance, a part of the appeal of companies like Microsoft and Wal-Mart is their domi-nance in the marketplace. Other organizations may be strong in other ways. Think tanks and nonprofit organizations, for example, may be effective at influencing public opinion or changing behaviors. Enter-tainment companies can emphasize the number of lives they touch, the effect they have on language and behavior, and so on.

A part of the appeal of start-ups is their speed and ability to get things done. Coupled with a healthy market and increased ability to pay, fast companies are luring more and more talent from the giants of industry. This is unfortunate for the giants, because they aren't as slow as they let on. A company can exude vitality in a number of ways:

o   By the speed of its product development cycle

o   By the rapidity with which it can open new stores or set up oper-ations in other countries

o   By its quickness at product delivery times

Many big companies have exciting workplaces, but they don't give themselves enough credit, and they do a poor job of convincing candi-dates that they really offer a dynamic environment.

Figure 3.3 provides a summary of some of the concepts introduced in this chapter relevant to employees' choice behavior. If you give employees good reason, they will come.

Organizational Entry

Fortunately for us, the wisdom of our elders often becomes codified as custom—making it harder to ignore them. One of the social conventions that our ancestors thought worthwhile to the preservation of good relations among newlyweds was a honeymoon. Knowing full well what lay ahead, they conceived of a transition period that enabled couples to adjust to their new social realities.

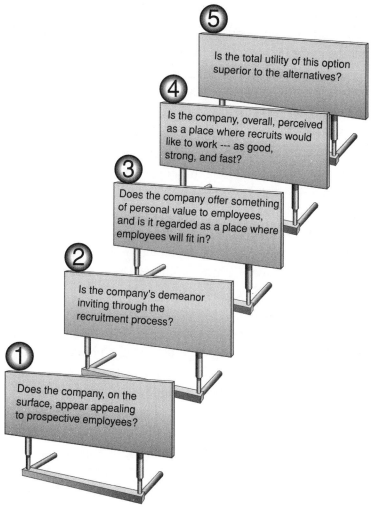

Figure 3.3 Choice hurdle.

A honeymoon is the interpersonal equivalent to clearing one's mind in yoga. It is a time when the ravenous disturbances from the outside world are deflected or suppressed. A respite from worldly demands affords the best chance for a couple to see that their decision was correct. There is no buyers' remorse or second thoughts with a great honeymoon. It also allows changes and interpersonal novelties to settle in within an environment that is unpressured and that offers unconditional positive regard (i.e., where you love the partner no matter what he or she does).

Many organizational newcomers are allowed about three months of experimental activities and screwups before toleration begins to fade — about the same amount of time that a married man has to learn to put the toilet seat down before polite warnings turn to serious questions about intellect. There is a period of acquiescence in most companies in which employees learn the ropes: the way things are done. However, barring the passive acceptance of minor transgressions and easier approvals for ideas and resources that under usual circumstances would be much harder to obtain, organizations by and large do not spend much time thinking about the first 90 days of employment.

Many new employees are greeted with indifference. The experience is something like: "Here's the key to your apartment. There are instructions on how to use the appliances in the cupboard. You can use the recreation room and pool during complex hours, which are posted. Washers and dryers are in the basement—there are no change machines. Any questions, call 555-HELP." Some new employees experience reality shock or are given a rude awakening upon entry. Their treatment from the onset borders on the physically and/or psychologically abusive. I have seen employees show up for work on their first day and have to face any of the following: they are told they have a new job; they find that their entire department has resigned—they are the new boss; they are asked to work a double shift; they're sent out alone on assignment without any training or supervision; they are informed that there are much bigger financial problems than anyone imagined. Most people rightly interpret these revelations as "worse things to come."

In contrast, Southwest Airlines has a welcoming party for new hires, celebrating entry into the family and everything that it signifies.[25] It gives recruits a chance to get to know one another as well as their new peers in a relaxed setting. It is a genuine welcoming that makes people feel valued and wanted, and it sets the stage for future, mutually satisfying relations. Too many companies reserve their celebrations for corporate exits versus more sublime events such as corporate entrances.

Some companies have instituted formal probationary periods; these should not be construed as synonymous with honeymoons or orientations. In fact, they are probably the opposite of a honeymoon. Probation suggests uncertainty on the part of the employer toward the employee. Additionally, these periods are generally associated with increased scrutiny, not less, and less tolerance of error, not more.

The practice of having probationary periods originated in union environments. Successful completion of the probationary period generally confers special status to union employees: employees can be discharged only for just cause and only after charges and appeals have moved through a formal grievance process. Employees, as specified in a collective bargaining agreement, also may be granted seniority and union membership rights once the probationary period expires.

Union and nonunion employers with probations may require employees to undergo additional tests, reviews, and assessments during this period: to make sure the employer hasn't made a mistake. Probationary periods are legal quagmires for a variety of reasons in which your legal departments are sure to be aware. In nonunion environments, for example, completion of probationary periods can give employees the false impression that they have greater job security than intended by the employer—which has created a rich history of litigation. Probations, as they usually are defined, are inhospitable beginnings; it is easier and less expensive to identify problems before hire rather than have to resolve them after hire. Whether you are a union or nonunion employer, it is better to start the relationship with the conviction that you have the right employee, and to treat him or her accordingly.

"Trial" relationships such as probations do not fare particularly well over the longer term. If cohabitation before marriage is any indication, then these relationships are not likely to last. Cohabitation before marriage is a good predictor of divorce according to The Marriage Project at Rutgers. Thus, rather than being a prudent rehearsal, "tryouts" appear to be primers for relationship dissolution. Practice runs may create a lingering aura of dispensability: the thought that termination always remains an option as opposed to the exercise of patience, perseverance, sacrifice, and compromise needed to rescue troubled relationships.

There are many formal and informal methods that companies use to assimilate employees into the workplace, including orientation programs, job training, mentoring, and coaching. All of these methods are intended to make new employees, even those who have been around the block a few times, more familiar with, and at ease within, the organization. The bare bones of an enculturation process should include the following:

Organizational overview. Includes a description of the benefits package [e.g., retirement plans such as 401(k), life and health coverages, vacation time] and compensation practices, including types of compensation (e.g., eligibility for bonuses); details on the performance assessment process and administrative particulars related to recording time, pay periods, direct deposit, and so forth.

Career guidance. Includes typical career progressions and criteria for advancement, as well as various developmental opportunities (e.g., training and outside courses available through educational reimbursement).

Health and safety. Includes any routine exams (e.g., physicals) or tests (e.g., drug testing) that may be required, use of health clubs, ergonomic training, and demonstrations on the safe operation of equipment.

Logistics. Includes location of facilities (e.g., cafeteria, library); assistance in gaining access to the building, the parking lot, the computer, and so on; ordering supplies; securing or borrowing telecommunications equipment; and other logistical necessities such as joining the credit union.

Policies and procedures. Includes familiarizing employees with all written and on-line documentation, such as the employee handbook, statement of professional ethics, and such; descriptions of special work-life options (e.g., telecommuting); procedures on completing special forms, such as expense reimbursement and such.

Job requirements. Includes learning the specific elements of the job and job interdependencies with other people and departments through formal and on-the-job training.

Neighborhood information. Includes information on transportation, restaurants, basic necessities (e.g., drugstores, cleaners), entertainment, and cultural/educational sites.

Employees need to know all of these things, and they are appreciative if they are introduced to, and periodically reminded of, corporate policies and offerings in an "edu-taining" way. Learning about the job, rules of conduct, benefits, and so forth, is important in that it can ease employees' anxieties and prevent them from feeling lost. However, getting employees to believe that they fit in requires more rigorous socialization.

As starters, it helps if employees are "primed" to be socialized. If employees enter the organization with the presumption of compatibility (with the company's values and with one another) and are enthusiastically welcomed into the fold, they will be more receptive to feedback and other influence tactics that encourage social integration. Employees, for example, must be willing to accept critiques of their behavior and performance in lieu of the prevailing norms. Some employees will adapt more quickly than others, but most require coaching in the art of corporate life.

For employees to connect to one another, they have to be socially and technically proficient. Social and ideological oddballs and blunderbusses are not going to find much interpersonal satisfaction in the workplace. Affinity usually depends on similarity: on acceptance of a common value system, on expressions of mutual interests, and on compliance to the same performance standards.

An emotional attachment to peers in the workplace is an important element to feelings of belonging, but mutual affection alone is not a sufficient condition to instill these feelings. To belong, there must be frequent, pleasurable contact.[26] An employee may like colleagues very much, but unless there is occasion for frequent and rewarding interaction, stronger feelings of belonging that can bind employees to the organization are unlikely to emerge. Companies intuitively realize this. They have summer picnics and holiday parties. They understand that employees are more connected to the company when they feel connected to each other. These events just aren't enough; sometimes, they are ugly failures when employees share no special fondness for one another.

Companies that want to build high levels of commitment look for innovative ways to build social solidarity through group activities at, as well as away from, work. It is tough to get a boccie court in Silicon Valley these days, for example, due to a resurgence of the sport and the number of engineering and software development companies that sponsor employee outings to such activities.[27] Similarly, Ingage Solutions, a Phoenix-based division of AG Communications, has kept turnover among software engineers to under 10 percent by building a strong social community in the workplace through leagues and clubs that bind people together.[28] The same social aims of bringing people together can be accomplished in many ways, including periodic training sessions, team projects, group problem solving, happy hours, and so on. Companies that care about the collective spirit and about engendering a sense of belonging make sure that there are plenty of forums for engaging and pleasurable employee encounters.

Social transience threatens one of the foundations of a productive workplace—friendships. There is a tendency for companies to underestimate the importance of friendships to commitment and the depth of these relationships. Recently, when an employee's kidneys began to fail and efforts to locate a match had been exhausted, it was a coworker who eventually stepped forward to donate one of her kidneys.[29] When we eulogize the good ole days, I believe it is this quality of corporate life we remember most fondly and long for.

Although we think of socialization as a means of assimilating newcomers into the organization, in truth it is a process that never concludes. Our connections need to be refreshed or renewed every now and then, particularly when they have been interrupted or changed by sabbaticals, stints overseas, transfers to new divisions and returns, and so on. Indeed, the high number of voluntary terminations of repatriated employees (about 25 percent leave the company within a year of completion of the assignment[30]) may be due largely to a lack of continuity and reassimilation plans. It is rare for people who have been away for a prolonged period of time to feel entirely comfortable upon their return. It takes a while to warm to the company and/or fellow employees. It is natural for us to think that employees who are being sent away on assignment, for example, will need some sort of psychological preparation. We sometimes fail to realize, however, that coming home can be pretty hard as well: It can feel like starting anew. In the end, if you allow employees to feel estranged from one another, they will tend to feel estranged from you—the company.

4

YOU'RE A PART OF ME

Status and Identity

When someone says, "I work for XYZ Company," or "I belong to Phi Beta Kappa," or "I am married to Martha," that person is not necessarily just describing a fact; rather, he or she may be expressing an attitude about how he or she feels connected to or associated with another person or entity. Indeed, how easily the statement rolls off the tongue says something about the quality of the relationship and one's emotional state. Try it. Say, "I work for [the name of your company]." Does that have any special meaning to you, or are you merely describing a state of affairs or a condition the way you would make any observation of fact ("It's going to be a hot one today.")? A statement that is empty of emotional content is telling too.

In many instances, who we are becomes inseparable from the relationships in which we engage. Extreme cases occur in couples when it is difficult to know precisely who one is talking to—the person has defined him- or herself almost entirely in terms of the relationship. Thus, questions directed at individuals are answered as "we": "We like to boat," "We vote for Republicans," "We like to vacation in Vermont," "We like to read nonfiction," and so forth. The emergence of union is one of the touchstones of close relationships. Indeed, the inclination to think and talk in relational terms is prognostic of interpersonal satisfaction.[1]

We have personal identities that distinguish us from others. We also have social or collective identities by which we define ourselves in terms of our relationships. We feel a part of a social unit, adopt some of the characteristics of the social unit, and feel good (or bad) about our membership. Thus, a couple may think of themselves as not only legally married, but as a pair, with each person acting to fulfill the needs and desires of their tiny group versus his or her individual interests alone. Two become one, and not simply because they share common perspectives and beliefs, but because it becomes increasingly difficult for them to conceive of themselves in any other way: they don't think of themselves as apart, as separate. They are transformed from unique individuals to group member.

Identification with a group (or a person) is like being enveloped by a psychological fence that shapes our social perspective. The fence psychologically demarcates a person's social meaning: "I am a part of group XYZ." Further, the fence can be high intensity and impermeable, or low intensity and porous (i.e., very weak boundaries), making it easy or difficult to pass through. Psychologically, the strength of the fence is determined by the degree to which a person has internalized the attitudes and values of the generic group. Psychologists refer to this as *self-stereotyping*, in which a person comes to view him- or herself as a prototypical member of his or her group. We'll discuss the possible routes by which this occurs in this chapter, but one precondition for internalization is that the group have something of value to offer employees. Accepting the group's value system and interests as one's own is getting a bit chummy—there has to be something worthwhile to membership for anyone to want to become this close.

It may be the ability to conceive (and categorize) oneself as a part of a social unit that is partially responsible for the trauma of loss (e.g., when a spouse dies or an employee is laid off or retires). The emotional and financial strains are trying in and of themselves. However, if you have come to think of yourself as Martha's husband or General Electric's engineer, then all the greater the loss. People who experience such losses feel a part of themselves is missing; in truth, it is.

There are practical reasons why identification is important in relationships as well as organizations. Considering oneself a *we*, as opposed to an *I*, has certain advantages:

○ *Promoting positive intermember attitudes.* Having a group versus individual orientation facilitates a group-centric bias—members of the group are presumed to have highly favorable qualities despite not having firsthand knowledge of all of the members' personalities.

○ *Promoting prosocial in-group behaviors.* The extent to which people consider themselves intimately connected to an organization, the more likely they will be to take the collective interests into account when acting (i.e., the goal isn't to pursue one's own interests to the exclusion of what is in the welfare of the aggregate).

○ *Promoting open communication.* A more inclusive definition of who *we* are tends to result in more open and candid discussions—greater self-disclosure of interests, desires, and so forth.

○ *Promoting organizational commitment, including reduced mobility.* Employees who define themselves partially in terms of their group membership are more integrated with their company and psychologically more insulated from opportunities that abound outside the organization's invisible walls.

Thus, to secure commitment, groups must not only satisfy employees' social need to affiliate and belong—to like and get along with the people with whom they work—as we discussed in the previous chapter, but must form a collective identity that differentiates the group from other groups as well. Members of groups that are ill defined or all inclusive lose their way—or rather, find their way to groups that have more to offer.

Before proceeding further, it is important to underscore what identification is not. First, it is not the same as affiliation and getting along with others. Although liking others may promote group affinity, it isn't a necessary condition. It is possible to feel like a part of a group and to never have met another member, as in chat rooms or virtual groups. Similarly, high-performing groups such as sports teams do not necessarily contain members who are universally fond of one another; however, they have a mutual connection and identification with the group—and they may be fiercely protective of fellow members on these grounds. More typically, identification creates closeness. I'm sure that you have had the experience of being introduced to another organizational member and developing instant rapport. The common identity with the group carries weight. The relationship starts with familiarity and the presumption that one will like a fellow member.

Second, identification is not the same as membership. A few dollars or a good resume will provide entree to most clubs and organizations. Membership offers you certain rights and privileges and imparts certain obligations. These are hard facts. Identification has to do with social facts. Do you *feel* like a part of the group that you joined? You can belong to a group in a formal sense but still not identify with it in any deeper way: The group has no collective meaning to you. It's like joining a pool club whose raison d'etre is each person's summertime enjoyment—the club's structure makes that possible, but it may be nothing more, experientially, than a holding tank for individual pleasure seekers.[2]

Degrees of Identification

There are degrees to which an employee can identify with the organization, ranging from "I hope no one finds out I work here" to "I can't wait to tell others who I work for." Specifically, employees can identify with companies in the following ways (arranged in order from low to high identification):

○ *Employees would never identify with the organization.* Employees distance themselves from the organization by engaging in behaviors that are countercultural or counternormative, making it known publicly that although they are currently employed by the organization, they do not consider themselves to be a part of it—and will remove themselves at the first opportunity. One restaurant chain I worked with believed that making the employees wear uniforms was causally related to turnover. Indeed, many employees would "forget" their uniforms (i.e., vests) or wear them backward as a joke. I convinced the employer that the employees wouldn't mind wearing the vests if they didn't mind working for the employer. A uniform is a symbol of identity and wanting to wear it or not is symptomatic of identity.

○ *Employees are indifferent to the organization.* Employees simply conceive the organization as a place of work—as a dispenser of benefits, with each individual exchanging time, effort, and contribution for those benefits.

○ *Employees identify strongly with the organization.* Employees clearly view themselves as part of an organization; due to socialization processes, subtle indicators of group membership and situational factors that foster mental constructions of *team,* employees tend to label themselves as members of the company. Employees mentally note that they belong to a social category of people.

○ *Employees self-identify strongly with the organization.* Employees redraw the boundaries between who they are with what the company represents—employees *self-stereotype,* or start to see in themselves, prototypical characteristics of the organization. The employee feels good about belonging to the company.

○ *Employees self-identify nearly completely with the organization.* Employees define who they are with reference to their organizational membership. A person does not believe he or she has distinctive qualities apart from the group. These extreme cases in which a person adopts the defining characteristics of the organization as one's own rarely exist in business settings. Extreme identification is characteristic of cults in which a person's identity, or self-concept, is tied primarily to what the organization represents. There is an outlook and value system that everyone shares with little left over for individual differences.

To advance to the highest levels of the identification continuum, two ingredients are required. First, a social boundary needs to be created that indicates that an identifiable collection of people of some sort exists. There is a group and it is possible to classify oneself as being in it or out of it.

Second, the group must assume some evaluative meaning. That is, for employees to grab onto a group and call it their own, the group has to offer something that the employee wants or needs. Most typically, this involves *status* as I describe it in a subsequent section: Being a part of the group can make a person feel good about him- or herself. Employees bathe in the reflected glory of some collective attribute, just as a spouse may vicariously participate in a partner's beauty or special achievements. The character and glory of kindred enhance one's own self-esteem through association: The employee is a part of a group with positive, distinctive attributes.[3]

The better-defined and the stronger the social categorization, and the greater the status associated with membership, the more likely employees will be to internalize, or assume, attributes of the group ("We are very creative here") and be proud of their association with the company. Thus, employees see themselves not only as belonging to a group, but they believe that they share the common characteristics of the group, and they value their membership. I have summarized the identification continuum in Figure 4.1.

Making a Group[4]

There are a host of cues surrounding us that are suggestive of the social categories to which we belong. These cues help to shape our sense of inclusiveness with certain groups. Thus, we may be Buckeyes, Catholics, or IBMers. We can be all of these or none of these. We can feel our membership more intensely or less intensely.

In this section, I will review the basic situational features that contribute to a sense of group membership. The more exposure that employees have to these features, the more likely they will be to feel like a part of a group and to incorporate that membership into their conception of who they are. The list is arranged alphabetically.

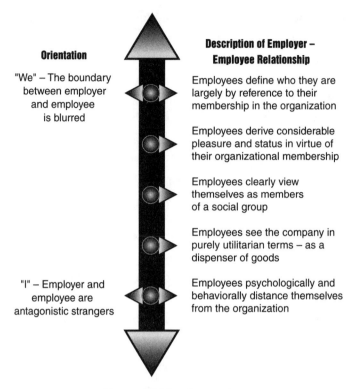

Orientation

"We" – The boundary between employer and employee is blurred

"I" – Employer and employee are antagonistic strangers

Description of Employer – Employee Relationship

Employees define who they are largely by reference to their membership in the organization

Employees derive considerable pleasure and status in virtue of their organizational membership

Employees clearly view themselves as members of a social group

Employees see the company in purely utilitarian terms – as a dispenser of goods

Employees psychologically and behaviorally distance themselves from the organization

Figure 4.1 Identity continuum.

Categorization

Minimal communication has been found to be sufficient in the formation of groups. For example, labeling a group of people as belonging together by giving them a common name ("All you people are 'Ones'") leads to social categorization. It is really quite amazing because the criteria for inclusion may be arbitrary. Nevertheless, people who are nominally grouped together come to perceive their group as superior to other groups, and they like their members more than the members of other groups. Thus, simply developing a companywide label or nickname for employees can be helpful in instilling identification with the company.

Common Experiences

Going through what others have gone through can nurture social bonds. Even silly, seemingly insignificant experiences can have this effect. Some companies, for instance, must bless the union between employees and employer by having new employees have lunch with an executive or, in smaller companies, the CEO. This demonstrates that the caring will continue after the courtship and establishes a historical precedence—everyone who enters the company must have lunch with Herb or George or Henrietta. It signifies the start of a new *relationship* and joins employees through a common experience.

Orientation programs, too, have the potential to bind simply by requiring all employees to pass through it—as long as the experience is meaningful. Some companies have very powerful orientations, as evidenced by employee comments that I have received over the years. When I reflect on those programs that I have seen to be most energizing and symbiotic, there are certain similarities:

○ *There is a pilgrimage.* Employees go somewhere (sometimes, just across a plaza) and they do not go alone—they travel in classes or groups.

○ *To a mystical place.* Like a trip to the Oracle of Delphi, it is a place that reveals great secrets (i.e., to previously unknown codes, processes, etc.).

○ *Where they will meet a charismatic leader (usually through remote video or videotape).* This person provides meaning and order (by having "the answers") and exudes a confidence in the future.

It is the corporate equivalent of a religious experience. Consider what PeopleSoft employees encountered when they joined on. They found a charismatic leader, David A. Duffield, who referred to himself as DAD and was referred to by others as "the legendary Dave Duffield." The company had a band called "The Raving Daves," sold luggage called "Duffield bags," and printed Mr. Duffield's image on coins called "People Dollars." The company also had a historian and employee pioneers of sorts who sported shirts that bore their employee number—people talked enviously of the "double digits"—the people who joined PeopleSoft in its infancy. They also had evil enemies (e.g., Oracle) and developed a suspiciousness of outsiders. The company engendered a quasi-religious fervor.[5]

Common Fate

Common fate implies that all employees uniformly share the same outcomes. Employees win or lose, succeed or fail as a whole—the fates among employees are inseparable. In business, common fate is usually expressed economically through profit sharing or availability of bonuses to the entire workforce (i.e., broad-based bonuses). If the company as a whole performs well, everyone will share its fruits. Thus, whereas programs like profit sharing are urged for their presumed motivational effects, one of the side benefits may be to foster group identification.

Some companies introduce *balanced scorecards*, which include financial (earnings per share) and nonfinancial (customer service) measures of corporate performance. Performance on these measures generally has material consequences to employees: Typically, performance determines how much money is available for dispersion to the workforce. A few companies turn this exercise into a game with scoreboards and comparisons with the competition on the relevant metrics as a way to give clarity to what is important and to emphasize total team effort in meeting goals. All of these programs, in one fashion or another, highlight winning, or losing, as a group.

Similarly, a oneness of community often results from crises or critical incidents that affect the whole organization. Crises remind people that they are jointly connected to events from which they cannot escape. "We are all in this together" is one of the most ubiquitous experiences people can have that brings them closer together and unifies them. A crisis also can pose one of the greatest threats to community, because people with greater power and influence often can avert personal misfortune by taking precautionary or remedial steps that are not available to others. A senior manager, for example, knowing that the company is having serious financial troubles, may defect to another company before employees at large realize what is happening.

Common Values

Most companies by now have gone through an exercise of developing their core values and fashioning a mission statement. Companies then plaster conference rooms with multicolored descriptions of these, which collectively depict what the company stands for. Companies sometimes believe that communities are borne through community edicts: that the simple act of posting one's beliefs is, in and of itself, transformational. It's a healthy start, but it's not an end-all. Corporate missions and values have to be motivating, believable, and consistently supported for them to be binding—thus, the role of vision and persuasion in leadership. It is important, then, for companies to gain consent on purpose and on values that are collectively viewed by employees as worthwhile and that are rigorously reinforced in the workplace through corporate policies and practices.

Values must also be divisive for them to be of consequence in the formation of a group identity. Not everyone should be able to agree with the value system advocated. *Freedom* binds Americans together, first, because our institutions give the word meaning and, second, because there are governments in the world that do not embrace this value. U.S. values and norms are recognizable in practice and strong enough to attract or repel.

Companies that timidly formulate values that no rational person could reject (Our mission is to profitably serve the customer) are doing themselves a disservice. To be an employer of choice that pulls people together, it must simultaneously be an employer of no-choice that pushes people out or away. Thus, for cultural values to promote inclusion, they also must be exclusionary.

Competition

Having a group identity requires the existence of mutually exclusive groups: There are people who are members and people who are different in some way who are not members. The distinction can be highlighted through competition where the collective *we* must band together to defeat the evil *thems.*

One of the things competition does is polarize attitudes. The in group begins to think of themselves more favorably and to think of the out group less favorably. Having an outside threat—someone who is out to destroy you—is instrumental in producing these changes in attitudes. Thus, employees of the in group come to think of themselves as being superior in some way: brighter, more responsive to the marketplace, more innovative, and so on. Whether advertent or inadvertent, there are some great corporate clashes that help to solidify employees' identity with their organizations: Sun versus Microsoft, for one. The danger, of course, with ethnocentrism is that a company may overestimate its abilities and its place in the marketplace (i.e., think more highly of itself than objective consideration of facts would warrant). However, being aware of the dangers of identification is a great safeguard against the lull of exaggerated self-opinions. One company in which I have worked, that has exceptionally high employee identification and is extremely successful, refuses to let itself be overtaken by thoughts of grandiosity. They adopt a position similar to the one I heard espoused by the great sprinter, Maurice Greene: "Think like you're number one, but train like you're number two."

Science fiction writers know that waging war against a common enemy from another world is a way of pulling the disparate countries of Earth together. Waging war in the marketplace can have the effect of pulling employees closer together: thus, Limited, Inc.'s, recent declaration of war in retailing—its new kill-or-be-killed strategy.[6] Limited's use of a battlefield analogy (showing employees war clips from movies such as *G.I. Jane*; holding motivational "battle summits"; providing "battle briefings" in the company newsletter, *Frontline*; and distributing bonuses as "battle pay") is intended to build cohesion among employees and to instill aggressive selling practices. The success of these tactics in increasing identification and productivity depends on the following:

○ *Accepting the implied culture.* Employees must come to think of themselves as warriors. Companies that have high employee identification tend to have very strong cultures and substantial self-selection—people who will be itching to get in because of the culture and people who will want out for the same reason.

o *Giving the enemy a face.* Effective wars are fought against specific enemies who must be defeated—not a diffuse, nameless retail marketplace, for instance. Opponent companies have to be anthropomorphized and vilified; they have to be perceived as a threat to one's way of life and survival; the personification of the company, the CEO, must be portrayed as bad.

o *Managing anxiety.* Wars aren't fun. They make employee-warriors suspicious and vigilant of the competition and create urgent and persistent calls to perform. This produces anxiety. Some anxiety is good—the arousal heightens performance. Too much anxiety produces too much emotional interference, however, which generally is accompanied by decrements in performance. Thus, the call to arms must be accompanied by attempts to moderate anxiety. A review of all of the possible anxiety-reducing techniques is beyond our present purposes, but common approaches include diffusing anxiety ("We're all in this together"), providing social support ("Don't worry, we'll help you"), or enhancing employees' sense of mastery and control over their environments ("You can do it").

Cooperative Interdependence

This is a fancy term used to describe working together to get things done. Some type of coordination is required: Workers have to align their efforts at a particular place or moment in time; exchanges of information and materials are necessary; and so on. The more interdependence, the more frequent the interactions, the greater the identification. In other words, an employee can't be successful alone—other people in a network of people enable completion of tasks. How vast employees perceive their network to be depends largely upon how the task is framed. Is the goal to satisfy the customer or to produce a widget? Each involves different networks of different sizes. This feature also highlights an issue that we will take up later in this chapter regarding the potential coexistence of multiple groups and memberships: department, function, business unit, company; marrieds, immediate families, extended families; city, county, state, country.

Distinctiveness

You have all heard the quip, "I wouldn't want to belong to a group that would take me." Indeed, groups that are not very selective will not be perceived as distinctive, because the corporate boundaries will be viewed as porous—anyone can get in. It is difficult to build identity with an organization whose membership guidelines are extremely broad or ambiguous. On the other hand, careful selection procedures in which employees must pass muster on well-defined attributes/criteria can create the aura of distinctiveness and the presumption of similarity and likability. Thus, employees who are selected believe they share rare attributes. Making entry difficult makes membership special.

Equal Status

Parity in status can create strong personal bonds and perceptions of community. Companies that try to do this tend to dismantle corporate trappings of power and privilege. Robert Shapiro, the CEO of Monsanto, and Andrew Grove, the CEO of Intel, sit in cubicles just like everyone else. Some companies try to downplay hierarchy by reducing the number of grade levels (or eliminating them entirely) or by linguistic slight of mouth. Managers at Eaton Corporation's small forge plant in Indiana are called vision supporters rather than managers to emphasize their connection to the organization and not their authority over people.[7]

Language

Anyone who has been around corporate life for a while has to smile at the special dialects that emerge. Outsiders cannot easily comprehend the word use, vocabularies, or idioms. "He's way out over his skis" (i.e., he's in big trouble). "The BPR of the CIT met with EOM" (a group from information technology, dedicated to issues related to business processes, met with the company's senior operations people). "We have 'associates,' not 'employees'—remember that." That is one that has gotten me on occasion and when I have slipped, I have felt like the poor human fools in the *Body Snatchers*—when the aliens shriek and point at them.

Having a common language is a way to distinguish *us* from *them*. It is one of the unifying and identifying aspects of cultures and groups. It operates like a secret handshake or pig latin (*igpay atinlay*) among a cohort of associates, putting a barrier between insiders and outsiders. Linguistic devices don't even have to be subtle. Employees of Scitor are "Scitorians" and those of American Management Systems are "AMSers."[8]

Physical Similarity

There is a Wall Street firm whose investment bankers all go to the same barber who cuts hair one way. They look a lot alike. There is a service company that requires their salespeople to carry the same style of briefcase. Some companies still have strict dress codes; others have uniforms. In all of these cases, the intent is the same: to create homogeneity of appearance so that who is "in" and who is "out" is unmistakable.

In addition to alerting employees to the commonalities among one another, shaping a common look is "deindividuating." That is, similar appearances not only promote a sense of oneness, but they erode a sense of "I-ness." This observation has not been lost in military circles where survival and success depend upon a powerful group ethic versus individual motives and preferences.

Proximity

Geographic boundaries and physical space help to define categories. A distinct boundary (e.g., a state line, a mountain range, or a river) helps to shape perceptions of nations, states, and so on. People who work within a defined area or who are spatially arranged as a collective tend to belong in the same social category. Romantically involved partners who live under the same roof are a couple. On the other hand, couples who live apart must contend not only with local enticements, but the separation itself may erode self-identification as a pair. Thus, the adage of "location, location, location" matters as to whether people characterize themselves as belonging to, and identifying with, a group. When the baseball team runs off the field, they sit together.

Employees who work in remote corporate sites typically do not identify with the company as strongly as those at corporate headquarters. There are many reasons for this. One reason is that employees in the field often feel put upon and pushed around by the corporate bullies at Headquarters. Another reason is that field sites are sometimes left out of corporate communications—or the communications are inadequate. There may be one poster with the corporate mission statement hanging beside the vending machines (next to the minimum wage laws) in the lunchroom. A final reason is that distance matters. There is some truth to "out of sight, out of mind."

I have heard employees liken their service in the field to being in a wilderness outpost or on a deserted island. Each metaphor suggests being cut off and isolated. Indeed, these same employees will tell you that they do not feel like they are a part of the company. It is not easy to close the distance gap. There is one thing I've noticed that helps, though: When executives and managers make it a habit to visit the remote sites, people in those sites are more apt to view themselves as being a part of the company as opposed to being an appendage. The general principle is to increase meaningful contact between employees within satellite offices and the corporate entity. A company could even run parallel activities as a proxy for spatial contiguity and contact: For instance, all locations can hold corporatewide activities on the same day, whether they are business (e.g., inventory checks) or nonbusiness (e.g., holiday party) related.

Representation Acts

Members of couples do things on one another's behalf. They sign documents, make decisions about child rearing, attend social gatherings, make purchases, and so on, on behalf of the couple. These acts bring couples closer together by promoting identification with the broader group (of two, in this case), even if one spouse is not altogether pleased with the other's decisions. In essence, one person serves as an agent for both by engaging in what is believed to be in the joint interests of the couple. Thus, one person is asked to publicly endorse the norms and/or opinions of the twosome through his or her actions.

Companies that ask employees to show the new people around, to tell a group what it is like to work at XYZ Company, to attend a trade fair, to interview candidates, to participate on a company-community committee, to speak at conferences under the company banner, are asking employees to be agents of the company. In so doing, employees are being asked to recite and act out a positive corporate story that they may internalize as their own. It is well known that attitudes affect behavior. Conversely, however, behavior can affect attitudes. Thus, employees who voluntarily act out behaviors that demonstrate their allegiance to the company will tend to espouse attitudes that support their fidelity (e.g., "This is a great company").

Symbolism

There are artifacts or activities that denote membership or union. In weddings, there is the unique dress, the recitation of vows, the ceremonial exchange of rings, and the kiss to cement the relationship. Organizations often miss the perfect opportunity to take an emotion-laden moment and make it positive and unifying by encumbering newcomers with sterile orientations and benefits booklets.

Tool manufacturer American Saw & Mfg. Company introduces new employees to the company a bit differently. Employees inscribe their names into wooden blocks that are visibly displayed on the Wall of Quality. When an employee retires, he or she gets the block of wood. The ritual itself—etching one's name in wood—is suggestive of permanence. Furthermore, everyone's names appear together on the wall of wooden blocks. This is a wonderful way to assimilate employees and to metaphorically incorporate them into the team. Posting employees' pictures on the cafeteria bulletin board, although not as novel, has some of the same effect as does creating an electronic bulletin board that holds the names, faces, and interests of the workforce. It's not a yearbook, but it's close.

Employees also often receive representations of the company, like company pins and personal identification cards, that they are asked to visibly display. I have seen both have great significance, positively and negatively, in the identification process. For example, when Society Corp. of Cleveland and Key Corp. of Albany, two regional banks, merged, they were unable to fully realize the potential of the new organization because of lingering differences in culture and identity. The in-group/out-group differences were so severe that some Society employees refused to wear their red-key pins—the logo of the new company, Key Corp.[9]

In another company, employees proudly display their company badges, which uniquely identify them as bona fide members. To get a badge is special, to the point that employees collectively reference themselves in terms of the badge's color. Employees are "blue badges." Other elements in the environment, such as rigorous selection procedures in which few people are chosen relative to the number of applicants, give the badge importance and augment the badge's ability to create identification with the company.

There may be many other symbolic overtures that heighten the employees' sense of identification with the company such as special entrances and exits for employees. Such devices signal *members only*. Employee discounts at the cafeteria or to cultural events in town also are subtle devices that enhance the salience and benefits of belonging to a group.

Status

Think about your favorite relationship partner and the qualities that you admire the most in that person. Take a moment to generate a list. When I ask employees to produce a similar "wish list" of desirable employer attributes, my guess is that list approximates yours.

Because certain characteristics are important to us, we want them in others. We want to be associated with people who have those qualities, because such an association elevates or reinforces our own sense of importance. It makes us feel better about who we are. Thus, we brag about the accomplishments of our children, spouses, or family members; we drop the names of famous or beautiful people we know; and we try to cozy up to the powerful. Our self-esteem and perceived social ranking is enhanced by the company we keep.

If an organization wants employees to identify with it strongly, it has to offer something special—something employees want. I generically refer to these items that elevate employees' self-perceptions as *status*— as you'll see, status comes in a variety of shapes and sizes. People prefer to associate with others (including companies) who make them feel good about themselves. Participation in relationships that contain status-enhancing attributes is a source of esteem and a part of the binding force of relationships.

These qualities have merit to employees in and of themselves because they involve conditions and characteristics that most people find desirable. They may take on added meaning, however, when it is known that other people outside of the relationship share their opinion of and enthusiasm for particular attributes. For instance, you may have a successful wife (or friend) who is pleasing to you. Knowing that others recognize his or her success and that they are duly impressed enhances the status that is evoked by the attribute, and it creates a stronger bond between spouses or friends.[10]

Corporate reputation and image have much the same effect: What outsiders think of the company influences how good (or bad) employees feel about their membership in the company. There are several ways in which a strong, positive company reputation may increase employees' identification with the company:

- ○ *Through social validation.* Others' opinions confirm employees' suppositions about the desirable features of the company, heightening employees' confidence that the company's value propositions are real.

- ○ *Through social reinforcement.* Others' positive attention is rewarding to employees (makes them feel special) and increases the value of the object (i.e., the company) that elicits that attention.

○   *Through reminders of supply and demand.* Others' opinions remind employees that positive corporate attributes are rare in the marketplace and not available to everyone, elevating employees' appreciation of their good fortune.

All of these may be factors to some degree. At any rate, here are a few of the common company characteristics that employees find most appealing.

Beauty

Gap, Inc., wanted a place that would attract top talent from the San Francisco area. So they created a special place with natural lighting and atriums, a full-service fitness center, lap pool, cafeteria (whoops, "restaurant"), and other work and nonwork amenities.[11] Novell recently invested $130 million in its new, Venetian-themed corporate campus that resembles a destination resort.[12]

The architecture of a facility can set it apart, give it a unique feel, and provide potential and current employees the impression that they are *some* place and not just any place. You feel a sense of awe, for example, when you walk onto PepsiCo's property—with the rare sculptures and well-groomed grounds. Employees take great pride at pointing at *their* building and saying, "That's where I work." I have seen some corporate buildings and complexes acquire special nicknames like the Cubes—a familiarity that humanizes the workplace. If you have the money and want people to come, building something magnificent, elegant, or beautiful can help.

Class

There are companies that have pizazz because they are "in" and cool, such as Internet/technology companies, including well-funded start-up companies such as Teligent (a provider of wireless local phone service) and up-and-comers such as Third Voice (providing Post-it Notes for the Net).[13] Some companies are presumed classy because they are in glamorous industries such as fashion or entertainment. Even though an employee may never see a model or star, the fact that the company handles or houses such talent often is good enough to lend glitz and status to the workforce.

Goodness

Some companies pursue missions that are recognized to be of social value. They support agreeable public policies or, in some measure, help us all to live happier, healthier lives. Merck and other pharmaceuticals, for example, are noted for their focus on the public welfare and craft strong mission statements to that effect. Some companies such as Corning and Herman Miller consider their broader social responsibilities and take active, prosocial roles in the general community. Part of the great appeal of many not-for-profit organizations are the purposes that they pursue. Many employees like to be associated with good companies.

Ben & Jerry's mission statement emphasizing linked prosperity illustrates a company's regard for the broader community. Doing business is placed in a social context. For example, "green teams" examine the environmental impact of its operations and the company purchases raw materials from places that benefit indigenous people—in the Brazilian rain forest, for instance.[14]

History

When you walk into Home Depot's lobby, there are antique tools hanging from the walls, with descriptions of their use. When you walk into Canon, U.S.A., you find a presentation on the history of cameras and other Canon innovations. Microsoft, Intel, and Chrysler similarly have stimulating exhibits that introduce visitors to their histories. These museums (or quasi-museums) are great ways of letting employees know the rich tradition of which they are a part—a part of good stock or lineage.

Intelligence

It would be nice to belong to a smart company versus the other kind. Working for a company known for resourcefulness and ingenuity, such as Enron, or for its raw intelligence, such as IBM or Lucent Technologies, is a plus for most employees. Thus, employees can point to new innovations and products, number of patents, Nobel winners and Ph.D.s, and such, as evidence of their mental prowess.

Enron is an interesting case study because it is in an industry that many people frankly think is—well—dull: energy services. Yet, they have no difficulty attracting talent from top universities because they have created a culture that permits people "to figure things out." It is a lively, engaging place that gives people with good ideas a chance to prove themselves.[15]

Popularity

There are companies whose products are immediately recognizable because of their brands and strong presence in the marketplace. Everybody knows these companies because they are exposed to their products and services through the media, usage, and symbols in the marketplace (e.g., golden arches). Automobile manufacturers, retailers, food and beverage companies, and communications companies all spend a great deal of money on their brand image. Some employees feel good about working for a company that everyone knows.

Power

It may be arrogance to the outside world, but it feels like status to insiders. Power relates to the ability to push the marketplace around a little because of the volume of transactions a company executes and its market share. These are dominant companies in their industry that others fear, respect, or loathe. Suppliers, for instance, don't mess with Wal-Mart, and I have seen the hint of exuberance within companies that are able to get their way.

Success

People like to be associated with winners—companies that are growing and prospering. They want to say they work for the best within an industry as summarized by profit or revenue growth, or both. There are countless other ways in which a company, or one of its divisions, may succeed. For example, each year *Industry Week* searches for the best manufacturing facility, measuring plants along a number of dimensions related to processes, customer focus, quality, cost, safety, and so on.[16] The plants selected, on average, have realized 64 percent five-year productivity increases (sales per employee), 21 percent five-year reductions in manufacturing costs (including purchased materials), and 15 percent plant-level return on assets. The employees at the winning plants (e.g., Lockheed Martin Tactical Aircraft Systems, Ft. Worth) should feel pretty good.

Wealth

There are some big companies with lots of assets or high market values, such as Citigroup and General Electric. Just being big can command respect. Employees and business observers alike can be quite enamored with the financial size and value of a company. This is the opportune time to raise two issues related to wealth and other positive corporate attributes. First, they don't last forever. Companies must periodically reinvent themselves and their value proposition to employees. Second, the luster of status-invoking characteristics can fade. You may have been attracted to the size of the company at first, but then find that size isn't everything it's cracked up to be. Thus, big and good and beautiful are better than just big because the former company has more status hooks that collectively will endure for a longer period of time.

All of these corporate attributes bestow status and prestige to employees who are fortunate enough to work for a company so endowed. Outsiders looking in are generally impressed as well. I have spoken to thousands of employees over the past 20 years, and I know that they like telling me about their companies and what their companies are known for or excel in. Sometimes, it's hard to get them to stop. They take great pride in their companies.

I am sure you can think of other corporate attributes that are of value to you and other employees. And that's the point. For high degrees of identification and employee-employer unity, employers have to have a corporate character with which employees care to associate. Consider descriptions of the following two manufacturing facilities. Which one do you think has the potential to inspire greater identification with the company?

Manufacturer No. 1. This facility has won numerous awards for the results of its quality improvement initiatives and process-engineering innovations. Repeatedly, it has been recognized as one of the most productive facilities in the United States.

Manufacturer No. 2. This facility produces its goods the same way it did 10 years ago and, as manufacturers go, is average—it meets customary quality standards and production quotas at acceptable costs.

The answer is clear. Just as in relationships, you are more apt to identify with someone with whom you can identify—people who have qualities that you admire. You certainly won't identify with people or companies who are repulsive.

Many of the ideas discussed in the previous sections are summarized in Figure 4.2.

Identification Processes

Let's review identification tactics by taking a look at those institutions that are masters at creating high-identity cultures to the point where we

Figure 4.2 Summary of ways to create identity and status.

go on paying into the institution years after we've left—colleges and universities. Granted, they are provided with pliable subjects who suddenly have been cut off from other communities with which they identify (e.g., family, friends), but colleges and universities make the best of the situation. They say repeatedly how selective and/or how good they are [they are particular about who they accept and find a way to be best in class at something (e.g., best medical school)]; they shepherd students en masse through a formal orientation program that is designed to alleviate their anxieties and teach them the way things are done (sometimes they are paired with a more senior buddy who guides and coaches them); they supply shirts, hats, mugs, and such, smothered with the university/college logo; they generate rivalries and competitions of all sorts in which students represent the school—and spectators share in the experience; they provide frequent contact with wise emissaries who share their secrets and visions of truth (i.e., faculty); they provide a collective benefit in which all members strive (graduation); and the list goes on. By the time the experience is over, it has become an everlasting part of you—a fundamental part of your persona that you proudly display on your resume and office wall.

Indeed, you never really cease to be a member of a university. The nature of your affiliation changes from student to alumnus, but the institution tries to keep its grip. Thus, there are quarterly newsletters, local alumni groups, special alumni events, reunions, and so on—designed to keep you connected and your identification with your alma mater high. The strength of identification lies in its trace effects—its power to persist even after formal disengagement. For example, alumni who have strong institutional ties and high identification attend more college-sponsored functions and donate more money. Similarly, employees who come from strong cultures to which they identify do not easily shake free from their roots. For example, once a GE'er, always a GE'er. Similarly, several consulting firms have alumni groups that meet monthly. Corporate experiences can become so ingrained with who you are, it is tough to let go. You carry your status with you.

Defining yourself in terms of the company in which you work can help keep the relationship together. Additionally, this may be an aspect of commitment that helps keep relationships together *after* they have ended. It enables the relationship to change its complexion without ending it. It permits students or employees to become alumni, and lovers to become friends. The relationship doesn't dissolve; rather, it changes form. That is good news for organizations, because it produces advocates in the marketplace who speak well of the organization.

In addition to *what* educational and other types of institutions do to foster identification, *how* they do it is critical as well. There are several processes that, taken together, have been referred to as *institutional socialization strategies*, intended to heighten organizational identification and commitment.[17] These strategies specifically orient employees to the collectively and help instill the corporation's ideals.

Collective Experiences

Information is disseminated to groups of employees who have been brought together rather than to individuals. Thus, employees participate in orientation, training, and other exercises in cohorts. In addition to the social benefits, education and instruction en masse underscore a group identity by burning in the image of the group and by providing common experiences through which all organizational members are known to have passed. The way to feel like a group (or a couple) is to do things as a group.

Training cohorts on occasion are given labels that imply membership to a larger organization and membership continuity (e.g., first-year class/employees). Contrast this with companies' tendency to name groups according to skill level or personal attributes (e.g., high potentials—HiPos). These labels distinguish employees from the rest of the company and highlight personal characteristics that are transferable to other organizations.

Ordered Experiences

These are sequential, often scheduled (either time- or event-driven) training, instructional, or developmental exercises that employees undergo with specific people as instructors. One effect this has is to recommit employees to, or ask them to rejoin, the organization through successive experiences. Educational institutions have class sign-ups every year and text-buying rituals. There is something the student has to do to remain engaged and a fully functioning member. There usually are no such renewal rites in corporations—like retaking of wedding vows. It would be interesting to know, if there were such rites, whether employees would pledge their commitment to the organization with the same conviction in years 2, 3, 4, and so on, as they would on the day that they were hired.

Scheduling various employee activities at certain times (or following certain events) with certain people demonstrates a corporate consistency that can pull a diverse workforce closer together. Unfortunately, some companies consider people in certain positions, such as trainers, to be fungible because they think the content is the important part. However, having solid trainers/educators that employees work with or are instructed by at particular times in their careers serves as an important rite of passage that facilitates integration into the organization. It's like having to meet crazy Uncle Al—it's a small step to becoming a part of the family.

Many ordered experiences are also *formal*, which is equally important to indoctrination—acceptance of group principles and practices—and subsequent identification. Formal socialization experiences are standardized, uniform, and required. The message to the target audience is, "This is the way it is done around here; this is the way everyone is expected to do it." Thus, formal training advances a shared-world view.

Modeled Experiences

While Odysseus was on his 10-year journey, the holistic education (moral, social, technical) of his son, Telemachus, was entrusted to his friend and advisor, Mentor. It was up to Mentor to groom, educate, and develop Odysseus' son and to provide counsel. Thus, a few of the key responsibilities of mentors are to be teacher, role model, and validator of organizational norms for their proteges. They instruct others on how to be successful within the broader social environment (e.g., organization).

Organizational mentors can have a positive influence on employees if mentoring is properly approached. First, the process must be approached deliberately: The pairings between employee and mentor must be thoughtfully developed rather than random or based on irrelevant criteria. The company has to help make the pairings an essential part of corporate life and not leave it entirely to incoming employees' own devices or choice.

Second, a precondition for mentorship should be that one is well-equipped to serve as a mentor. Many organizations assume that anybody can do it, or they expect managers, who sometimes are having a hard-enough time managing, to fill that role. A mentor's job is not only to transmit technical or operational knowledge; it is to offer support, encouragement, and constructive correction when needed, and to model the attitudes and behaviors of a good citizen. They are what a company should want all employees to be. What more important role could there possibly be?

Third, the mentor must believe in the institutional attributes and norms that he or she is upholding. In the argot of this chapter, if the mentor doesn't identify with the organization, he or she can't serve as a mentor or, at least, be effective at it.

There is certainly much more to establishing mentoring programs than we can cover here and now (e.g., goals and duration of the program, the number of programs within a given company, means of rescuing mismatches).[18] However, if identification with the company is important to you, mentoring plays a crucial role. Consider the experience of Foodmaker, the parent of the Jack in the Box chain. They established an "on boarding" orientation for senior managers that included mentoring as one of its chief ingredients. Only 2 of its 24 managers who have gone through the program have left within the last four years. In contrast, a survey conducted by the Corporate Leadership Council, a Washington, D.C., association, found that about 50 percent of top managers leave within three years of hire.[19] Mentors help new employees to get on and stay on the proper corporate path.

These institutional process tactics help to build a strong culture and high identification with the company. In addition, they clarify employees' organizational roles and convey specific expectations about corporate life. Both of these give employees a greater sense of place and enhanced job satisfaction.

Identity Problems

Corporate identities aren't fixed. First, corporations are large enough to have multiple social units with which employees may identify. Second, companies, like people, change. A discussion of these common identity problems follows.

Multiple Memberships

Many social categories with which people identify are hierarchically clustered: One category is subsumed by another. Thus, the defensive unit is a part of the football team in the Central Division of the American Conference of the National Football League. What is the most meaningful categorization from the perspective of the player? With which social unit does the player identify most closely? The same concerns arise in organizations where one category (e.g., a department) is clearly nested within others (e.g., a function).

Social categorization matters primarily because it affects organizational cooperation. Many companies—I'd say most companies—that I have worked with have struggled with coordination among units that have nurtured identities of their own. Getting the units to provide one another with more than superficial assistance becomes a long and agonizing process. That is because companies ask people to get along with each other without first changing the organizational unit with which they identify by using many of the tactics that are described in this chapter. Companies assume that cooperation will occur upon request. Many employees, however, have strong ties to their units and derive a good amount of self-satisfaction from their current membership. Indeed, I have seen attempts at cross-divisional or unit initiatives heighten intergroup animosities and solidify existing social identities when forced interactions highlight differences—companies make matters worse! The "Can't-everybody-just-be-friends?" approach doesn't work without social boundaries first being dismantled and then reassembled in the manner that one wants.

Social categorization also matters for the now-obvious reason that it keeps employees connected to the organization. The efficacy of that identification depends on its strength and stability. Although a company will have to work more diligently at creating global (i.e., company) rather than local (i.e., work unit) identification because ready influencers such as proximity and spatial arrangements are more pronounced at the local level, broader social identities are more likely to be stable and permanent. Corporate identity will be affected less by everyday situational factors: People come and go and they are reshuffled in endless company moves. Employees whose identities are anchored to the company will be less susceptible to these occurrences.

At any rate, there are several factors that determine the social grouping with which employees most closely identify.

○ *Salience.* This is the social unit that is most prominent to employees, based on how the company (intentionally or unintentionally) directs their attention. For example, pay programs can emphasize unit or corporate performance. The organization can be designed to promote interunit contact or to isolate units, and so on.

○ *Perspective.* When you go to France and someone asks you where you are from, you are likely to say the United States and not Ohio, for example. You assume a grouping unit that is of greatest interest and meaning to the listener. Similarly, employees look at the company the way others outside the company are likely to view them. With an emphasis on the point of view of shareholders, whose interests lie with the organizational gestalt, employees may be encouraged to think of the relevant social unit as the corporation. If employees see the world through the eyes of competitors, they may be more inclined to group themselves by product line (e.g., by business unit or division).

○ *Opportunity.* People seek out social meaning and status and are not simply passive bystanders; they are active in the process. Thus, in the absence of any situational variables that lead employees in one direction or another, they will try to find their own way. Personal identification tactics will be likely to take place at the local level (e.g., search out people who are physically and attitudinally similar). Most employees will join and identify with a group. Left to their own devices, this will be with fellow employees within their work unit or department—and it may not be altogether wholesome. For example, groups of corporate rebels may spontaneously form: employees who belong to a group bound by a common antipathy toward the organization.

Tightly knit internal groups also often form around employees who perform "dirty work"; that is, work that has a physical, social, and/or moral taint, where these are defined as follows.[20]

○ *Physical taint.* Occupations that are associated with garbage, waste, pollutants, death, and so on, or that are performed under noxious or dangerous conditions.

○ *Social taint.* Occupations that involve regular contact with undesirable or stigmatized populations, or whose duties are suggestive of subservient relations with others.

○ *Moral taint.* Occupations that are regarded as sinful or on the fringe of virtue, or that involve the use of deceptive, intensive, or confrontational methods that are generally perceived as being in violation of norms of civility and manners.

Most jobs of this ilk are low also on occupational prestige, which relates to indices such as educational requirements and income. Whereas most people regard dirty work as essential, most people also view it as distasteful—for someone else to do—even by fellow employees. Thus, employees may refer to other employees who are doing tainted work as "rivet heads" or "grease monkeys" or "shop rats" and occasionally ask them self-ingratiating, rhetorical questions such as, "How can you stand it!?"

Needless to say, the stigmatized employees tend to band together and separate themselves from a population that clearly wants them to stay away and keep out of sight. The existence of organizational factions is not good for companies that rely on unified action for success; besides, it's unnecessary. In addition to the identification tactics discussed throughout this chapter, it is essential to treat all work, including dirty work, as integral to the operation of the company. This can be achieved by the following:

○ Underscoring the social value(s) fulfilled by jobs

○ Emphasizing the special skills and endowments required to execute a job, such as dexterity and strength, as opposed to the outcomes

○ Pointing out the unique benefits that the job specifically provides to others (outside the company) and the times when it made a difference to others

○ Describing the connectedness of the job's work products to other endeavors inside the company—how they make other things possible

I am not playing games here or being cute with language. This is how people who perform dirty work conceive of their jobs—or try to conceive of their jobs despite others' reminders that it really is pretty disgusting. How can you expect employees to feel like they are a part of a larger team if you are unable to appreciate and respect the work they do?

Mergers and Acquisitions

It is now a truism that corporate marriages that look awfully appealing on paper fail miserably in practice because the interpersonal dimensions of the union were not fully appreciated. Hindsight can be revealing but, really, a little foresight couldn't hurt. Putting people together on the bold presumption that the business rationale will prevail and everyone will live happily ever after is myopic, particularly given the high anxiety that accompanies these events. Arranged marriages only work by luck.

There are countless examples of corporate mergers that never obtained the synergies sought because of culture clashes and powerful, existing allegiances. Before the work of business can be done, employees need to see themselves as belonging to the same club. This requires fending off natural inclinations to see one's own group as better and purer than other groups whose individual members are perceived as foul and inferior (e.g., "we're more artistic," "we're more productive," "we're smarter," etc.). It also involves resisting temptations to do what one can do because of economic power: Thus, acquiring companies descend like barbarians on vanquished foe (who are often perceived as too stupid and ineffective to deserve their independence any longer) and decimate the conquereds' jobs and resources. If employees who are involved in mergers and acquisitions sometimes feel like second-class citizens, that's because that is precisely the way that they are treated. Unions require thoughtful, social identity plans to overcome the stubborn obstacles that interfere with cooperation.

Organizational Change

Companies have identity crises, and employees are sometimes asked to accept qualities in their "partner" that they didn't know would ever be displayed. Companies, for example, may feel weighed down by the past and, for the sake of future prosperity, attempt to break away. In doing so, they may chisel away at beliefs that no longer hold up under scrutiny (e.g., the company is no longer the best or the biggest). They adopt a new name, put on a fresh public face, and forsake its past. The problem, of course, is that many employees feel connected to the past and revel in old glory. They do not want to give up a part of themselves so easily.

Employees' initial reactions to this aberrant corporate behavior is to dismiss it as situational—It is a phase that the company is going through. Sooner or later, it will come to its senses and employees decide to wait it out. If the changes persist, the employees next try to reconcile old with new. For example, it's not so much that the organization is different, it has simply changed its exterior—changed the name on the clubhouse entrance. Deep down, it's really the same organization that it always was. If the change persists, some employees will fight it, some will flee from it, and some will adapt to it.

The nature of change and employees' responses to it are beyond the scope of this book. My intent here is to point out why it can be so hard. It is because, in the process of change, companies not only ask employees to explicitly accept what it has become (or wants to become), but implicitly to reassess who they are.

5

PROMISES, PROMISES

Trust and Reciprocity

Imagine a spouse who drains all of your financial accounts, liquidates some of your valuable holdings, and runs off with a younger person, all the while confirming his or her love for you. You would know at once what it feels like to have your trust seriously violated, and you would wonder how you could ever allow someone who could do so much harm to get so close. The reason we let others "in" is because we need people to be close to provide or nurture those things we care about. We depend on others to help us and to benefit us in ways that we can't achieve on our own. We trust others because sometimes we need to and sometimes we have to. Thus, the person who can do so much good is the same person who can cause us great pain. It is this hand-wringing, nail-biting precariousness of trust that gives the topic color, great literary value, and puts it at center stage in organizations where trust and sound interpersonal relations are essential for success.

According to recent surveys, trust in corporate America continues to decline.[1] In its place are anxiety, insecurity, and ambiguity regarding employees' jobs and their futures. Reengineering, layoffs, and mergers and acquisitions have all conspired to create an uncertain workplace. Employees are uncertain of their futures; corporations, fixated on quarterly earnings reports, are reluctant to make any long-term promises.

In terms of a relationship, companies and employees both seem to have one foot in and one foot out—hardly the type of standing one needs to build trust. The "trust gap" between employers and employees, which *Fortune* explored 10 years ago, seems no closer to being filled and is not easily resolved by cosmetic treatments such as unsubstantiated value statements about corporate integrity.[2] Yet, despite the prevalent view among human resource managers that distrust is a barrier to quality employee relations and healthy corporate functioning, the once conventional platitude, "What we need is more trust," is seldom spoken, or spoken softly. Discourse on trust in the workplace often feels awkward or is greeted with suspicion. Its currency has been so eroded that it is easy to change the topic whenever it arises.

The Benefits of Trust

Trust is the social equivalent to air and water. It is what makes rewarding social interactions possible. As a thought experiment, imagine what life would be like without trust: a world of deception, bluffs, distortions, exaggerations, and lies. Not only would our personal relations falter, our social institutions would buckle as well.

Without a presumption of minimal trust, even basic social encounters would be trying. Right now, for example, you can call for pizza and be reasonably assured that you will get it on time with the toppings you want. You also trust that the cook won't add ingredients that you would find objectionable, as a joke perhaps. The business, in turn, trusts that you really want the pizza and will pay when it arrives. There are varieties and degrees of trust, as I will soon discuss, and ordering a pizza is not among the more perplexing social transactions that require much of it. However, if each party (and individuals and businesses more generally) assumed nefarious or malicious motives—that is, distrusted rather than trusted each other—the set of transactions would work much differently. The process would be more complex, more costly, and would take much longer to execute to the point that no one would bother ordering pizzas at all. Even the exchange at the door would be complicated and filled with intrigue: "Hand me your money." "Let's see the pizza first."

To demonstrate the benefits of trust and the costs of distrust, allow me to relate a true organizational story to you. It illustrates an extreme case of social decay due to rampant distrust among all quarters of the corporation. If the story sounds familiar to you, it is time to start rebuilding trust in your organization.

This is a company, with over $5 billion in revenues, where no one trusted anyone. Unsurprisingly, the presenting complaint that brought myself and a team of others into the company was high turnover and related issues. We were taken aback by initial directives to exclude certain executives from meetings and to disregard their opinions, even if decisions that were made affected those executives. When others' ideas from outside our workgroup were offered, they were minimized as being out of step or old-fashioned.

Many departments and business operations had created duplicate services. Most of the various business units had their own staff departments (e.g., information technology, human resources), even though corporate groups with overlapping responsibilities toward the businesses existed. Every decision, no matter how trivial, required multiple approvals within and across departments and units: checks and balances ad nauseam. Those approvals were hard to get, first, because no one really knew whose approvals were needed and, second, because agreement among warring parties could never be reached. There were cliques and cabals, good guys and bad guys; never was there agreement.

Actions that were taken were threatened either by behind-the-scenes shenanigans (e.g., propagating falsehoods, instilling fear in others, and engaging in outrageous acts of self-preservation: "No one ever told me about this. Had I only known . . .") or vigorous opposition ("It will never work. We did this before—it failed then and it will fail now."); or by creative derailment ["This is very good, but it requires much more study and analysis"; "This is very good but what about . . ." (change the subject and get everyone onto another topic—bonuses were a popular diversion)]. As soon as an idea had been planted or the results of a decision activated, it fell quarry to social vandalism.

Amazingly, the vandals were not confined to the executive suites. Self-interested hooligans could emerge from anywhere in the organization and popped up at any meeting. I refer to this latter phenomenon as the 30-person syndrome: 5 people were invited to a meeting and 30 showed up with not one person being able to recite the meeting's objectives. They were present for entirely personal reasons: they were fearful that their interests would not be fairly represented or that they would be blamed unduly for something if they were absent. Each person could inflict great damage to a project through a number of subversive means: for example, feigning not to understand how something worked, overstating the implications of a decision, mentioning someone else's (one of the few people who were not at the meeting) difficulties with the recommendations, telling woeful personal stories with similar approaches in the past, and so on.

Throughout the project, employees called me directly to let me know how things really were or to ask for progress updates: employees who were remotely connected with the project calling me for a status report! There were no organizational boundaries, no clear lines of authority, and no specific accountabilities that could be pinpointed. Each person diligently tried to carve out his or her own isolated existence, safe from the intrusions and demands of others. Maybe that was okay for them, but it wasn't for us. Several employees throughout the project presented themselves to us, or were presented to us, as project directors. It was never clear who was in charge, and when we asked who was, "I am," "I am," "I am . . ." was the echoing reply.

To make matters worse, two of the departments with whom we were dealing had two heads trying to win the allegiance of the organization the old-fashioned way—through money, political favors, and titles. The employees were justifiably confused: Not even they knew to whom they reported or the expanse of each of the department head's duties. One department head might be global, the other domestic, but there was no clear delineation.

Detailed project plans were redrafted no fewer than 20 times during the course of the year as a vain attempt to reconstitute reality as a "living document." The company managed the only thing it could: paper and text. Mostly, meaningful interventions sat idle until someone blamed the consultants. Like bad theater, this scene played over and over again: define the project steps, assign accountabilities, do the work, wait until nothing happens, blame the consultants; refine the project plan, reassign accountabilities, do more work, wait until nothing happens, blame the consultants; revise the project plan, describe new procedures, redo old work, do more work, wait until nothing happens, blame the consultants.

Meanwhile, I attended so many team-building/strategy retreats with this company that I thought that I was at summer camp. It seems that the employees could not get enough of the business advantages of teamwork "in the new millennium." I suppose if you're starving, you think a lot about food.

I could go on, but you already see that it is a very troubled organization. Needless to say, this publicly traded company is not one of the darlings of Wall Street. Not all of their problems, of course, can be attributed to distrust, but it made an unhealthy contribution. The symptoms of distrust were evident in many of their daily transactions, ranging from a robust antipathy toward one another to ardent attempts to detach oneself from the rest of the organization in an effort to avoid distrust's reach. There was dysfunctional conflict that was either avoided or handled immaturely. Unlike secure and trusting persons in healthy interpersonal relations who acknowledge distress in their relationships, take responsibility for their actions, and engage in constructive remedial actions, people in this organization either became more detached from the conflict or hypervigilant to every slight. In the former case, the distress of conflict was ameliorated by suppressing its existence ("We're all one happy team") or sidestepping from any potential confrontation. In the latter case, employees tended to ruminate on causes and meanings and to focus on negative aspects of the relationship—about why the company is a bad place and about the countless things it does wrong.

Of course, there was the hallmark of distrust: lack of cooperation within and between departments and units. Each department in this organization was hopelessly locked in a duel to outdo one another as they cast one another as unresponsive incompetents. Some departments, as previously mentioned, felt compelled to replicate the services of other departments.

The results of distrust are measured not only by the social harms inflicted, but also by hard business results. In this and similar cases, the destructive consequences of distrust to the business are:

○   The results achieved take longer.

○   The results are of poorer quality and higher cost.

○   The implementation of outcomes is less effective.

In contrast, the benefits of trust are evident.[3] First, it reduces the transactional or social costs associated with interpersonal interactions that otherwise would have to be expended in managing less trusting relations (e.g., additional time spent dissecting motives and meanings; extra effort required to overcome languid or incomplete responses for fear that one's work will be ripped off, misused, or misrepresented by others; increased costs due to increased vigilance and surveillance; and more frequent conflicts attributable to miscommunications).

Second, trust promotes acceptance of organizational initiatives. When an organization must move quickly and without the benefit of complete information, it will not find progress stalled by second-guessing, adversarial challenges, and, in extreme cases, refusals to act. With trust, employees are willing to suspend judgment and defer to the authority of others—to temporarily put oneself in another's hands.

Third, trust permits organizational flexibility by promoting "spontaneous sociability." Let's go back to the pizza delivery person. Upon receipt of the pizza, imagine saying, "Thanks, I'll pay you later," or "Would it be okay if I take what I owe you and donate it to charity?" Neither would be permissible because the relationship's operating premises are *immediacy* and *specificity*: It's now and for this. This is standard for relationships that have little stock of trust. Altruism and extrarole behaviors are pushed out because these classes of behaviors presuppose time delays and a tolerance for ambiguity. With high trust, a payback need be neither immediate nor of an equivalent value—frequently, it need not be made at all. In addition, the give-and-take is systemic, not individual. I may help another person with the implicit understanding that he or she will, in turn, extend the same courtesies to others. Reciprocation is achieved by adhering to the moral code of the group.

Companies tend to underestimate the extrarole behaviors that are necessary for corporate success, thinking of them as little remainders to employees' job duties. They are, however, at the heart of civic engagement: the voluntary responsibility acts that employees take for the benefit of the group—some of it performed on one's own time and much of it performed outside the watch of the employer.

Taken together, trust helps to build the social capital of the firm, whereby social capital is an attribute of the community, an asset embedded in relationships, that results in many of the public goods we discussed earlier. Social capital can be measured by the character of social relations within the organization, and it is undergirded by trust.[4]

Definitions and Varieties of Trust[5]

The value of trust in exchanges has not gone unnoticed by the countless people and organizations who want yours. After all, shouldn't you:

- Trust your car to the man who wears the star? (Texaco)
- Trust your health to the people who "build trust"? (Invacare)
- Trust your baby's care to the "face you can trust"? (S.C. Johnson & Sons)
- Trust your money to a company with a "tradition of trust"? (Merrill Lynch)

Evidently, trust sells. What is it that you are supposed to buy, though, when someone says, "Trust me"? What does it mean to trust and to be trusted? Certainly, there are varieties and degrees of trust, depending upon the nature of the relationship and the items being entrusted. You can trust someone to watch your briefcase for a moment or your child for the night. You might trust a given person with the former but not the latter because your interpretations of risk will be much different in the two situations. There is more to lose in the one situation than the other. Accordingly, betrayals in the two situations won't instigate an equivalent emotional response.

Interestingly, in both cases, and with many cases involving trust, the trust is not literal. That is, generally there is considerable discretion about what precisely is being entrusted to another. If I ask you to watch my briefcase, I also expect that you will not search through it while I'm away. Similarly, I wouldn't expect you to polish the leather or to vigorously protect it from armed robbers. Thus, when you trust someone, there are certain limits and extensions implied as well—you can do too little or too much.

Employees, for instance, look to employers to provide training. Let's say the company provides it but only offers it on the employee's day off or following a 12-hour shift. I've seen both versions and neither produces much fellow feeling between employees and their employers. In other words, the caring acts that normally would enhance trust are important, but so are the social graces that surround trust—like interpersonal understanding, tact, and good sense. A company's heart may be in the right place, but the company also has to exercise diplomacy and common sense to not undo its good intentions. One of the hardest parts of building trust is to handle what is entrusted in precisely the right way.

The interesting question is, What kind of trust do employees expect in their relations with their employers, and is there a version of trust that is more likely to produce commitment? In what follows, I will briefly explain the primary forms of trust, the kind of trust employees want from their employers, and the types of things employees believe they have entrusted—for good or ill—to management's care.

The most common definition of trust from the social sciences goes something like this:

> Trust is a psychological state whereby a person is willing to accept a condition of vulnerability based on the positive behavioral expectations of others.[6]

Thus, the key attributes of trust are as follows:

- ○ Trust involves a relationship between two or more people.
- ○ There is the assumption of risk and the possibility of betrayal.
- ○ One person holds the belief that another will behave as expected.

Until now we have been very cavalier about the proper use of the word *trust*. In fact, we often use the word *trust* when we probably mean something else. The various meanings of *trust* are clarified below and summarized in Table 5.1.

———— *Table 5.1* ————

Type of Trust	Description	Label
Trust as arithmetic judgment	Others do what is expected because the benefits of compliance are greater than the costs of betrayal.	Cooperation
Trust as dependability	Others do what is expected because their character predisposes them to act in such a way under specific conditions and circumstances.	Trustworthiness
Trust as emotional reciprocity	Others do what is expected because they consider the needs and interests of others before acting.	Trust

*This sequence of types of trust is largely based on the work of R. Lewicki; see R. J. Lewicki and B. B. Bunker, "Trust in relationships: A model of trust development and decline," in B. B. Bunker and J. Z. Rubin (eds.), *Conflict, Cooperation and Justice: A Tribute Volume to Morton Deutsch* (San Francisco: Josey Bass, 1995); R. J. Lewicki and B. B. Bunker, "Developing, maintaining and repairing trust in work relationships," in R. Kramer and T. Tyler (eds.), *Trust in Organizations* (Thousand Oaks, CA: Sage Publications, 1996).

Trust as Arithmetic Judgment

One of the reasons we often can trust others is because the relationship is highly regulated by salient costs and benefits. The benefits of behaving according to the social script are greater than the probable costs of defection. In essence, it is to everyone's material advantage to play by the rules. Indeed, as we might loosely construe these situations as involving trust, *cooperation* may be the better word.

In most social encounters of this ilk, it is reasonable to presume that everyone will perform as expected because there are benefits to be attained and strong deterrents to violations of expectations. The costs of violating a trust are perceived to be higher than compliance. This is a calculated form of trust (and some psychologists refer to it precisely in those terms). To return to an earlier example, your pizza will show up because they want their money; they will make it the way you want because either you won't pay or you'll tell your friends they're no good. Remove the incentive for compliance, however, and life suddenly becomes very scary.

Thus, we often depend on the context of our relationships to hold them together. We depend on the evenhandedness of the exchange, our laws, peer pressure, and so on. It should be self-evident that this is not the form of trust to which we should aspire in our deeper relationships, nor is such a form of trust comforting to employees.

These are high-maintenance relationships, both socially and economically. They have to be regulated by things outside of the relationship itself, either by finding people who will act a certain way regardless of the quality of the relationship or by putting in safeguards to protect corporate interests. The former mechanism is a *hire-and-hope* strategy. Companies hire employees whom they hope won't cheat, lie, steal, leak secrets to the competition, and otherwise engage in activities detrimental to the company. Thus, through routine reference and background checks (e.g., for criminal records, telling the truth about such things as educational experiences), drug testing, personality screening, and such, companies hope to find employees with the "right" character traits.

Even so, when the thread that holds the relationship together is an even economic exchange (i.e., the benefits of the relationship must be at least equivalent to the costs), then paying employees the "right" amount becomes of tantamount concern, as does minimizing corporate exposure to employee abuses. Thus, companies (or departments) in this position find incessant pressures to pay more and more to keep employees situated and compliant, and require more and more controls (e.g., video cameras and more managers, punitive absenteeism policies, and "sniffer" packets to look at employee electronic transmissions) to guard against aberrant employee behaviors in case employees view the relationship as inequitable. In the extreme case of no trust, lousy work, and low pay (and no other redeeming features of the workplace), vigilance is often high to ensure proper work effort and ethics. For example, it was recently discovered that some California retailers lock their janitorial contractors in the stores overnight so they can be searched when the store opens in the morning.[7]

Sometimes, employers and employees do not understand what type of relationship they have. Several years ago, a well-liked and well-known newscaster received lucrative offers from other television stations. Knowing that it was a fickle industry where youth and looks matter, she was tempted to take the money and run. Her present station, however, assured her that there would always be a place for her there. On the basis of this intangible benefit, she elected to stay with her current station for less money. When ratings dropped in subsequent years, so was she.

The newswoman accepted the station's assurance that they would grow old together as evidence of a particular type of relationship involving a specific form of trust (discussed later). In fact, it was an economic relationship predicated on her continuing high performance as an anchor. Once her performance became an issue, the relationship as it existed was no longer viable.

Employees who have suddenly realized they have mistaken one kind of relationship for another generally can kick themselves for being so stupid and vow never to let it happen again—and keep all future engagements at an arm's length. I have heard many employees, including senior-level human resource directors, say, "Never again." This is a problem because you cannot be deeply committed to someone (or something) whom you don't trust beyond the immediate economic costs and benefits of the relationship. To understand how it feels to be discarded, consider a woman whose husband unceremoniously dumps her once her fortune is spent and her looks have waned. There is a price tag hanging from the relationship and once the economics are no longer sound, the relationship perishes. Employee performance will always be an issue for employers in organizations. It is in many kinds of relationships, including families, but it is possible to develop deeper, trusting relationships without excusing poor performance.

If everyone mutually understood the rules of the game, one could be more tolerant of a breakup. However, neither party ever openly advertises that the kind of relationship one really wants is built on immediacy and utility. People have shallow relationships, but I haven't seen many people who actually invite and welcome shallow relationships. Companies sometimes give strong hints by suggesting to employees that they maintain their employability through continuing education, self-help, and other means. They further argue that it is up to employees to solve the riddles of their careers and find their own way through the organization. In other words, stay fit and look out for yourself.

Trust as Dependability

Trust frequently means *predictable*. It means that you can be counted on to act in a certain way so that others know what to expect. Managers expect employees to complete work on time, to exert an appropriate amount of effort, to be available when needed, to meet quality standards, and so forth. Managers who trust their employees are more willing to place themselves at risk—to give the employee more latitude to act without direct supervision.

Employees, too, expect their managers to be dependable, or in a word, *trustworthy*. I have found through employee interviews and investigations into employee trust that there are six general attributes that managers can display to prove themselves to be worthy of another's trust.[8] These are:

1. *Reliability.* This means there is surety that certain things will get done and get done well because the manager is perceived to be competent and takes the obligations of his or her position seriously. It is hard to build trust if you are incapable of executing your job or are nonchalant about your responsibilities. Reliability also means being temperamentally even—not emotionally labile or abusive.

2. *Integrity.* This is simple—tell the truth and keep your promises. Integrity also means being forthright, not evasive, and following through on what you said would be done without undue delay. Furthermore, integrity also means acknowledging when you have made a mistake or were wrong about something, and adhering to socially acceptable norms of behavior (e.g., not denigrating an employee in public or casting insults in areas that are personal and sensitive).

3. *Discreetness.* When you give someone privileged information, you assume two things—that the person will not reveal the information to others and that he or she will not use the information against you. Maintaining the confidences of others is a prerequisite for gaining trust.

4. *Openness.* Information is power and there is great temptation to withhold information to bolster one's standing—to know something others don't but should. Openly sharing information is one way to ensure the trust of others. It communicates that you find others worthy of the information, and it shows that you have nothing to hide. Closed doors tend to generate suspicion and rumors.

5. *Support.* At a minimum, it means empathy with another's predicament. I have found this to include pitching in when the workload gets heavy or a deadline approaches, protecting employees from political fallout and standing behind them (but not too far behind) when there are difficulties, and actively searching for solutions to employees' problems.

6. *Fairness.* Fairness generally means being evenhanded in dispensing one's duties—for example, being objective when evaluating performance. It also means making business decisions that are based on business criteria and not showing favoritism toward certain individuals (e.g., some people have a better chance of getting an assignment versus others based on criteria unrelated to broader business considerations—the manager just likes certain people); giving due credit to employees for their ideas and work versus portraying others' work as one's own; and objectively holding one accountable versus falsely and harshly accusing and blaming.

Thus, the untrustworthy manager, for example, is unreliable, fails to keep his or her promises, betrays confidences, keeps information close to the vest, is never there when needed, and treats others' ideas as his or her own. It is frightening to think that there are some managers who are really like this. Chief executive officers should likewise be alarmed.

Most companies assume that such managers are rare and their effects localized to their specific relations with their employees. Thankfully, it has been my experience that managers are, by and large, trustworthy; however, it is incorrect to believe that the acts of untrustworthy managers remain isolated incidents. The organization itself is blamed by employees for failing to intercede in the employees' behalf when there have been clear violations of trust.

Employees view themselves as belonging to an organization that has a set of rules and expectations. In anthropological terms, there is a perceived network of "kin." If a manager breaches the trust of an employee by, for instance, claiming ownership of an idea widely known to belong to another employee and is not sanctioned by the larger community, it is the organization that is held accountable. By failing to redress an obvious violation of trust, employees often feel that the organization itself cannot be trusted. In effect, employees perceive the broader community as tolerating acts that contradict normative expectations. Vicariously, the distrust is experienced by many employees. When employees say, "I don't trust this company," they are often unable to supply their own personal reasons of why; instead, they cite others' experiences of trust violations that have gone unchecked. This is yet another reason why good management is central to the vitality of an organization: Each manager's effects on the organization are widespread and not confined to their own corner of the world.

Trust, as dependability, is the underlying basis for many successful social encounters. Organizational exchanges are successful because we expect the people with whom we are dealing to be honest, fair, open, discreet, and so on. This form of trust, though, does not eliminate the risks of trusting, because it is conditional. I refer to this form of trust as the appliance-conception of trust: The car will start as long as it doesn't get too cold; the toaster will work as long as its slots are not jammed full; managers are dependable as long as everybody is making money. There may be slippage in trust if the circumstances change.

You can expect to see trust as long as certain conditions are met. However, what if a product line fails, sales are down, your company is acquired, a business is reengineered, new automations are introduced, and discussions of outsourcing proliferate? Also, what if an employee's interests change: They want to relocate to another office, they want to move to another function? How much support can they rely upon now? Can they still predict what management will do or are all bets off? Trustworthiness is an attribute of a person that suggests, but does not guarantee, that trust will prevail in the relationship.

Relationships do not have to change when contingencies do. For example, a regional supermarket had introduced new automation into the meat-cutting function, which would potentially displace many of its employees. The CEO, through a video, assured workers that no one would lose their jobs: Job retraining would be provided for anyone who wanted it. Admittedly, this company had the luxury of growing and, therefore, was creating new jobs for people to fill. Nevertheless, what the employees saw was a company that provided unwavering allegiance to them. They felt a trusting bond that moved beyond mere dependability. Conditions weren't as agreeable at Apache Corp., an oil and gas concern, whose values of integrity and investing in people were tested by a decline in oil prices. The company continued its training programs and avoided layoffs as signs of its continuing commitment to employees.[9] Similarly, R. Arthur Gentry, president of Excel Computer Store in Excelsior, Maryland, says, "My employees give one hundred ten percent because they know in low times I'm going to stick by them."[10] It is this constancy of behavior that can elevate the relationship to a new level. It gives rise to a type of trust most employees would relish.

There are many occasions, or moments of truth, when companies have the opportunity to reveal themselves. A manager recently hired a new employee who was to begin work the next Monday. As it happens, his mother died and he would be unable to start on the appointed date. The company had a choice: It could say, "No problem, we'll just rearrange your hire date to the following Monday." The other option was that it could acknowledge that it has a policy that grants time off to employees to attend funerals but that his start date (and pay) would commence as planned. (They chose the latter course of action).

Trust as Emotional Reciprocity

Trust as dependability works because everyone subscribes to the same social norms of integrity, fair play, and so on. Indeed, for there to be trust, there has to be a common belief system as the basis of the relationship so that the basic rules of conduct are understood. Trust in close relationships, however, goes far deeper than having a shared value system and a predictable partner. It means knowing that one person will consider the interests of another before he or she acts. Often, that will be the only thing that matters.

When my father died many years ago, his final words to me were, "I trust you." He needed emergency surgery and I briefly described the procedures he would undergo. His response said something profound about the nature and quality of our relationship. When he said, "I trust you," he was not just commenting on my good nature or sense of fairness or eliciting fond memories of common values. At his most vulnerable time, he knew *his interests* were the only ones that mattered *to me*. Furthermore, he knew that I would conscientiously act in accordance with those interests, pursuing them on their own terms.

I did not pause to ask my father, "What will you give me in return?" Nor was he concerned about my dependability in time of need. The primary form of exchange was emotional. No one was counting or measuring what was being exchanged or how often. This variety of trust involves an inexact reciprocity in which the needs and interests of one another are mutually considered over time. The relationship is sustained through reciprocal feelings of good will, which only appear to be in disequilibrium at the extremes: when interests and needs are seldom or always satisfied.

It is hard in organizations to develop the same depth of trust in their relationships with employees; no one would fault managers if they didn't—unlike married couples or families. There are, however, degrees to which others' interests can be entertained. A manager or a company that never does what is in its employees' interests would be considered by employees to be acting in bad faith—not to be trusted. It would be difficult to develop trusting relations if the only acceptable course of action is what is in the company's benefit, in general, and to the manager's benefit, in particular. As you can imagine, it would be difficult to trust someone who *never* looks at the world from your point of view or who demonstrates a complete lack of regard of your interests. A recent *Wall Street Journal* column tells the story of an employee who was forced to fly to a distant city, even though his wife was pregnant and overdue. During his trip, his wife required an emergency cesarean section. The employee never forgave his employer, left the company, and he and his wife remain so distressed by the experience that it is difficult to discuss to this day.[11]

Strong leadership is helpful (to say the least) in shaping the interests of employees to be more aligned with the interests of the company. A good leader is able to get employees excited about the mission of the company and he or she can instill a passion for the work at hand. To the extent that the corporation develops communal interests among employees, individual interests become much easier to satisfy. That is, a strong leader can take a band of employees with disparate interests and unify them behind singular goals.

Nevertheless, employees will always have unique needs. The extent to which they are attended to gives rise to interpretations of trust: "As an employee, I'm confident that my interests will be taken into account in my relationship with my employer." With this form of trust, motives are important. Nothing will be gained with regard to trust if I appear to do something for you that in fact enriches me. In its basest form, "consultative selling" may be viewed in this light. At times, the real motive is to disarm the buyer so that the seller can get what he or she wants, not what the buyer wants. The concern is disingenuous because, at its root, the relationship is utilitarian: I feign to consider your interests only because that will help me get what I want.

Some things that companies do for employees are utilitarian acts. These are thoughtful gestures but knowingly self-serving. Gratis dinners after 7:00 P.M., free sodas, dry cleaning pickup and drop-off (and other concierge services), car repair, and bring-your-dog-to-work days are conveniences for employees that are designed to help them work longer hours. Indeed, there seems to be no end to corporate ingenuity when it comes to these little luxuries. Everything is done for employees and they don't even have to leave their offices.

Don't get me wrong, employees say they appreciate these items; they would rather have them than not. However, providing these items does not arouse feelings of trust nor does it generate long-lived feelings of satisfaction; no employee has ever told me he or she stayed with the company because of the free coffee. These conveniences are perceived as tit-for-tat exchanges of time for small pleasures. It's just another business transaction.

There are three general conditions that lead employees to ascribe positive motives to employers, which serve to heighten feelings of trust:

1. Employer actions are in response to a special circumstance or need; programmic actions that apply to everyone do not elicit feelings of trust, even though these programs may be perceived as good for employees. For example, telecommuting for everyone may be great, but allowing a specific employee to temporarily telecommute, for example, because of a special family circumstance or personal injury that makes travel difficult, instills trust.

    It is instructive to note, however, that the reverse unfortunately does not appear to be true. Programmatic actions with adverse consequences to employees (or certain populations of employees) may create a sense of betrayal. For example, when IBM and other companies announced that they would replace their traditional defined benefit retirement plans with cash balance plans that would lower retirement payouts for older workers by as much as 50 percent, employees cried "foul."[12]

2. The employer does not have to grant or provide the benefit: It is not mandated by law or done out of a matter of policy. That is, the actions are perceived as voluntary. The one exception I've seen is managers who coach employees to use laws and policies to their advantage (e.g., show employees how to take full advantage of a disability program). Thus, what is eventually done had to be done, but the company was helpful in getting the employee there in the first place.

3. There is no immediate and obvious return for the company's actions; indeed, sometimes the company incurs a cost or exposes itself to loss. That is, the company accepts a measure of risk. On the other hand, the company that refuses to take risks with employees often puts itself at a disadvantage as illustrated in the following story. An employee who works for a multidivision company learned that his division wanted to keep a cross-division promotional opportunity secret from him because they didn't want to lose him. A flattering thought but a poor gesture. They probably have a greater chance of losing him now than before—this time to another company! The employee informed me that his trust in the organization went down a notch following this experience.

I believe there are four areas of concern that, if positively addressed, boost employees' sense of trust in the employer, again, particularly if personalized in some fashion. These are growth, work-personal integration, individual accommodation, and health and safety.

1. *Growth.* Most people have a fundamental desire to get better— to become more proficient in their vocation or discipline. The individual attention and investment that a company dedicates to an employee's development is a good way to instill trust. The

amount of training and education that a company makes available and encourages employees to use is one measure of the company's commitment to employee growth. A willingness to properly deploy employees to engage their interest and stretch their capabilities is another. Proper deployment doesn't necessarily mean an upward promotion, but it does mean fitting what a specific employee can do to the responsibilities of a role or a position. Moving employees around sometimes results in short-term inefficiencies as the organization adapts to the reassignments; however, again, organizations that are willing to make short-term sacrifices so that employees have a chance to use and develop their skills tend to build trust and commitment.

Psychologists refer to this relationship strategy as maximizing joint outcomes: Couples act in ways that yield the highest collective returns for themselves, even though either person may generate greater benefits for him- or herself through more self-serving actions. Companies that do what is beneficial to both parties, versus maximizing its own outcomes, will create a greater and deeper sense of trust among employees.

Some companies offer concentrated growth and learning experiences through paid sabbaticals: time off to pursue further training and study in a specific area. Although many in the academic community have argued that these programs are instrumental in creating a sense of reciprocity and commitment,[13] not many companies have embraced them primarily because of the cost and lost productivity of key workers. Employees, too, worry about taking them—even when sanctioned—believing that they can sidetrack careers. Companies clearly see the importance in building employee capabilities, but they also realize the immediate productivity implications of taking someone off-line. A fundamental part of developing trust is learning how to balance interests that are sometimes in conflict.

2. *Work-personal integration.* By most accounts, the workweek is getting longer for most Americans. Most people feel pressed for

time and zapped of energy. One thing that employees wish companies would allow is greater personal time when needed. Indeed, a good number of employees say that what they want most is time — and they are even willing to trade money to get it. This typically involves scheduling flexibility and special work arrangements, such as job sharing, working from home, and devising special part-time schedules. Successfully blending work and personal times also implies abstaining from recurring intrusions into personal time by forcing overtime without sufficient prior notice, requiring work on weekends without relief, and so on — hours that make it difficult to coordinate activities with friends and family and to live a balanced life. Work-personal integration is also related to stress and job satisfaction, issues that we take up in Chapter 6.

The central issue for trust, again, is taking the time to discern or listen to an employee's special need and trying one's best to accommodate it — not merely making programs available. For example, I have seen companies create special schedules for parents with sick children and for employees who perform community services. These companies actively worked with employees to solve their problems versus asking them to deplete their annual resources such as vacation time. A major study by The Families and Work Institute found that such employer support was related to higher employee commitment.[14]

3. *Individual accommodation.* Personal accommodation can take a variety of forms. For example, this may entail allowing a pregnant employee to perform light work.[15] I also have seen companies pay the college tuition of a deceased employee's son, pay for home care and equipment for an employee's newborn triplets (so they could go home from the hospital sooner), and pay all medical expenses related to an employee's breast cancer. There are countless stories of corporate benevolence toward employees. These acts were not advertised nor was anything expected in return. These companies thought it was the right thing to do. Employees don't forget, either.

4. *Health and safety.* It would be hard to trust someone if they placed little value on your health and safety and, indeed, asked you to engage in hazardous activities without first minimizing the dangers. Additionally, companies that neglect worker complaints or fire or discipline employees who report injuries can't be trusted.

Companies that make a concerted effort to guard employees' health and safety are more likely to be trusted than those who consider safety precautions unnecessary expenses. Demonstration of trust-evoking behaviors may involve providing the proper equipment, clothing, and related items to each employee, given the unique demands of the job; assuring that instruction is duly given on health and safety procedures; and working with employees to redesign jobs for safer execution. For example, Sequins International has been installing new equipment and furniture to prevent musculoskeletal injuries, and Perdue Farms and textile manufacturer Fieldcrest Cannon—tough employment settings—have been praised by the Labor Department for their health and safety practices.[16]

There are some things that a company will be able to do and some things it will not. Every need cannot be satisfied in every relationship; in many respects, that would be as unhealthy as complete inattention to those needs. The key to trust is that one not lose sight of another's interests, not that every need be met.

If you think about a close relationship in which you trusted one another in this way—where you knew that your interests mattered— you would feel secure in that relationship, which is an important by-product of trust. One of the great myths of contemporary business, however, is that this is a bad thing. Security somehow is believed to drain the life force from employees and to make them comfortable and stupid. Security is associated with complacency and an aversion to risk.

The kind of security that I am talking about is one in which employees are confident in the benevolence of their employer, who is ready to respond when called upon. Self-reliance, innovation, and experimentation require interpersonal trust and a firm sense of security—a reservoir of goodwill is necessary for risk. People feel the most daring when they feel secure. The employer is like a military base that sends out expeditionary forces who can retreat to the base if necessary. It is because the commanding officer of the expeditionary force is confident that his home base is secure that he or she dare press forward.[17]

The ultimate I have seen in stagnation and unhappiness came in a sales organization known for its "drive-by shootings" in which unsuspecting employees were unsystematically eliminated. Because there was no clear pattern to the "killings" (performance, challenge to authority, and being a suspected troublemaker all qualified as potential reasons), the employees were immobilized. Creativity and risk were furthest from their minds. Employees stealthily attempted to leave the organization, always fearful of discovery. Employees rightly perceived that the company had no personal interest in them.

Breaking the Trust: Layoffs

Many companies I speak with believe it is impossible to have trust and commitment in organizations today because lifelong work can never be guaranteed. Indeed, given the 400,000 to 700,000 layoffs in each year since 1991, there appears to be some truth in this. Many of these employers regard themselves as "employment-at-will" companies in which permanent employment is not a given. Employment-at-will employers can fire employees at any time *for any reason* under at-will provisions, unless one of the following conditions applies: employment is subject to written or implied contracts (including union contracts), employees belong to a protected class and discharge may entail discrimination, or employees live and work in Montana where employment-at-will does not have legal status.[18] The point is this: Most Americans do not work under contract and even if we did, there is no guarantee that commitment between employer and employee would be any better. There are never guarantees in any relationship. Often, both parties simply have a common understanding that the relationship will endure indefinitely and that each will try their hardest to preserve it.

Through layoffs, companies often have to overcome prior assertions ("We are a family," "Our people are our most important asset," "Our competitive advantage depends on our people") and false communications ("The company is having a banner year," "There is no intention of selling the company," "There is no plan for layoffs"). Indeed, company communications and annual reports tout the dedication and commitment of the workforce while simultaneously eliminating massive amounts of jobs and people.[19] As Robert Reich aptly observed, it is not so much the layoffs themselves that undermine trust; it is everything that surrounds the layoffs and the way they are conducted that matters.

> *The real question is how downsizing is done rather than whether to downsize. Companies that downsize through buyouts and attrition, that help their workers get new jobs, and that sometimes provide outplacement services, end up much better positioned than companies that simply wield the ax. The first group of companies has a better chance of retaining the loyalty of the surviving workers. Trust is one of the most valuable yet brittle assets in any enterprise. I talk to many employees who no longer trust that management cares about them or feels any loyalty toward them. They say to me, "How can management expect us to go the extra mile when there's no reciprocal loyalty?"[20]*

Every organization has crises, and sometimes, some organizations must reduce their workforce, hopefully with no pretense that this constitutes a strategy that will have a positive impact on earnings. Studies have found that it doesn't—companies that downsize also have lower morale and a higher incidence of disability claims and wrongful termination suits.[21] The way the company and the managers face these crises will say quite a bit about the kind of company it is and the decision makers within it.

Layoffs are not easy, because everyone knows that many of those who are let go will find it difficult even if they quickly secure new jobs. Often, the new jobs are for less responsibility and less money. Some employees encounter marital and financial difficulties and have bouts of depression and substance abuse. By and large, however, people are resilient and adaptive. Those directly affected by downsizing, as well as the surviving employees, have a better chance of withstanding the adverse effects of layoffs if conducted humanely. I have seen layoffs that were carried out very poorly. Employees resembled parolees: They were herded up, handed their personal possessions, and ushered out the door by an agent of the organization whom they never met. You can imagine the confusion and isolation of these employees as they heard the corporate doors swing shut behind them after many years of service.

Consider what you would want to happen if, as an employee or spouse, your relationship was on the ropes.

- *You'd want to know that there is a problem.* Withholding relevant information that would profoundly affect you is dishonest. (It's at least a questionable practice; admittedly, the ethics surrounding layoffs are complicated.)[22] In addition, it's offensive. It denotes that you may be unworthy of the trust or unable to cope with it. Also, it may suggest that others want to see you (or the relationship) fail since giving you vital information would give you a chance to save it. Alternatively, letting you know something is wrong in advance just may make life uncomfortable for others who have made up their minds that the relationship will be dissolved.

  In some instances, workers must be notified ahead of time. The Worker Adjustment and Retraining Notification Act (WARN) requires (among other things) that employers give employees 60 days' notice of a reduction in force for "mass layoff" or "plant closure." The rules pertain to all forms of businesses, public and nonprofit, who maintain staffs of 100 or more full-time employees or 100 or more full- and part-time employees who, in the aggregate, work at least 4,000 hours per week, not including overtime.

- *You'd want to be part of the solution.* You would want to do what you could to make things right and not be labeled as part of the problem. For a company, this may be a massive cost-cutting campaign in which everyone participates. I have seen companies turn these campaigns into games that unite people—that pull them closer together. People like to have some control over events in their lives; if they are going to go down, they prefer to go down fighting.

Several years ago, I consulted to a division of a huge diversified financial services company that was widely rumored would be closed down. After about a year had passed, it eventually was. In the meantime, employees spent hours drinking coffee and shopping in a nearby mall, which clearly hastened the fall of the division. The employees I spoke with felt helpless and resigned—they had given up, unaware of what they could do to help turn the division around.

○ *You'd want to know that all possible actions to stem a problem have been taken.* You would want to take all prudent steps to contain the problem and resolve it, if possible. These steps may include hiring and salary freezes, across-the-board reductions in pay and benefits, unpaid time off and shortened workweeks, job sharing and job loaning (i.e., temporarily sending employees to a supplier or customer), eliminating overtime, and asking for voluntary separations (e.g., through early retirement). For example, Hewlett-Packard's managers recently took a temporary pay cut to save jobs.[23]

○ *You'd want to know that there are no hidden agendas.* What is a problem for some might be a blessing to others. It is possible to reap benefits with others' misfortune. When I lose my job and income, will you get a bonus for having cut costs and increased profits? There has been the occasional high-profile case in which layoffs and executive bonuses have been announced around the same time. During retrenchment, it is important to know that everyone's intentions and values are aligned—that people want, and are working toward, the same ends.

○ *You'd want candor throughout the process.* It is tempting to justify a painful experience not only as necessary but as just. The common metaphor is: "We had to clean house," which suggests that one is ridding themselves of dirt or vermin. It is a good way to alleviate guilt but a poor way to send off friends and colleagues of survivors. This becomes all the more problematic when workers who have been laid off are rehired.

○ *You'd want your own and others' dignity preserved.* There are no pleasantries in layoffs, but they are sometimes far uglier than they have to be. They are unceremonious and abrupt, unlike other life events that involve rites of passage: marriage, divorce, birth, woman- or manhood, death, graduation, and such. We create rituals around changes of states so that we can celebrate, mourn, renew, rejoice, honor, and more than anything, adjust. Yet, employees are often expelled before coworkers ever realize it because one version of wisdom is to lay off workers on Friday afternoon or the day before a holiday. Instead, the company may want to reserve some time to thank people who have worked hard in the company's behalf.

○ *You'd want to know about the future.* There is a search for meaning following most crises and frequently the need to change behavior. Employers should be prepared to paint a vivid picture of the future and the direction in which the company is heading. It should also carefully reexamine the way work will be done with fewer people and make changes accordingly. In essence, there must be a reconstruction plan that is understood by the workforce.

○ *You'd want everything possible to be done to soften the impact of layoffs on those who are most affected.* Simply helping to spruce up the resume and providing a telephone is inadequate and qualifies as "progressive waste management."[24] Surviving workers want to be assured that a reasonable safety net exists for those who have been (and may be) let go. This may include severance (one or two weeks of salary per year of service is typical, three weeks of salary per year of service would be considered generous); outreach to agencies that may provide assistance (e.g., training centers); subsidies to help workers make a transition into the not-for-profit world; continuation of benefits for a specified period of time; and so on. Levi Strauss, for example, provided laid-off workers with three weeks' severance for each year of service, extended medical coverage, enhanced early-retirement benefits, and a maximum of $6,000 per person for training and education expenses—they correctly perceived that goodwill can be extended to others, even when the relationship is ending.[25]

In late 1995, textile producer Malden Mills burned down. Owner Aaron Feurstein kept his 1,000 employees on the payroll while the factory was rebuilt. It cost him $15 million to do that. Contrast this with a restaurant chain that lays off workers, without pay, for two to four weeks while restaurants are refurbished. Seriously, for whom would you rather work? The turnover rate at Malden Mills is about 5 percent, and, over a 14-year span, revenues tripled (in constant dollars) and the workforce doubled.[26] The restaurant chain experiences from 200 to 300 percent turnover.

The generosity displayed at Malden Mills is not an isolated industrial incident. When a fire gutted one of Worthington Industries' metal-pickling plants, the company offered jobs in other locations to every employee affected.[27] When sales of a product line slip, rather than lay off employees, Hallmark Cards reassigns them to another unit or allows them to perform community services at full pay. How can this not produce goodwill? Indeed, employees lucky enough to work at Hallmark rarely leave.[28]

Barriers to Trust

There are certain features of the relationship that may make it more difficult for trust to develop and thrive. Following is a discussion of each.

Depth of Trust

Some relationships are more fragile than others because they lack many of the essential ingredients we have already discussed or are relatively new and unproven. The more passionately you trust another, the more resilient the relationship: If you trust someone, you are more likely to make benign interpretations of transgressions (e.g., "The manager didn't assign me to this project but I'm sure she [or he] has her [or his] reasons") versus thinking the worst. There is a broader interpretive frame of reference that enables people to see others' faults and foibles in the context of what is good and positive about the relationship: You evaluate what you don't like in the context of what you do like.

Additionally, when trust is violated, two things are more likely to occur the closer the relationship. First, the transgressor is more likely to apologize. Second, the victim is more likely to empathize with the transgressor and forgive. In a sense, building trust is iterative or episodic: With repeated experiences that another, in fact, will consider your interests, and vice versa, the relationship continuously renews itself and becomes increasingly resistant to isolated incidents in which either party is disappointed by the other.

As relationships develop, so will expectations. Repeated or severe violations of trust will elicit more vehement responses—the higher the top, the longer the drop. For this reason, some companies I have worked with over the years hesitate to develop deeper relations with employees fearing that the company will not be able to keep their part of the bargain and elicit harsh reactions: Companies that adopt this anti-Shakespearian position (i.e., 'tis better to have never loved at all) should realize also that they will reap what they sow. First, these relationships are extraordinarily easy to sever. Second, these relationships are extraordinarily difficult to repair because there is no goodwill or affective foundation for mending them. To edit Justice Oliver Wendell Holmes' famous remark, people will be more inclined to feel kicked versus stumbled over.

Power Differences

There is a clear power differential between managers and employees. Most notably, managers have control over employees' pay, career opportunities, and the nature of their work (e.g., assignments). Social scientists refer to this as a *punitive capability*. This power imbalance often makes it difficult to develop trust. Indeed, there tends to be less information exchange, greater conflict avoidance, and lower levels of cooperation and trust when one party clearly has the upper hand. Often, employees are fearful that their interests will be arbitrarily thwarted or dismissed and, therefore, plot a more secretive course. Given the unilateral nature of the relationship and employees' susceptibility to executive whim, they are reluctant to openly express their ideas and needs.

Managers who do not use their authority irrationally or to threaten and punish (i.e., who have the power but exercise restraint) are more likely to develop cooperative and trusting relationships with employees because they will create a more open and inviting atmosphere. The managers who are able to instill trust are those who are able to relate to employees as if the playing field were level and who do not resort solely and arbitrarily to the authority of their positions to force cooperation.

Corporate Culture

Companies have personas that they create through their actions. Companies that are willing to cheat or mislead customers, for example, may find it just as easy to be dishonest toward employees. Employees I have spoken with think so. Indeed, employees seem to be suspicious of employers who seem willing to engage in dishonest practices. As one employee said, "If you're going to be deceitful with the people who are giving you money, think what they'll do to the people who are costing them money." Thus, purposely filling customer orders with cheaper products, watering down fruit juices, falsely fortifying cars for crash tests, and using illegal means to collect on credit card debts have potential effects beyond customer reactions; it may have a systemic effect on employees' trust in the company as well.

Structure

If you were an anthropologist studying your company as you study other civilizations, what evidence would there be about the existence of trust in your "society?" Without asking, could you tell if the inhabitants trust one another or not? One area to explore would be whether managers and employees protect themselves against their vulnerabilities. That is, the extent to which either side is willing or reluctant to take risks in their relationship may be seen as an indicator of the amount of trust that is present. People who don't trust one another want assurances that expectations will not be thwarted. The greater the distrust, the more vigilance and safeguards required. In turn, the more vigilance and safeguards, the greater the distrust, and so on in a deescalating cycle.

The more signs of distrust in the workplace, the harder it will be to build trust because the messages being sent are *Trust at your own peril.* Often, employees try to protect themselves and their interests by forming unions, for example, in which the things upon which they are dependent (such as pay and promotions) have solutions that are collectively bargained versus left to the benevolence (or malevolence) of others. Also, employees may avoid putting forth extra time and effort that they believe will go unappreciated and unreciprocated. Fearful that a company will attempt to exploit them, they try to minimize their exposure.

Employers may closely observe employees, carefully and regularly noting their performance and whereabouts. There may be elaborate sign-in and sign-out procedures and a gauntlet of permissions for exceptions, days off, and so on. Each party is afraid of being taken advantage of by the other and each takes precautions against it. The relationship itself becomes heavily contractual and regulated—most behaviors have an if-then quality: If you do x, I will do y, with each side understanding the consequences of noncompliance. If two people do not trust one another but still have to associate, something external to the relationship (e.g., written agreements) is necessary to choreograph their behaviors—thus, relationships in which there is little trust tend to resort to a plethora of agreements and counteragreements. In essence, trust and opportunities for expressions of trust are driven out: The most salient and unflattering reason to do a good turn is because one must.

This is not to suggest that contracts (or formal agreements) ought never to be used; there may be an appropriate time and place for them. Furthermore, this doesn't suggest that the use of contracts or formal agreements necessarily undermines trust. In fact, contracts that are drafted appropriately will help to preserve trust. Relational uncertainties cause the use of contracts, but the use of contracts will not necessarily undo trust.

Successful companies are able to build structures that facilitate trust in the corporate system—that suggest to employees that their faith in the company, as well as in one another, is well placed. This may involve putting employees in situations that require their trust and that enable the organization to demonstrate that it is up to the task. Newcomers to the Minnesota Mycological Society (mushroom afficionados), for example, are treated to a feast that includes mushrooms gathered by members.[29] The neophytes are hopeful that their senior brethren can discern eatable from uneatable varieties. After surviving the feast, newcomers progressively learn of the rigorous training and instruction that ensures the competence of all members. The supreme lesson is not simply that one should trust in the expertise of one's fellow man; it is to believe in a system that permits the expression of trust—a system that assures members that their vulnerabilities will not be exploited or end in ruin.

The Completeness and Duration of Trust

Often, trust is discussed as if it were a switch that has an on (complete trust) or off (complete distrust) position. This is seldom the case—one need not trust wholly or distrust wholly. Trust doesn't require that one put one's guard down entirely or suspend common sense. It doesn't have to be a binary decision. Indeed, people who trust others completely (regardless of the circumstances, the depth of their relationships, etc.) are often considered foolish—or if that blind trust is abused by others, suckers. There are gullible people who unjustifiably trust and paranoid people who do not trust at all.

To illustrate the continuum of trust, consider a self-service bookstore. Typically, customers are invited to take the books they want and to deposit the proper amount of money into a container. The container is nailed to a table and has a slit on the top that is large enough for the money but too small for a hand. It is an honor system with certain built-in protections—demonstrating how trust and distrust can coexist.

Customers would undoubtedly think that the special precautions were reasonable. Besides, the customers would not think that the precautions were aimed at *them*; rather, they would think that they were intended for those who are not as honest. Customers most likely relish the convenience and the faith that the proprietors have in people. Conceivably, customers could take the books and not pay anything at all. The owner assumed some risk. However, he or she also assumed, one would think, that a given loss would be restricted to what a person could carry or read within a short period of time and that the evident exposure would reinforce the very norms that he or she hoped would prevail—that by trusting others to act in an honorable way, they would.

Employees expect to trust the people with whom they work, and the organizations in which they work, because they expect trust in any social relationship of quality and substance. Furthermore, feelings about trust can be both passionate and enduring. The American Airlines pilot "sick out" of a year ago cost the carrier many millions of dollars (the specific number was disputed by the Airline and the pilots' union). Many observers traced the dispute back to lean years when many pilots had made wage and benefit concessions or were forced through reorganizations to start over at the bottom of the career ladder for a new airline.[30] The expectation was that someday when times were better, the Airline would reciprocate with sacrifices of its own. When, in the pilots' eyes, the airline did not, the pilots responded. To be sure, the strife was about economics, but the emotional intensity of the reaction indicated that it also was about much more. Issues regarding trust and distrust, sacrifice and betrayal, can last a very long time.

6

HEART AND SOUL

Finding Satisfaction at Work

Over the years, I have asked employees to rate the attractiveness of a variety of hypothetical organizations that contain different characteristics. Inevitably, I find corporate attributes that make the workplace more emotionally appealing lead to higher ratings of satisfaction. In turn, employees say they will exert more effort on behalf of those companies and stay longer. In a nutshell, there has to be an emotional connection between the employer and the employee to achieve the highest levels of commitment.

The place of passion in commitment is so central that it is easy to mistake it for all of what it means to be committed. It gives the relationship its closeness, excitement, and durability. People who are deeply connected to one another are happy in their relationship.

Furthermore, happiness tends to beget happiness. First, relationships that are emotionally satisfying have a built-in protective element. They are resilient because people who are emotionally close make favorable interpretations of ambiguous events—inferring the good intentions of others. There could be no continuity to close relationships if each party constantly challenged one another's motives. Second, satisfying relationships reduce the likelihood that a person will explore alternative relationships. Somewhere in the world there is a better friend, mate, or company, but you don't go on an endless search. Most people use decision strategies that yield outcomes that are the best among the acceptable options. That is, if you get what you want, you stop looking. Otherwise, the investment costs of time and money associated with endless searches would be extraordinarily high and you would never be truly happy. Third, people who are happy are adaptive. They are able to take flexible actions that keep the relationship moving in the right direction over the long haul—and to quickly correct course if necessary. Emotional bonds make this easier because you are apt to view the relationship from multiple perspectives. Conversely, it is very difficult to carry on a lengthy, mutually rewarding relationship with two selfish partners involved—each with his or her own unique point of view and response set. This would severely limit behaviors that are constructive (such as taking the time to discover what the other person wants) and that are effective in managing conflict (such as compromise and cooperation).

Most people are aware of what makes a relationship satisfying. There are satisfiers particular to the relationship itself and a surrounding set of conditions, such as family, friends, and work, that are instrumental to relationship satisfaction. Thus, whereas a relationship may be more or less satisfying on its own terms, the total satisfaction that one feels is inseparable from the social context of the relationship. The relationship doesn't exist apart from the people and events that surround it. One of the most important tasks of a relationship that hopes to be successful is to figure out how to make the best of one's circumstances: how to live happily together given extrarelationship demands and constraints that may be placed on the relationship.

Said differently, marital (or other relationship) satisfaction is a particular species of life satisfaction. Other domains of one's life affect the quality of the relationship, and vice versa. Most people have experienced this indivisiveness of life. In addition to all of the intrinsic factors that make a relationship pleasurable (e.g., mutual caring), partners must integrate with their environs and eliminate or temper outside threats (e.g., dissatisfaction with one's job, economic hardship, an intrusive in-law, odd friends).

Employees' work lives are much the same. There are certain features of the job that contribute to an employee's satisfaction. However, there are extrajob influences as well. A job—and one's relationship with his or her boss—is practiced within a broader social context. A person may have a perfectly enjoyable job but have too many distractions outside of the job (e.g., elderly parents) to be fully satisfied at work. Similarly, a person may be too fully consumed by his or her job to find pleasure in it: being prevented from enjoying a richer, more fulfilling life. Therefore, to have emotionally rewarding experiences at work, or work satisfaction, two ingredients are necessary: a good job and a situational context in which it can be enjoyed. Each of these is discussed in the ensuing sections as *job satisfaction* and *work-life satisfaction*.

Job Satisfaction

More has been written on job satisfaction than any other organizational topic with the exception of leadership. Its place in the literature is well deserved. How happy we are on the job has profound effects on the quality of our lives and behavior, including commitment.

Employees who enjoy their jobs work harder and stay longer with their employers than employees who don't. Whereas greater effort often yields more and better results, the link between job satisfaction and performance isn't altogether clear.[1] First, other factors are involved in the satisfaction-performance association. That is, satisfaction only leads to greater productivity under certain conditions. We can speculate on what those might be: having personal goals, talents, appropriate reward contingencies, and organizational supports such as adequate resources.

Second, there are organizational actions or interventions that are intended to elevate either productivity or job satisfaction levels but that have the unintended consequences of deflating the other. For instance, process-oriented areas of companies (e.g., claims processors and telemarketers) often have production quotas or their equivalent (e.g., take a certain number of phone calls per day) and introduce corresponding incentives to reinforce activities that support production. These corporate actions often diminish the more satisfying elements of the job by routinizing the work and by demanding a level of production that cannot be sustained over longer periods of time without placing significant mental and physical strains on the employee. The job becomes less and less satisfying, and short-term productivity gains may be lost in the long run.

On the other hand, common practices of making jobs more satisfying by expanding their scope (job enlargement) or adding new, desirable features (job enrichment) often result in short-term losses in productivity. It takes time to learn and adapt to new duties with near-term deficits in performance. Interventions, then, designed to improve either productivity or job satisfaction can sometimes undermine the other.

Third, conceptions of job satisfaction often are incomplete or overly narrow, making the satisfaction-performance relationship less pronounced. The common approach to job satisfaction is to construe a job as having a set of component attributes or features that, if present to a sufficient degree, will be gratifying to employees. Indeed, this is one aspect of job satisfaction, but that isn't all there is to it. I think of the formation of job satisfaction as analogous to the development of a sound social partnership.[2] For the relationship to be emotionally rewarding, it has to confer certain benefits. First, it has to be satisfying based on the things that individuals want and need. Second, it has to evolve and grow: to remain as, or to become more, satisfying by staving off habituation (e.g., losing interest in one another by doing the same old stuff over and over) and, in the case of close relationships, by becoming increasingly privileged in one another's life's (e.g., by providing special access to personal thoughts and experiences). Third, it has to facilitate or enhance each other's social effectiveness. You might be funny, which I like. However, does being with you make me funny—which I want to be and think I am? The same person can be interesting or boring, funny or humorless, lively or inert, depending on whom one is with.

A satisfying job has the same three properties:

1. It has intrinsically enjoyable features.

2. It provides an opportunity for growth and development.

3. It makes employees feel effective in the execution of their duties.

I refer to these, respectively, as inward, upward, and outward satisfaction. These are graphically depicted in Figure 6.1 and summarized hereafter. Fuller descriptions are presented subsequently.

○ *Inward satisfaction.* Satisfaction derived from the intrinsic features of the job.

○ *Upward satisfaction.* Satisfaction derived from technical and intellectual growth experiences and with progress in one's career.

○ *Outward satisfaction.* Satisfaction derived from employees' belief that they can positively influence organizational outcomes.

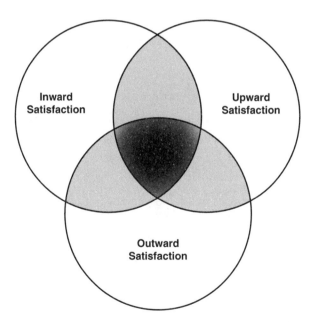

Figure 6.1 Varieties of job satisfaction. *Note:* The more elements that are present in a job, the more satisfying the job is, as represented by deeper shades of gray.

Inward Job Satisfaction—Intrinsic Satisfiers

This is the customary view of job satisfaction—satisfiers driven by the nature of the work that is performed. A satisfying job typically has the following components:

- ○ *Clarity—employees know what to do.* Employees' jobs are well defined and their specific roles in the organization are clear and purposeful—they know what has to be done and understand its importance.

- ○ *Interest—employees find the work to be energizing and fun.* Employees' jobs are stimulating and involving because they are consistent with their interests; because of the variety of tasks that must be combined and acted upon (versus repetitive work); and because the work is challenging (relatively complex, involving novel situations, and/or expected to meet rigorous and/or precise standards of excellence that require employees to be proactive problem solvers).

- ○ *Discretion—employees have some discretion in how the job is performed.* Employees can make decisions commensurate with their experience—they have authority to act without undue constraints and controls; also, they can openly express ideas and opinions that others will seriously entertain.

- ○ *Feedback—employees are appreciated for the work they do.* There is timely acknowledgment and recognition of the effort put forth and of the results obtained—a note of thanks appropriately given.

These job attributes are made possible by managers who are able to provide more or less of each. Thus, the quality of relations with managers affects employees' job satisfaction as well. Managerial features that employees judge particularly highly in this regard are decisiveness, openness to new ideas and experiences, and good two-way communication. These are traits that enable managers to provide definition and direction in the workplace but to act flexibly within those overall aims. They also form a basis for understanding and reacting to what employees want and need.

The degree to which desirable job qualities are available to employees partially is dictated by the nature of the job. Whether these qualities are perceived positively or negatively by employees depends on the person in the job. Clearly, more of each job feature is not necessarily better. First, the job itself will impose its own natural constraints based on the work to be done (e.g., an auditor will not have unlimited discretion). Second, even within the normative range of these attributes for a given job, it is possible for there to be too much challenge, for example, given an employee's current capabilities. On the other hand, too little of these qualities may yield confusion, boredom, and, ultimately, dissatisfaction. The challenge for organizations is to optimize the person-job fit through recruitment strategies, job design, and training.

Overall, companies devote much of their attention to the technical or skill requirements of jobs and whether a given employee has the requisite abilities to satisfy them. This is an important exercise but it often obscures the bigger picture: Does the job itself deeply interest the employee? Is the employee engaged in an activity that fundamentally makes him or her happy?

Many times, we don't really know the answers, first, because employees are seldom asked about what truly excites them and, second, because it is assumed that performance is an index of their pleasure. As long as the employee is doing well, we suppose they must be wonderfully happy also. High achievers, however, will perform well whether they like it or not. They just won't do it for very long before seeking out other job opportunities.

For employees to reach the highest levels of job satisfaction, they need to be matched to jobs that allow expression of their passions. This implies taking care during the selection process so that employees who are hired are placed in jobs for which they are psychologically suited. It also implies crafting jobs and structuring developmental progressions to take maximum advantage of employees' natural inclinations. There are eight common business activities that serve as outlets for many employees' basic underlying cognitive and social interests. Satisfied employees in many disciplines will have one to three of these built into their jobs.[3]

1. *Application of technology.* People who are intrigued by the inner workings of things and who are interested in finding better ways to use technology/machines to solve problems.

2. *Counseling and mentoring.* People who like to teach and guide others and who derive satisfaction from observing others' development and success.

3. *Creative production.* People who gravitate to the unknown or unconventional—who enjoy invention (making something out of nothing) and the creative process.

4. *Enterprise control.* People who enjoy being in charge and having decision-making authority—to have control over the course of events.

5. *Influence through language and ideas.* People who love language and the act of communication—of putting thoughts and ideas together and expressing them orally or in writing.

6. *Managing people and relationships.* People who enjoy working with groups that have a clear focus on achieving a definitive end result—they find pleasure orchestrating people to those ends.

7. *Quantitative analysis.* People who use numbers as a method of inquiry and discovery—they find mathematics and statistical analysis to be fun.

8. *Theory development and conceptual thinking.* People who enjoy thoughtful consideration and discussion of theory, abstractions, and models.

It is interesting to note what happens to inward, or intrinsic, job satisfaction with the passage of time. The answer seems to depend on when measures are taken. Parallel findings have been observed for marital satisfaction and they go like this:[4] When a cross section of employees (or marrieds) are assessed (i.e., people who have been with an employer for various service periods are evaluated at the same point in time), a horseshoe pattern emerges with the greatest satisfaction occurring with newcomers (or newlyweds) and longer-service employees (or golden-agers), and the least satisfaction with short- to medium-term employees (or marrieds in child-rearing years). With respect to marital satisfaction, these findings have been attributed to cohort differences (i.e., the reason that long-term marrieds are so happy is that dissatisfied couples have deselected: separated or divorced). I suspect that the same reasoning can be applied to observations of job satisfaction. Longer-term employees are the corporate survivors; the most dissatisfied employees have left. I also suspect that as it becomes more difficult to leave a company (i.e., when employees are older), employees may either try much harder to satisfy themselves or become much more artful in convincing themselves that they are.

When, however, the same group of people are followed over time, the results are different. With respect to marital satisfaction, there is a steady decline during the life span. I would expect similar results for job satisfaction for similar reasons: At the inception of the relationship, the fit between partners or between employees and their jobs is relatively tight, but it progressively loosens over time with personal and environmental changes. Relationships move from as-good-as-they-get to less good. Job duties also may normalize over time and become less interesting. This pattern is true in a collective sense; individual employees may have distinct experiences than run counter to this trend—particularly those employees whose interests and talents are recalibrated to the job through periodic promotions and reassignments. Nevertheless, the probable long-term, downward course of intrinsic job satisfaction for many employees generally urges periodic change and renewal—relationships occasionally need to be refreshed. Otherwise, there is a tendency for them to become disconnected and stale.

Upward Job Satisfaction—Personal Growth

A host of psychological perspectives converge on the common notion that people are preprogrammed to strive and grow. In business settings, the most popular of these theorists has been Maslow, although several others including Adler, Allport, Fromm, and Rogers have posited similar innate tendencies. Consistent with these positions is the belief that people have a natural desire to fulfill their potential. Thus, employees who are given the chance to develop, who are asked to consistently

enhance their base of knowledge and skills, and who are encouraged to
try out new ideas—to learn and to grow—will be most satisfied.

Thus, the advent of learning organizations may be deeply rooted in
one of our most fundamental needs to realize our full capabilities. The
concept of collective learning is predicated on individual initiative and
personal mastery.[5] Put simply, if individuals don't learn, neither will
the company.

For some people, growth means developing in one's vocation or discipline. Employees are attached to their line of work: They are dedicated to it and derive substantial satisfaction from perfecting their craft.
Companies that can help employees in ways that other companies cannot are particularly seductive to employees with high career aspirations. In particular, companies can hold out the following:

- ○ *Collegiality.* Having a cadre of talented, knowledgeable employees who share enthusiasm for a vocation/discipline.

- ○ *Unique opportunities and resources.* Providing access to technologies, customers, materials, and so on, that are unavailable
  elsewhere.

- ○ *Specialized training and expertise.* Expending time and money
  to keep employees current.

- ○ *Support for professional norms and standards.* Conveying strong
  expectations that the norms and standards that pertain to a field
  will be upheld (i.e., shoddy practices will not be tolerated).

Commitment to career often is used to express employees' commitment to their line of work, and despite attempts to draw parallels with
organizational commitment, it is not the same.[6] In fact, *commitment* is
a misnomer in this instance: *dedication* is more accurate—goal-
directed behavior aimed at excelling in one's vocation/discipline.

Career commitment can invoke desires that can be so singular
and consuming to employees that little else matters—the organization is measured largely by its ability to feed professional ambitions.
Some organizations (e.g., academic institutions and law firms) and
disciplines (e.g., medicine and engineering) have employee populations with strong career/professional work ethics. Career is such a

fundamental part of their life's satisfaction that it constitutes a central place in what it means to be satisfied on the job and committed to the company.

In addition to heightening satisfaction, employees have told me that nourishing their career aspirations increases their sense of indebtedness to the company. One of the best things a company can do for an employee who is heavily invested in his or her career is to help him or her get better. It helps in the formation of commitment in two ways: to increase employees' satisfaction and sense of obligation.

It is surprising, then, when I see companies covertly discourage personal improvement in employees for fear the employee will leave them—it presumably is better to keep your significant others dumb. Companies fail to realize that such practices undermine their own competitiveness. Good employees who care about their development also recognize the personal disservice imposed by a corporate orientation toward the status quo—they end up leaving. Companies need employees who are dedicated to their careers. Ironically, employees are more likely to stay with companies that will help them to learn and grow, allow them to test and ply their skills, and offer tangible evidence of success and progress (e.g., promotions).

Outward Job Satisfaction—Personal Effectiveness[7]

People make assessments of how effective they believe they can be in a given situation: of their capacity to influence or to affect outcomes or the course of events. Feeling that you can be successful in dealing with prospective situations is self-satisfying. It means that you are optimistic about your operative capabilities to act and react. This belief in one's capabilities is known as *self-efficacy*.

Self-efficacy has great functional value. Beliefs about our effectiveness regulate the choices we make. We are unlikely to engage in or persist at activities that we believe will conclude with failure. If we think a situation calls for a response that we will be unable to make, we won't respond and will find imaginative ways of avoiding those situations in the future. On the other hand, if we believe we are self-efficacious—if we believe we can successfully execute behaviors that will produce desired results—we will

○ Exert the effort required
○ Persist in those efforts, despite potential obstacles and temporary setbacks

Not surprisingly, people in organizations who think they can cope with a particular task or situation perform better. Put simply, people who expect to succeed, do—although people, at times, may overestimate their true capabilities or have no incentive to pursue outcomes that they are certain that they could achieve.

It is important, then, that companies create the proper spirit of expectation among employees that leads to assured, opportune actions and good feelings about one's endeavors. There are four primary ways of building employees' sense of efficacy:

1. *Performance accomplishments.* Successive, progressively difficult accomplishments build skills and experience in effectively handling diverse situations. Mastering tasks, especially when that mastery is attributed to one's personal abilities, is critical to an employee's confidence in meeting future demands. The best way to feel effective is to be effective. Thus, allowing employees to succeed on their own and to notice performance improvements that they themselves enacted, while guarding them against the debilitating effects of failure, is instrumental to self-efficacy.

   There are many callous managers who have been undone by corporate concepts of freedom and empowerment, so before calling for "the hook," allow me to make the following crucial clarifications:

   ○ Self-efficacy does not imply that employees' successes be achieved through a process that is both unplanned and uninstructional for those accomplishments to be construed by employees as self-made. On the contrary, asking others to proceed unattended on a task for which they do not have the requisite capabilities or serviceable skills and strategies for overcoming barriers is a prescription for personal disaster as well as organizational failure. Mastery involves an ongoing process of testing/deployment and practice/training. It requires the discipline to give employees the latitude that they need to exercise their skills and to experiment with new behavioral repertoires without being unduly restrictive or permissive.

o   Self-efficacy does not imply that employees be insulated from failure. It suggests that managers help employees learn how to rebound from failure and to set an environmental tone that prevents employees from generalizing their inadequacies to other situations in which they are not applicable (i.e., keep employees from thinking of themselves as losers).

2. *Vicarious experience (modeling).* Watching others perform a task in which the behaviors for success are clearly demonstrated is another way to enhance self-efficacy. Observers come to believe that they, too, can execute the necessary sequence of actions that would improve their task performance. Thus, having a peer or supervisor who is proficient in some area and who takes the time to show "how it's done" can be instrumental in elevating the satisfaction and productivity of employees.

    Often, modeling is performed in a perfect world—under controlled, ideal conditions—the way training sessions are frequently conducted. However, in most real-life situations, employees also need to acquire effective ways of dealing with adversity. Thus, good models not only show others *what* has to be done to attain performance goals, but *how* it is done within environments that are not always hospitable.

3. *Verbal persuasion.* One of the least time-consuming and, unfortunately, one of the least effective means of building another's confidence in his or her ability to effect a particular outcome is through suggestion or exhortation. Telling an employee that you believe that he or she is capable of doing something can raise his or her self-efficacy, but this sense is easily overridden by subsequent confirming or disconfirming evidence. An employee's per-

sonal accomplishments carry much more weight. Verbal persuasion, then, has short-lived effects; demonstrations and personal enactments are needed to build a stronger sense of efficacy that will not extinguish easily.

4. *Self-management of emotional arousal.* Performance situations (e.g., giving a speech) often create physiological responses such as anxiety. The way these internal cues are interpreted and/or moderated has a lot to do with employees' expectations of success. Emotional states that are self-interpreted as normal are unlikely to interfere with performance. On the other hand, arousal that is viewed as a sign of one's unpreparedness and deficiencies is likely to impair performance. People who are able to reduce their anxieties through various self-administered techniques such as relaxation or by making harmless cognitive attributions (e.g., "I'm not frightened, I'm excited") will preserve feelings of self-competence. Actually, there is some circularity to all of this. Employees who are able to remain calm in trying situations and who are able to prevent negative thoughts about their abilities from invading their psyches will perform better—which reinforces their perceived competence, buttresses positive expectations, and generally yields more benign psychological states. One of the things that good managers do is help employees to make accurate interpretations about their abilities and their performance.

Most companies I have visited have a collective sense of efficacy, which reflects the general social milieu. Ultimately, for people to feel like they can succeed, they have to experience success. In some companies, try as they might, employees never seem to be able to meet their goals, to serve the customer, or to produce quality results because of poor leadership, corporate obstructions of one kind or another, or the personally crippling effects of repeated failures. When employees' efforts are continually thwarted by an environment that is unresponsive, those who are able to maintain a sense of competence will ultimately desert those environments and ply their efforts elsewhere. The remainder of employees, resigned and apathetic, will stay behind. The pathological condition in which people refrain from making adaptive responses in new situations because past attempts have failed is known as *learned helplessness.*[8]

Local management plays a key role for all elements of job satisfaction—and I've mentioned several contributions that direct supervisors can have throughout this section. However, I also have observed that job satisfaction requires sound leadership at the macrolevel. Employees are more likely to enjoy their jobs when they understand the direction of the company and are confident that senior leadership in the organization is able to meet objectives designed by strategy. In essence, the leadership is perceived as competent: leaders who clearly shape and communicate the strategies and objectives of the organization and take action. They say and they do.

The first time I noted that strong management who lead by example appeared to be associated with all aspects of job satisfaction, I passed it off as a chance relationship. However, I have seen it since and consistently, and I am led to speculate on why leaders, who are millions of miles from the average employee, matter. I believe that it is because effective leadership conveys three messages:

1. "We know what is important."

2. "We will succeed."

3. "We can make plans."

The focus and confidence of leadership trickles through the organization and allows local management and employees to be more thoughtful and proactive about jobs and careers: how to structure work, how to train, how to deploy, how to build a base of talent, where to promote, and so forth. It is difficult to do these things well in uncertain, chaotic environments where people and jobs are in constant states of flux. In addition, effective leadership contributes to employees' optimism about the future and to their belief that their work efforts will yield meaningful results.

Work-Life Satisfaction

According to the Bureau of Labor Statistics, 41 percent of U.S. families have children under the age of 14, and of these, more than one-half are families with two wage earners or single working women. More than 60 percent of mothers of children under age 6 are now in the workforce.

In addition, given our continuously aging population, more and more employees are responsible for the care of elderly parents and relatives. When the United States was founded, the life expectancy of a newborn was 35 years. Today, it is around 76 years old. Twelve percent of the U.S. population is now over 65, and that percentage is expected to grow to 20 percent by 2050. As a consequence of these trends, about 65 percent of employed workers now say they provide some form of unpaid care to a friend or relative over the age of 50.[9] This care entails activities of daily living such as walking and bathing, as well as instrumental activities of daily living such as money management, transportation, and housework. The toll on lost productivity due to late arrivals, early departures, lengthy lunch breaks, and workday interruptions such as time on the phone is estimated at between $11 billion and $12 billion annually.

If managing domestic responsibilities hasn't become hard enough, the length of the workday for many employees and the technical reach of the corporation to off-site and to after hours continue to get longer. As a result, discussions of work-life issues have become more fervent, and companies are making more concerted efforts to be family friendly by introducing a host of programs intended to ease employees' many burdens.

According to a recent (1998) survey cosponsored by Bright Horizons and William M. Mercer, the typical company sponsors an average of about 30 initiatives that may be classified as *work-life*. These can be categorized as follows:

   ○   *Flexible work arrangements.* These predominantly include various work options such as part-time versus full-time work schedules, compressed workweeks (e.g., four 10-hour days), job sharing, and flex-time arrangements (e.g., come in earlier/later, take off a block of time in the afternoon); also, telecommuting can be subsumed in this category.

O *Child care.* These include flexible spending accounts that allow employees to make tax-deductible contributions to child care as well as the many child care options that have emerged over the years: referral services, on-site child care, backup care, after-school care, summer camp, and so on.

O *Time-off policies.* These include the programs that govern employees' time away from work such as sick days, holidays, and vacations, as well as leaves for special purposes or events (e.g., maternity, adoption) and sabbaticals—whether these days are paid or unpaid.

O *Elder care.* These include provisions for long-term care, support of community-based adult day care services, on-site care, and similar programs.

O *Health care.* These include flexible spending accounts for medically related expenses, wellness benefits such as on-site fitness centers, special health-related accommodations (in addition to those mandated by the Americans with Disabilities Act) such as nursing rooms for mothers and provision for alternative lifestyles (e.g., medical coverage for same-sex partners).

O *Information and counseling.* These encompass a wide range of services, including legal and financial counseling, nutritional advice, stress management, and employee assistance programs.

O *Convenience services.* There is no limit to these, but they generally include free or subsidized meals, employee discounts at area stores and/or museums, on-site banking, and subsidies for public transportation.

O *Community services.* These include public giving campaigns in which companies engage, such as the United Way, as well as matching donations to employee charities, assistance in placing employees on local councils and the boards of charities, and support of volunteer programs including release time for employees to participate.

This list is by no means exhaustive, but it captures the essence of corporate offerings.

There is plenty of evidence that suggests that work-life programs make good business sense. Although the idea of putting employees first is anathema to many publicly traded companies that are more attuned to shareholders, there are payoffs:[10]

○ Arnold S. Porter, a Washington, D.C., law firm, instituted backup child care with an estimated savings in absenteeism costs of $800,000.

○ By allowing employees to return to work part-time following family leave for childbirth, Aetna cut attrition rates in this population in half and saved more than $1 million in recruiting and hiring costs.

○ Hewlett-Packard's Financial Services Center in Colorado Springs, Colorado, offered employees compressed workweeks (four 10-hour days) that resulted in productivity gains—an increase in transactions processed per employee.

○ First Tennessee Bank found that business units that ranked highest on favorable work-life attributes such as flexible scheduling as determined through surveys, had 7 percent higher customer retention rates.

Despite these successes and evidence that shows corporate support of work-life initiatives heightens employee satisfaction, work-life programs remain out of reach for many employees. Frequently, the most "family-friendly" companies provide benefits that are underutilized. There are several difficulties surrounding the use of work-life benefits. First, companies remain skeptical about the benefits of work-life programs, generally perceiving them as costly intrusions into productive time. Subsequently, even though companies have the benefits, they do not actively encourage their use. Second, work-life programs are viewed as career killers. Someone who makes use of these programs presumably also can't be serious about work. Without supportive management, many employees won't take advantage of their company's offer of work-life benefits. This observation is confirmed by surveys that reveal employees' fears of taking advantage of work-life initiatives.[11] Third, work-life issues are generally perceived to be, well, unmanly, feminine. There remain cultural barriers to the use of work-life benefits, particularly for men. Some men I have spoken with lie about their whereabouts to employers. They would rather tell an employer that they are working a second job than coaching a daughter's t-ball team, for example, for fear of appearing "soft." Fourth, many employees, especially single workers, believe that work-life benefits are irrelevant to them. The general perception is that these benefits are for married employees with working spouses. Some companies do little to dispel this notion by creating women-with-children-first policies, forgetting that whereas not everyone has children, everyone does have a personal life (bigger for some, smaller for others).

The pervasive metaphor for work-life benefits is still one of *balance*, as shown in Figure 6.2a.[12] The problems inherent in this depiction are clear from the illustration:

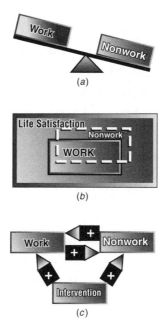

Figure 6.2 Relationships between work and nonwork. *Note:* The + in picture (*c*) denotes a positive effect between one variable, or domain, and another.

o   There are two spheres of life connected by an underlying dimen-
    sion (usually time) such that more of one implies less of the
    other. This conception of work-life issues has been referred to as
    the "Taylorization" of people, in which people's lives are nicely
    fragmented into the two parts of work and nonwork selves, the
    combination of which is a whole person. The illustration depicts
    a classic zero-sum game (a gain in one sphere of life necessarily
    results in a decrement in the other) and it suffers from two fal-
    lacies. First, it suggests simple, unidimensional solutions to work-
    life dilemmas. Employees, for example, are seen to be victimized
    by time; if only they had more of it, everything would be well. If
    it were that simple, all of our problems would be solved by now.
    There are multiple options that need to be weighed against a
    variety of potential outcomes such as organizational results, psy-
    chological well-being, and family functioning.

    Second, it suggests that less of one is *better* for the other. This
    is the greedy-institution theory, which suggests that work and per-
    sonal lives are necessarily in conflict. If an employee reduced his
    or her work commitments, his or her personal life would sud-
    denly take off—a condition that many of us have found to be
    untrue. Indeed, more time on our hands away from work can
    make our personal lives *more* stressful and *less* satisfying.

o   The concept of balance also leads us to believe that there is an
    equilibrium point—one, right answer. This is the false quest for
    a perfect state that only exists for a lucky few. Finding work-life
    satisfaction is an ongoing search for, and experimentation with,
    many options that change as our needs change.

Let's look at other ways of depicting work-life issues. I have included
two other illustrations in Figure 6.2. They suggest other ways of framing work-life dilemmas. Figure 6.2b denotes integration or fit. Work
and life are not distinct arenas; they are a part of a whole integrated person. Robert Deutsch, the founder of General Physics Corporation and,
more recently, of RWD Technologies, has his philosophy of work-life
integration printed on the back of his business card: "Work should be
an enjoyable part of a well-rounded life."[13] With this scenario, it makes

as much sense to ask: "How can we make your personal life more satis-fying?" as it does to ask "How can we make your work life more satisfy-ing?" Both questions are inseparably bound together.

Figure 6.2c shows that it is possible to intervene on work-life issues with satisfactory results for both home and work. Both areas can be improved simultaneously. I was recently working with a computer com-pany on work-life issues and was engaged with an internal interdiscipli-nary team: we were jointly listing the benefits of being an employer of choice, which included being a work-life-friendly organization. We were in a business setting and our brains naturally focused on business results (e.g., lower turnover, greater productivity) until someone chal-lenged our narrow point of view and called out, "Fewer divorces." At once, we were reminded that the best companies are capable of fulfill-ing business and personal needs by refusing to compartmentalize them as distinct issues. The best companies find ways to satisfy both.

Indeed, it reminded us that an employee's experiences in one domain of life cannot be isolated from other experiences because of:

○ *Contagion.* An employee's general attitudes, regardless of where they emanate, have pervasive effects—negative or positive expe-riences at work or home can influence one's broader life experi-ences; one's emotional life cannot easily be turned on or off depending upon location.

○ *Spillover.* An employee's experiences at home or at work can moderate experiences in the other: Having a rich personal life can reduce stresses at work, for example, and vice versa.

Given the continuity of life that we all intuitively understand, it remains surprising that we persist in our attempts to create boundaries between work and family (e.g., one should leave one's personal prob-lems at home) that are destined to fail. It also highlights the shortcom-ings of managers who believe what is happening away from work is irrelevant to what is happening at work. To be sure, we admire the courage of people who perform outstandingly despite adversity in their personal lives, but we don't insist they do this regularly and forever.

The customary approach to tough problems is frequently to add more programs. This has a cleansing, self-satisfying feel to it. Create the programs and transfer responsibility for employees' personal affairs to the employee—just don't let it interfere with work. Many employees with whom I talk feel squeezed by companies that tout whole-life programs but who stand apart from the solutions. In essence, companies that just create programs and policies, dangle them before employees, and do nothing more may be making matters worse by elevating employee frustrations to new heights.

Companies that truly help employees to live productive, well-rounded lives do two things exceptionally well. First, they develop a culture that supports work-life initiatives and the expectation that these benefits will be used. They know that there is good reason to use them. Companies such as Sun Microsystems, Nielson, and First Tennessee Bank have noted that work-life issues play a prominent role in employee satisfaction and that employee satisfaction relates to customer satisfaction and behaviors.[14] All are realistic in acknowledging that their companies must make money, but they also acknowledge that increasing profits entails a satisfied and committed workforce. Thus, the top executives of these companies communicate, "This is something we want."

Second, they are actively involved in developing work-life strategies in tandem with employees and are prepared to make individualized responses to employees' needs if necessary. This involves understanding employees' personal and work needs and constraints; understanding the outcomes to be optimized (i.e., what the business must accomplish and what the employee personally hopes to achieve); and understanding that active experimentation with work-life strategies is required to mutually address business and personal goals. Sometimes, there are no completely satisfying solutions. Baxter Export International has dramatically changed the way it organizes and schedules work to accommodate employees' needs, with 30 percent of the workers telecommuting, sharing jobs, or working part-time.[15] These measures haven't entirely removed the chaos from people's lives, but a deliberate, collaborative attempt between employers and employees to do something about it heightens employee commitment and makes good business sense.

Stress

Work satisfaction has a valence (positive or negative) and an intensity. The more satisfying your job is and the better the resolution of your work-life dilemmas, the higher and stronger your work-life satisfaction will be. There is no harm in trying to make everything right about a job and the work environment so that all is as satisfying as possible, but it will never be quite that simple. There is no definitive recipe for work satisfaction, because there is no certainty to the events and conditions employees will face—and how successfully they will face them. Sooner or later, each employee will be challenged by events (states of affairs or conditions) that are aversive. Potentially, these events will have a grave impact on the emotional well-being of employees. The extent to which their negative influences on the employee can be tempered by the company or by the employee him- or herself will go a long way to preserving employees' satisfaction.

Stress may be defined as a discomforting adaptive reaction to events or situations that place special mental or physical demands on a person.[16] A person's emotional response to an event, or to a stressor, is a signal that something in the environment is amiss and action is required. Inadequate reactions that fail to reduce or eliminate the stress coupled with chronic conditions (i.e., persistent stressors) generally cause *burnout*, a condition typified by emotional and physical exhaustion and by a loss of motivation.

Stress is of keen interest to organizations because of its relationship to health-related costs and productivity. Consider the following facts:[17]

- The employees who suffer from stress-related illness lose an average of 16 work days per year.

- The employees who are under stress are less productive and more likely to cut corners on quality: 7 out of 10 employees say stress has negatively affected their productivity; 1 in 5 say they miss work because of stress; and 1 in 3 seriously consider quitting their jobs (between 10 and 20 percent do).

- The national health expense of stress-related disorders (e.g., gastrointestinal problems, mental disorders, and substance abuse) amount to $200 billion annually.

○ The average corporate cost of rehabilitating an employee who has been disabled because of stress is $1,925; the average corporate reserve for disability payments for unrehabilitated employees is $73,270 per person.

Depending upon the survey, anywhere between 25 and 60 percent of workers report extreme stress on the job and symptomatology of stress: most commonly exhaustion, anger or anxiety, and muscle pain.[18] Thus, at least one in four employees perceive themselves as working under conditions of severe stress.

Lower work satisfaction and higher stress levels are bound to have organizational side effects: avoidant or escape behaviors (e.g., absenteeism, prolonged disabilities, turnover), increased conflicts (e.g., grievances, communication breakdowns, workplace aggression), faulty decision making and decreased output. The typical sources of stress are related to the areas of work satisfaction that we have discussed. These potential stressors are:

○ *Intrinsic to the job.* Job attributes that make a job enjoyable or unenjoyable for employees. These include the nature of the job (e.g., challenge, congruence with native interests), the conditions in which it is exercised (e.g., time pressures, zero tolerance), employees' role in the organization (e.g., its clarity and purpose), and the relationship that employees have with their boss.

○ *Linked to conceptions of career.* Actions (or inactions) that nurture or undermine employees' career aspirations. These include deployment decisions, career development, and promotional opportunities.

○ *Related to perceived effectiveness.* Able (or unable) to produce timely and meaningful results in accord with one's system of values and standards of excellence.

○ *Concerned with work-life issues.* Strategies and programs whose application either allows or does not allow employees to lead well-integrated lives. These include scheduling flexibility/control of hours, alternative work arrangements, and various familial supports.

Because people are motivated to reduce aversive states, people will actively seek ways to alleviate stress, whether the company chooses to be an ally in this effort and whether these self-styled methods are in the company's interest. In general, companies try to help employees in two ways. First, they try to eliminate stress by improving the fit between an employee and the job/work environment. Second, they try to mitigate the intensity of stress through a variety of measures and techniques, including stress management, respites, social support, and environmental control. Each of these is discussed in the following sections.

Fit

When we speak of *fit* with respect to work satisfaction, we generally mean that an employee's personality, interests, motives, values, and capabilities are compatible with the job and the lifestyle afforded by the job. Thus, vocational counselors are matchmakers. They help people understand how their psychological makeup and skill sets mesh with careers that have many of the same underlying values and attributes.

When companies think of fit, they often think of technical fit. Companies analyze jobs to determine technical requirements: They describe what employees have to know and do to achieve the desired results. The company then requests resumes that summarize what employees know and what they have done before. The closer the fit between the job specifications and employees' knowledge, skills, and experience, the better—or so some companies believe. In fact, they believe it's better in three ways. First, they think that these people will be better performers. Second, they think that these people will be happier. Third, they think that these people will be more committed.

Before you think these things, ask yourself the following questions: What are the attributes of the best performers I have ever seen? What makes people successful in their chosen vocation or discipline? What makes people happy with their work? I think you will conclude that technical fit is a limited conception of compatibility. The broader, socioemotional characteristics of the employee have to fit, too (companies often refer to the nontechnical attributes of a person and job as competencies). Thus, *fit* doesn't imply one peg and one hole; rather, it means that many pegs have to slide into place for work satisfaction. A school bus driver, for example, may be great at operating large vehicles, but he or she most probably will not be regarded as a very good driver if he or she doesn't like the cargo in the back. You can imagine the stress of a bus driver who has no affinity for children. As a former child and bus rider, I have seen it. The point is, people have different psychological tolerances for various aspects of their work that make them more or less suited for their work and more or less susceptible to the stressors in their environment.

Increasingly, companies are beginning to think of fit more globally and are creating job profiles that contain both technical requirements and competencies. This is good news and altogether appropriate. Beware, however, it is hard to find certain combinations of attributes. For example, an increasingly popular job in information technology departments is that of relationship manager. Typically, these people are programmers by trade who are responsible for satisfying the needs of a particular client base. The latter requires significant social skills; however, many programmers are introverted and analytical and are socially awkward. Thus, obtaining an ideal fit for some positions is like chasing gold dust through a sandstorm. In this case, companies do the best they can in selecting and deploying employees based on characteristics presumed to be most critical to performance and/or the least easily acquired on the job. For example, a company may select based on competencies that are enduring and resistant to change and on technical capabilities that take time to master but train on skills that readily can be learned.

There also is a temporal dimension to fit. Employees' capabilities, for example, change over time and companies need to keep employees' talents calibrated to the nature and complexity of the job. There are a host of mechanisms by which this is done, with advancement through promotion being the most common. Responsibilities are added as abilities mature. There are occasions, however, when the opposite occurs: when corporate policies have the unintended effect of misaligning employee capabilities with the demands of the job—and elevating stress to new highs. For example, many operations have seniority systems in which the most experienced and longest-serving employees are able to select the most advantageous times to work. That leaves the least experienced employees working at the most disadvantageous times: in manufacturing, when the machines run at capacity; in retail, when there are the most customers; in transportation, when there are the most riders; in service organizations, when there are the most callers; and so forth. This is the corporate version of the stress-o-matic: Tender and unworldly employees are placed in tough situations and shredded.

Stress Management

Stress management is, in reality, a combination of methods such as relaxation techniques, rational emotive therapy and cognitive restructuring, social skills and assertiveness training, and other coping skills strategies. The thrust of these techniques is to interpret situations or events more benignly to prevent overreactions, to be more attuned to one's emotional states and to attenuate arousal, to be more confident and effective in handling stressful situations, and to self-manage behavior in more productive ways (e.g., divert attention to other activities).

Companies, observing the costs and travails of stress, have taken action. Many offer stress management clinics to employees. Public Service Electric and Gas, a New Jersey utility, has a psychologist on staff to assist with stress. The e-business area of IBM provides employees with massage therapists (touch has stress-reducing properties) and with a host of recreational releases such as Ping-Pong and pinball.[19]

Respites

Time out from stressful conditions is one way to recover or recharge. In any relationship, a little elbow room, time for reflection, and self-indulgence can be purifying. Vacations have been the traditional form of respite, but they are losing their effectiveness as temporary havens as employees use more and more vacation days to meet demands in their personal lives and as communications have enabled easy remote access to work while on vacation. Indeed, about 82 percent of executives say they work while on vacation.[20] Working on days off does not constitute a reprieve. Neither does working during time off inspire confidence that a company can function independently of its key contributors—the company has done a poor job of developing "bench strength." As the saying goes, you can't work 52 weeks in 52 weeks, but you can work 52 weeks in 48.

There are other respite methods that primarily vary by the pattern of time on and time off. Sabbaticals, extended periods away from work for self-improvement in an area of interest to the company, last from three to six months and generally occur after an employee has been on the job at least five years.

Tours of duty permit employees to opt out of an area through temporary reassignment. I have seen applied engineers, programmers, and technicians do stints in research and development departments and processors and customer service providers be taken off-line to learn a related area of the company. In this instance, an employee is "on" for two to three years and "off" for two to three months.

Respites can be more frequent, however. Practices in which employees work three 12-hour or four 10-hour schedules divide time on with time off on a weekly basis. Such schedules are commonly believed to enhance satisfaction and productivity because of the extra time it gives employees to attend to needs and interests outside of work. For some jobs, however, these schedules also may be beneficial because of the time they afford away from work.

Finally, jobs are often rotated daily within teams. Assignments are varied based on individual and organizational need. Thus, a given employee who needs a break (i.e., a cushy day's work) may be given one if the team's goals can accommodate it.

Social Support

One of the best ways to moderate stress and maintain employees' satisfaction at work is through social support. The simple provision of material aid won't do. The stress-reducing properties of support require someone "to be there for you."

From your experiences, you are undoubtedly aware of the positive assistance that can be lent by a friend or partner. Indeed, it is impossible to conceive of any relationship that would be satisfying and enduring without a relationship partner who lends some form of social support. If you think about the best managers that you have ever had, I am confident that one of the most important attributes that would emerge is tied to the provision of support of one kind or another.

Specifically, the forms of support that a manager, or close other, can offer are the following:[21]

○ *Emotional.* Empathic regard for another's predicament; felt understanding.

○ *Confirmation of worth.* Interpretations and explanations that make a person feel better about him- or herself.

○ *Security.* Information that a person will not be abandoned and that others can be counted on for assistance.

○ *Guidance.* Insight and advice on problems.

All are helpful in alleviating stress, and all are used in all kinds of relationships, including between manager and employee. I will sidestep the delicate matter of when and how to be supportive, trusting appropriate actions to the instincts of managers. The general goal of managers, however, should be to provide employees with some emotional relief when they need it, enabling them to muster a capable response. That is, a critical role that managers fill is helping employees contain immobilizing affect so that employees may effectively deal with the stressor.

Social support can operate in subtle ways and is one of the most overlooked or underestimated elements within the work environment. Simple maneuvers that encourage support can have profound effects. The phone work in call centers, for example, can be highly stressful, given the unrelenting volume and the unpleasant natures of some of the callers. Yet, most of the time, employees are isolated in cubicles—everyone has his or her own trench. Instead, if employees were organized in a way that permitted emotional support among one another (i.e., eye contact coupled with the ability to make quick verbal exchanges regarding tough calls), some of their stress might be relieved.

I found in one retail organization that employees who were hired through the referral of a friend or a relative were 50 percent less likely to turn over than employees hired through advertisements or as walk-ins to posted help-wanted signs. There are several explanations of why referral programs work, but one viable explanation is that there is someone in the organization from day one with whom the employee can confide. Referral programs provide built-in social supports.

Environmental Control

Control repeatedly emerges as a central theme in organizational life: as an essential ingredient to work satisfaction. Consider a job with incessant demands, constant time pressures, and a lot to lose (or organizational punishers or sanctions) if one slips up—and working conditions that contain unpredictable events or critical work processes that are outside of one's control. No matter what you do, getting the results you seek is outside of your grasp. Welcome to the world of high stress and low control—a world of high accountability or importance, where the personal consequences are great, but where individuals do not believe they can readily influence results.

Control is the belief that you can influence events to reduce their psychic toxicity.[22] Control can be exercised either by doing or thinking:

o *Things that you can do.* You can avoid stressful situations, you can escape from them, you can reduce the probability with which a stressor will occur, lessen its intensity, or modify its onset or duration. Understanding the myriad of ways that people use to reduce stress helps to explain a range of behaviors such as absenteeism and on-the-job absenteeism (e.g., feigning to be working, volunteering for errands/tasks that mysteriously take an inordinate amount of time to complete). These may be the *adaptive* responses of escape artists versus the *maladaptive* behaviors of lazy employees, as commonly believed.

  There are parts to most people's jobs that just are not any fun and, in some instances, are extremely painful. Paperwork, for example, can be highly aversive for some. However, you might be able to automate or delegate some of it, or to choose when and where it gets done—you can make it more tolerable. It's the ability to anticipate and regulate aversive conditions that can promote a healthier and more satisfying work environment. The ability to anticipate stressors is just as important as the ability to terminate them. This is because if you never know when you will be hit with a stressor, you will never be able to relax. This is why air traffic controller jobs are so stressful. They don't have the luxury of knowing when a potentially stressful event will occur and, hence, when it will not occur.

○ *Things that you can think.* There are cognitive strategies that can influence the felt aversiveness of an event. There are strategies, for example, that divert attention away from the stressor — whistle a happy tune, so to speak. Some assembly line workers are able to be miles away while at work or are able to dissociate from the monotony.

Some cognitive strategies focus on the arousal stirred by a stressor and either try to attenuate the arousal through a variety of stress management techniques (e.g., relaxation) or by attributing the arousal to benign causes. If you are aroused before giving a public speech, that arousal will be stressful if you interpret the arousal as fear. On the other hand, if you conclude that your feelings are just normal jitters that everyone experiences, your arousal will quickly dissipate once you go on. Actors and actresses get the jitters, not stage fright.

Also, people can prospectively or retrospectively change the meaning of the event ("I'm not working on an assembly line, I'm earning a living for my family"; "What I do is what I do — I play the cards I was dealt"), or reappraise a threatening event as nonthreatening ("The upcoming meeting with my boss about quality problems is an opportunity to learn" — which reduces anticipatory stress).

People typically welcome a modicum of stress in their lives. It means things are interesting. However, people will actively try to manage extremely stressful conditions by exercising some form of control. People are motivated to reduce pain, and they will do it in ways that are, organizationally, either healthy or unhealthy. Thus, it behooves companies to build environments/jobs in which employees are able to manage stressful events and that encourage employees to remain confident in their ability to make effective responses.

7

THE TIES THAT BIND

Economic Interdependence

One of the most distressing aspects of relationships is that exciting and hopeful beginnings often dissolve into drab and pessimistic endings. People start out their associations with positive expectations. Indeed, that is why people marry, join various groups, and become employees: They believe the utility of the union beats the alternatives. It is better, for example, to be married to *this* person as opposed to being single or married to somebody else. Dissolution occurs when, through unexpected events and the accumulation of new information, the anticipated benefits from the relationship are no longer as attractive as the available options.[1]

The utility of a relationship is not all about love. To be sure, the psychic rewards are important, but so is the materiality of the relationship. Unsentimental items like hard cash play a role in the connecting power of relationships. Unions in some cultures are predicated on the joint preservation of material advantages. To dispel common notions that love conquers all, take a look at a few facts on relationship stability and divorce.

O Divorce rates have increased exponentially over the past 150 to 200 years.

O Between one-half and two-thirds of all first marriages end in separation or divorce.

○ People are most likely to divorce within the first few years of marriage (i.e., the first five years).

○ Second marriages are more likely to end in divorce than first marriages.

○ The absence of children is associated with divorce, particularly in the earlier years of the relationship (premarital births increase separation).

○ Lack of accumulation of joint assets, such as home ownership, is associated with a higher incidence of divorce.

○ Economic independence measured by wages or employment status by either party increases the likelihood of divorce.

These patterns reveal two things. First, marriages tended to last longer in times when it was harder to get out—versus our contemporary no-fault culture. There were only two petitions for divorce in all of England from 1800 to 1850! The more difficult it is to disband a relationship and the greater the negative consequences of dissolution, the more those relationships will persist.

Second, the stability of relationships is partially contingent on growing investments in children, property, and each other. There are positive outcomes from the relationship that can be obtained only by being in the relationship. There is a division of labor and economic interdependence that makes sense and that is satisfying to both parties. Both are better off (financially and otherwise) inside rather than outside the relationship. Additionally, discovery of the potential relative rewards of marriage occurs early in the relationship. People determine within the first couple of years whether the advantages of staying together are likely to be greater than the advantages that are presented by the alternatives.

The same mechanisms are at work in organizations: Employees stay with companies because there are constraints against leaving and incentives for staying. Money, and money equivalents, happen to be a part of that equation. This helps to explain why people choose to stay in relationships with which they are not particularly happy: There are economic/structural barriers and incentives that prevent dissolution.

Clearly in the limiting case of a company that offered no economic benefits and posed no barriers to exit, no employee would either join or stay. We know, therefore, that these elements are important. The task for organizational professionals is to set them up in the right amounts and in the right ways.

There is nothing inherently bad in "making" people stay. In fact, companies might be faulted for taking too long to establish special inducements or barriers. Creating financial incentives and constraints in some companies is akin to watching paint dry: By the time they get around to it, half the organization has already departed. The key is to structure the economics of the relationship in a way that won't obstruct commitment or the seemingly voluntary nature of the relationship. There are employees in organizations and in other types of relationships who have a large economic stake in the continuance of the relationship, but who sail merrily along without a second thought about it. The association is not perceived as confining or forced, even though there are very material reasons for its existence. When the financial character of the relationship is salient, it is structured in a way that preserves the relationship. Specifically, the economic arrangement is viewed as equitable, and it supports (or does not undermine) positive emotional experiences, particularly around feelings of self-determination. That is, participants in a relationship will not necessarily feel oppressed in that relationship simply because it is held together partially by economics.

Barriers to Leaving

In later sections, we will discuss specific mechanisms that companies use to retain talent. In this section and the next section, we will concentrate on some of the underlying concepts, looking first at barriers and then at incentives.

Sunk Costs and Investments[2]

If you have ever waited for a ride that was late in coming, you would have an intuitive sense of the hardening effect of time on your behavior. You think about abandoning the ride and striking out on your own, but given the time you have already put in and the imminence of good things to come, you stay—often, until it is no longer rational to move (e.g., the only possible way to make your appointment is to wait for the ride).

The investments we make to a company become part of the binding power of the relationship, particularly if two conditions are met:

1.   The investments are irretrievable.

2.   The investments are relationship-specific.

These are investments that irrevocably would be lost if employees choose to move to another company. The *sunk cost effect* (or *Concorde fallacy,* named after the supersonic jet because work continued on it even after its financial prospects were viewed as dim—the countries involved "threw good money after bad") specifically seems to be due to people not wanting to waste an investment made or to abandon a course of action that they have chosen; otherwise, they might appear inconsistent and incorrect.[3]

Time and energy, for example, are irretrievable investments (although the latter can be replenished). The more of these that an employee sinks into the relationship, the costlier it will become to walk away; otherwise, the employee will have wasted so much. Additionally, the longer employees delay leaving, the more likely they will be losing out in other ways as well, such as careers that have been built and reputations that have been made.

The costs of leaving are even higher if the investments that employees have made are firm-specific. Like a couple that decides to have children, these types of investments are more valuable inside rather than outside the specific relationship. Employees may be asked to learn about machines, technologies, methods, and processes that are relatively idiosyncratic to their companies. Employees also are generally required to become increasingly knowledgeable of the company's particular operations, markets, strategies, values, and so on.

Companies depend on employees to learn their ways, and employees who do are revered. Employees, however, do not want to invest in company-specific knowledge unless they expect the relationship to last. They don't want to sink time and energy into goods they can't readily transfer (i.e., that tie them to the company). It is more important to do things that make one more attractive outside the company if the relationship is viewed as ill conceived and/or short term.

There is a cyclicity to these causal events: Employees won't invest in the employer if the prognosis for longer-term gains is poor, and the prospect for gains will be poor if the employee doesn't invest. If you, as an employer, can't convince employees that there are longer-term advantages to staying, employees will be reluctant to make the necessary down payments that make the relationship stronger.

Difficulty of Termination

It is self-evident that making it harder to terminate relations prolongs them. Blocking retreat may have unintended consequences as well. First, it may create a more thorough and thoughtful search and selection process by employees: If termination is believed to be difficult, employees may be more careful in making sure that their skills, values, and interests match those of the company. Second, it may change employees' attitudes toward the company: If you feel that you can't leave, psychologically, you may try to make the best of the situation (i.e., "I really like it here").

There are a number of factors that potentially affect the ease or difficulty of exit. Several of these have been shown to be instrumental in keeping close relationships together, and it is interesting to contemplate the parallels.[4] Following is a brief review of these factors:

○ *Penalties and forfeitures.* Some companies require employee givebacks within a specific period of time (e.g., of relocation expenses) and other possible forfeitures (e.g., of stock options) at any time for terminating employees. Employees also may see themselves as giving up other tangible (e.g., choice location of employer) and psychological (e.g., the nice people with whom they work) benefits if they were to move.

○ *Availability of options.* Naturally, the perception that one has no viable alternatives is a constraining factor for the existing relationship. Conversely, termination is easier when there are suitable options to the current relationship (e.g., when there are many employers searching for talent in tight labor markets, when an employee's skills are in high demand, etc.).

○ *Peer pressure.* Some organizations build strong cultures that border on cults, and leaving not only may induce personal feelings of guilt and betrayal but may elicit attempts from peers and executives to retain employees. These attempts may include counteroffers as well as oral influence tactics in which the benefits and working conditions of the company are praised and the competition is derogated. I recall the employee who likened his employer to a used-car dealer—the employer dogmatically proclaimed its advantages while trashing the competition. These may be seen as mate-guarding tactics, intended to make the current relationship as attractive as possible while characterizing the alternatives as unworthy—such tactics also may contain implicit or explicit threats directed at either the partner (e.g., "Of course, you would lose your stock options if you left") or the suitor (e.g., "We will take legal action against you—this is a thinly veiled means of stealing our secrets"), or both.

○ *Policies.* Some companies make it a practice not to rehire employees. When you go, you're gone, so all decisions are final. Other companies will take employees back; not only will they take them back, but sometimes the company will circumvent normal hiring and selection procedures (e.g., forgo interviewing) and pay returning employees significantly more than they previously earned with the company—creating an incentive for separation. In addition, companies vary on the way they handle the benefits of returning employees. Government rules have much to say about pension vesting and participation. However, companies have considerable discretion about what to do with such items as vacation time, health insurance, life and disability benefits, and other perquisites. Some companies reinstate benefits in full when an employee returns within a particular time frame (one year, for instance), whereas other companies may treat returning employees as new and reset the clock. Still other companies will restore most benefits but only after the returning employee satisfies a waiting period of, for instance, six months. The interesting aspect of these different policies is not just how enticing they are to potential rehires but how instrumental they are in retaining existing employees.

o *Perceptions outside the company.* Employees may perceive excessive exit costs if the move comes in the wake of other successive moves [and may raise questions in the labor market about the his or her work stability and propensity for commitment (e.g., "He or she is a job-hopper")] or at an inopportune time that leaves the company vulnerable (and leaving prematurely may damage one's reputation in the marketplace, particularly in industries in which everyone knows everyone).

o *Practice.* Like most things (including marriage and divorce), leaving gets easier with practice. If you quit once, it becomes easier to quit again. There are two related reasons for this. First, employees discover that the experience of separating is not as aversive as they imagined and they become more acclimated to the process. Second, employees may become more cynical about expected gains from employment the second, third, fourth . . . times around — if not more cynical then at least more realistic rather than idealistic. There has been some conjecture that the teen job market is a fertile training ground for learning about the perishable nature of work relationships: Entry and exit barriers are so low in many teen jobs that kids never learn to stick with jobs in which there are disagreeable features. They simply quit and move on.[5]

Incentives for Staying

I will review the specific methods that companies use to induce employees to stay in the next section. Our mission in this section is to conceptually describe the mechanisms at work. It is rather straightforward. Companies try to increase employees' net benefits to a level that surpasses those offered by similar companies to which employees are likely to look.

Now, let me complicate this formula a little. The perceived net benefits can get tricky because their value depends on a number of factors:

○ *Nature of the benefit.* Employees merge financial and nonfinancial costs and benefits into an overall evaluation of the good they receive. Thus, for example, a meaningful and satisfying job may partially offset the need for greater pay.

○ *Importance of the benefit.* Employees who are at different periods in their careers (e.g., starting out versus nearing retirement) or who are demographically dissimilar (e.g., married versus single) think about benefits differently. For example, a married employee who can obtain health coverage through a spouse may not place as high a premium on insurance as a single employee who has no other coverage options. An older employee may place greater value on retirement benefits.

○ *Immediacy of the benefit.* Benefits that are immediate versus delayed have greater value, all else being equal.

○ *Magnitude of the benefit.* Bigger or more is better.

Most companies use money as the main vehicle of attracting and retaining employees because it can be flexibly administered (both the amount and timing are readily adjusted, unlike many corporate benefit programs that are subject to government rules and must be applied uniformly) and has universal appeal.

The formula can be complicated even further. The quality of employees' alternatives may vary by circumstance as well. Employees have more or higher-quality options depending on their demographic profile (e.g., younger); education, training, and experience; the supply and demand of their particular skill sets; the amount of contact they have with the outside world such as vendors, customers, and the competition; and economic conditions and unemployment rates. Thus, when companies allocate benefits among their employee population, they should specifically consider employees' options outside the company, given this array of factors. For example, some companies supplement the salaries of employees in "hot" areas to counterbalance marketplace demand.

Financial Retention Mechanisms

One of the reasons to stay in a relationship is because it is economically prudent. One becomes accustomed to a lifestyle that can't be easily obtained elsewhere, given the expected benefits of remaining in and/or losses of terminating the relationship. Thus, one of the reasons people stay connected is because it makes financial sense to do so. The economic payoff makes continuation of the relationship worthwhile—in a word, there is mutual dependence.

One crucial component of commitment is *dependence* in which one party's personal satisfaction and enjoyment is contingent (or depends) on what the other party says and does. In the case of organizations, employees' well-being rests on their involvement with their employer. If employees can obtain more favorable, work-related outcomes independent of the company, there is little reason to remain engaged in the relationship—employees' fulfillment is mutually exclusive of the relationship.

Thus, there are two sources of dependence:

1. The degree to which the relationship gratifies employees' most important needs

2. The degree to which the employees can obtain as high, or higher, satisfactions outside of the relationship

Taken together, employees are dependent on the employer to the extent that the employer furnishes or enables personal rewards that cannot easily be satisfied elsewhere. Thus, an employee is highly dependent on the employer-employee relationship when he or she derives a high degree of satisfaction from the relationship that would be very hard to secure in other ways. Whereas dependence is not the same as commitment, it is hard to imagine anyone who would be committed without also being dependent—the relationship is necessary in some way. However, it is easy to conceive of instances in which a person is dependent but not committed any more deeply than that. The person subsists through some form of free ridership: He or she collects on what the relationship does have to offer (e.g., the financial piece) while expending little effort on the other. For example, an employee may elect to remain with an employer but actively expand his or her interests outside of the place of employment—to hobbies, family, and friends.

Companies that add on benefits, then, are establishing the foundation for richer forms of commitment by producing a need for the relationship (i.e., creating dependence). Following, I explore the major financially oriented programs/methods that companies use as ties that bind. Other retention devices are examined in an ensuing section. Table 7.1 summarizes the retention devices that will be discussed.

Table 7.1

Common Retention Devices

Financial measures	
Sign-on Bonus	Bonuses that are staggered over a period of time
Base Salary	Salary levels that are highly competitive
Variable Pay	Bonuses that are used expressly for retention or paid out at a future date based on specified criteria
Long-Term Plans	Payments of stock and/or cash that are made at a future time—depending on years of service and/or performance
Benefits	Benefits that may increase in value with the passage of time
Other measures	
Contracts	Agreements that penalize employees who terminate
Ancillary Benefits	Benefits that can raise employees' perceived total reward
Offsets	Rewards that are used to preserve the value of employees' benefits

Sign-on Bonuses

Sign-on bonuses are what they sound like they are: bonuses paid to employees who elect to say yes to a company's offer to join. These bonuses generally range in value from a low of 5 percent of starting base salary to a high of 25 percent. For executives, the amounts can be much higher. The actual percentages offered depend on the industry and the employee's discipline, as well as on the specific talents of the individual. Often sign-on bonuses are bundled with relocation assistance—at least in the employee's mind. Companies offer various forms and amounts of financial aid to help recruits move to and settle in their new homes.

Sign-on bonuses are thought of most often as attraction devices: ways to get sought-after talent such as MBAs from top schools in the door. Some smart companies, however, spread these payments out over the course of the year (and maybe throw in a little extra to compensate for the time lag). The employee, then, has to stay to collect the full amount. Alternatively, the entire sum may be paid up front, but the company asks employees to sign a carefully worded agreement that stipulates they have to pay back all or a portion of the sign-on bonus if they do not remain with the company for a specified period of time.

It is a good idea to provide employees with some inducement to stay during their first year—when they are most at risk of leaving. If you are going to use a financial incentive, most psychologists would argue that a reinforcer for staying (rewarding the behavior you want) is more powerful than punishing separation (punishing the behavior you don't want). Giving employees something will produce better results than asking for your money back which, in most states, is precisely what you have to do—you can't just take it. Some companies, such as Arcnet, a designer and builder of wireless communications, gives employees newly leased BMWs with the completion of one year of service. They claim that benefit is more highly prized by employees than traditional bonuses but is less costly to the company.

Base Salary

Companies adopt different philosophies about the level of base compensation they are willing to pay employees. Most companies are 50th-percentile payers, meaning that they set their compensation at about average levels compared with similar organizations. Some organizations, however, set their compensation levels much higher, typically at the 75th percentile. For a given job, then, the company is willing to pay more to their employees than those employees are likely to find elsewhere in the labor marketplace. Indeed, on average, only 25 percent of employees with similar duties will be earning more outside the company. This tactic gets people in the door and it holds them because it will be difficult to find as good a deal someplace else. If money is important, companies with this pay philosophy are good places to be.

Variable Pay

As a part of their pay philosophies, companies generally advance a position on bonuses/incentives. Companies decide such things as whether to offer bonuses, which employees are eligible to receive them, the size of the award, the type of bonus plan, and the conditions and criteria for payouts. Bonus plans can be seductive to eligible employees if:

○ The amounts that can be earned are high—that is, these payouts can be truly enriching if the criteria established for the payouts are met (some companies set their base compensation at the 50th percentile, but their total cash compensation—base salary plus bonus—at the 75th percentile, putting much more into the variable piece of pay).

○ The probability of getting a sizable award is good either because the employee can control the outcomes through his or her intelligence and effort, or because the company always pays the bonuses.

There are many different kinds of bonuses: profit sharing, gain sharing, and broad-based incentive plans, to name a few. Project-based incentives also are proliferating, particularly in areas where there are longer-term projects and it is essential to keep a team of people together for the duration (i.e., Y2K was a common theme for project incentives in IT departments). Project-based incentives have the same form and function as other types of bonuses. Employees earn extra money that is paid out at a future date. If the employee is still with the company when payouts are made, the employee collects.

Some companies make no pretense of their intentions and introduce retention or stay bonuses, typically to keep employees over a 6-month to 3-year time period. Often, these bonuses are in response to events that heighten employees' risk of employment. These events include reductions in force, plant closings, mergers and acquisitions, and divestitures. Industries that are undergoing change (e.g., industry consolidations) are most likely to provide retention bonuses to key employees as a means of establishing a modicum of stability during business transitions. Most companies offer retention bonuses that are pegged to base salaries: for example, 10 percent of base salary at the middle-management levels and 50 percent at executive levels. Some companies expressly base the bonus on length of service during the retention period (e.g., one week's salary for every two weeks worked).

A few companies may pro-rate employees' share of the bonus money if they leave prematurely. For most companies, however, being present on "bonus day" is a condition of receipt; otherwise, the bonus is forfeited. Thus, the prospect of healthy bonuses can both lure employees in and entice them to hang on. Employees will hang on but, if they are not committed, just long enough to collect their bonus.

In general, the dissolution of relationships often corresponds to external events (e.g., following payments of the bonus, after the holidays, at the beginning of the year, when the baby is born, after a move). Some events help instill a sense of completion on one hand and a preparedness for a fresh start on the other. *At the beginning of the year* not only signifies a new start, but also a closure on the past. Some events simply make dissolution more convenient and easier to convey to people who may not be overly receptive to the separation: "Now that we've moved, I have found another job closer to home." There are occasions when people have had enough and their departures are not coincident with any reference to time. However, employees on the cusp, by setting their internal alarm clocks to sound at a particular time or following a particular event, are taking a step closer to the door. It is imperative for companies to recognize these high-risk moments—like following a bonus distribution—and to manage them well.

Benefits

Various types of benefit plans mean a great deal to employees. Choosing to remain with or leave the company may determine the ultimate value of the benefit or whether an employee will be able to keep it. Health care and retirement benefits are two of the more valuable benefits from employees' perspective. Most employees believe that good health insurance that includes sizable employer-paid contributions is a benefit worth having and holding on to. Employees who do not have backup coverage through a spouse will have to think very carefully before moving to a company that either does not provide health coverage or that leaves employees exposed for a prolonged period of time—although the Health Insurance Portability and Accountability Act limits waiting periods for preexisting conditions to one year. In general, the Act addresses "job lock" by ensuring uninterrupted health benefits for employees who move from one employer to another. However, companies that do not provide coverage are not required to start. As a fallback position, the Consolidated Omnibus Budget Reconciliation Act (COBRA) rules allow employees who separate from companies to continue their coverage for up to 18 months, but this usually will be at their own expense.

Although retirement benefits do not seem to have much appeal to younger employees who still have their lifetimes to save, most middle-aged to older workers give these benefits considerable thought—and second thoughts. Job hopping is not good for building a retirement nest egg. For one thing, if an employee leaves his or her job, he or she may be leaving retirement benefits behind on the table. Many plans have vesting schedules for employer contributions. Employees may have to remain with a company for as long as seven years to be entitled to 100 percent of the proceeds from the plan.

Second, some types of retirement plans, such as defined benefit (pension) plans, often compute final monthly benefits based on years of service. The fewer the years of service with a company, the lower the monthly benefit.

Third, when an employee moves to a new company, he or she must reenroll in benefits programs. However, an employee might have to wait a considerable length of time before becoming eligible for a particular savings/retirement plan such as a 401(k) plan. Depending on the hiring dates of employees and the rules of the plan document, employees may have to wait as long as two years to get in. One to two years of foregone employee, and matching employer, contributions is a lot of money to give up over time, particularly as one considers the lost accumulations due to compounding interest. For these, as well as other, similar reasons, it becomes increasingly difficult for older employees to jump ship.

Long-Term Plans

More and more employees are being included in cash and stock arrangements that offer payouts after a given time: either when a performance cycle is complete, a certain period of time has elapsed, or a particular event such as retirement has occurred. Program time frames typically range from one to five years, but they can last much longer.

There are many different types of long-term plans, each with unique functions, advantages, and disadvantages. They go by different names: stock options, restricted stock, performance unit plans, deferred compensation, phantom stock, and so on. (Stock option plans are the most prevalent long-term retention devices.) The actual mechanics of these programs are not germane to our discussion here.[6] For our purposes, these plans are similar in that some delay of gratification is required: Employees have to wait to get the goodies.

The plans differ along three dimensions:

1. *The specificity of the wait time.* Some perquisites, such as restricted stock or deferred compensation (which is often used as a means to supplement retirement income for executives), have a definite time when employees can get at, or have constructive receipt of, their money; other benefits, such as stock options, may have a minimum wait time such as a year, but the actual wait time depends on when the benefit accrues value and when employees decide to cash in.

2. *The personal control that employees have in securing the benefit.*
   At one end of the spectrum, employees are masters of their fate,
   and at the other end, they are subject to conditions beyond their
   control such as the health of the economy, consumer spending,
   and so on. Thus, at the former end of the continuum, there are
   certain things that employees can do to obtain the pot of gold at
   the end of the rainbow. These usually involve fulfilling certain
   performance and/or service requirements. At the other end of
   the spectrum, the circumstances are less personal and subject to
   factors outside of one's immediate control. Any benefit that is
   tied to movement in the company's stock price, for instance,
   will be subject to the vicissitudes of the marketplace to a
   degree — try as one might to remove all risk.

3. *The predictability of the benefit value.* Sometimes, employees
   will be able to anticipate the value that a benefit will have after
   a specific time, given that all other conditions attached to the
   benefit have been met. The expected payout of bonus plans
   with three-year life cycles can be well anticipated if the history
   of the company's performance is consistent over time. Even the
   future benefits of stock-based plans such as options may be reasonably estimated. Many large companies have predictable
   stock patterns. I have listened in on the musings of employees
   about their stock: "Every year it goes up to $70 per share and
   splits." Conversely, some stocks are so volatile or the performance criteria that have been set are so rigorous that it is hard
   for employees to project the value of their benefit; there is much
   greater uncertainty.

Highly probable benefits that employees have a high amount of control in securing at a specific time are pure retention devices. The
employees know what they will get, what they have to do to get it, and
when they will get it. All they have to do, then, is still be at the company when it's time to collect. Restricted stock in a blue-chip company,
with years of service as the only restriction, is a close approximation to
a pure retention vehicle. In this case, an employee is promised a certain quantity of stock (and is reasonably assured of its value) as long as

he or she remains with the company for a period of three years, for instance. The larger the award, the more certain the award (e.g., because preconditions are easily satisfied) and the shorter the time frame, the "stickier" the program (i.e., employees are more likely to stick around). Companies that relax these conditions will loosen the retention power of the program—but the company, then, may be wanting to achieve other ends, such as motivating employees to work harder instead of staying put.

More and more companies foster dependence (ahem, "ownership") primarily at the executive levels by establishing minimum ownership guidelines (executives must have a certain amount of their total remuneration in stock) and through mechanisms that encourage continuous holding of stock. Restoration, or reload, stock options is one such mechanism; stock options are fully replenished if they are purchased with already owned shares of stock. In essence, to get more stock, an employee has to make sure he or she owns stock.

There are many variations on retention devices that use stock and cash. For example, restricted stock may be used in stock purchase plans that give employees the right to purchase company stock at a 15 to 20 percent discount, typically through payroll deduction. Receipt of the discounted stock is subject to fulfillment of a service period. If an employee leaves before the required stay time (usually a year), he or she is forced to accept the lesser of the amount paid or the current fair market value of the stock. The employee loses the benefit of the program.

It should be duly noted, in concluding this section, that unless the financial and nonfinancial net benefits are out of reach from competitors, those competitors have little difficulty "seeing and raising." For example, if money (or stock) is the primary bond between employees and their employers, other companies simply buy out the amount of money that will be lost through forfeiture or cancellation. They offer, for instance, sign-on bonuses, stock options, concessions on benefits (e.g., crediting extra years of service), and so forth, that make up for what is being left behind. If they want an employee, they will get him or her unless the current relationship is too lucrative and/or too deep.

Thus, to sustain employee allegiance, economic benefits must be periodically either replenished and/or supplanted by other, less consumable rewards.

Additionally, employees often don't know what they have to lose or gain by leaving or staying with their company, respectively. Although every company spells out the conditions under which it makes special dispensation, that doesn't mean employees know what they are. A common refrain in every relationship is, "If only I'd known." Believe it or not, many employees are not aware of the total value of their financial benefits or of the strings attached. As such, the power to retain is lost.

Other Retention Devices

In addition to financial retention mechanisms, let's consider other methods that employers use to retain their employees.

Contracts and Severance Agreements

Companies sometimes try to restrict employee mobility (and associated knowledge about trade secrets, special processes, formulas, etc.) through postemployment contracts, most notably, noncompete agreements. These agreements, also known as restrictive covenants, noncompetition agreements, and covenants not to compete, prohibit employees from working for competitors (sometimes, but not always, within a particular geographic area) usually for six months to two years following separation—regardless of the circumstances surrounding separation.

In addition to the legal prohibitions these contracts create, terminations can trigger financial penalties. Noncompete clauses are sometimes inserted into long-term plans, such as stock option plans, and may include "payback" or "bad boy" clauses. These clauses stipulate that if the noncompete contract is violated, the employee may have to repay past gains on exercised options (for a specified period of time) and forfeit all remaining unexercised options. Sometimes, similar clauses are attached to sign-on bonuses and other hiring expenses such as relocation costs: If an employee leaves the company within a certain time frame, bonus monies and the company's recruiting costs must be repaid.

Thus, contracts are used to place restrictions on where and with whom a key employee can work and to impose penalties for defections. Taken together, they are designed to curtail separation from the company by limiting available options outside the company and by elevating the financial costs of termination. Like going AWOL, there's nowhere to run and you'll be shaken down when you're found.

Other types of contracts impose other forms of costs and burdens on employees, primarily by limiting employees' use of business-specific knowledge and expertise outside the company—thereby reducing their immediate value to others. For example, nonsolicitation agreements prohibit employees from soliciting business from a former employee's clients or from recruiting employees away from a former employer. Nondisclosure agreements, or confidentiality agreements, prohibit employees from revealing trade secrets or other proprietary information, such as manufacturing processes, during or after employment. Both types of agreements require suitors to live without the full benefit of an employee's knowledge for a period of time, for instance, until the contractual obligations expire or information becomes publicly available. In essence, an employee can run into another employer's arms, but they can't be intimate.

Companies will sometimes negotiate "prenuptial" agreements (i.e., employment contracts) that outline the terms and conditions of employment and one's property rights upon termination. These early understandings are needed in some disciplines, industries, and organizational levels because employees won't go into a company unless they have a good way out—just in case things don't work out. Employees in high-profile positions, such as executives, or employees in creative areas, such as writers and producers within the entertainment industry, are highly exposed—and there is some possibility that the relationship will not be mutually fruitful. These employees need assurances against the financial risks that they may be assuming by moving. Thus, these contracts typically stipulate that employees are entitled to severance if they are terminated without cause. Conversely, if employees leave without good reason, these severance benefits are canceled. Employees are appropriately motivated to fulfill the life of the contract.

Ancillary Benefits and Expenses

Employees also consider and incorporate less obvious costs and benefits into their perceived net returns from employment than those afforded by direct cash and stock outlays. Work involves an entire complex of behaviors and related expenditures. Employees prepare for work (e.g., need an appropriate wardrobe), travel to work (e.g., need a means of transportation), and oversee domestic duties while at work (e.g., need to make sure their children are cared for). These entail expenditures of time and money. There are potential costs, for example, associated with clothing, commuting, eating, child care, yard work, and such: activities in which employees incur costs either directly in the course of pursuing their careers or indirectly because they no longer have the time to do it themselves because of their work.

These potentially can increase or decrease employees' perceived net benefits with a given employer. For example, a shorter, less costly commute to Employer A that enables an employee to be home for longer periods of time is better than a long, more expensive commute to Employer B that, because of the added time away from home, forces the employee to outsource more domestic chores—all else being equal. Many companies try to defray the financial and inconvenience costs of work-related activities by introducing on-site services (e.g., health club, car repair, dry cleaning pickup/drop-off) and through subsidies (e.g., for child care, transportation, lunches). Costs also may be reduced through alternative work arrangements such as telecommuting, compressed workweeks, flexible hours, and job sharing. In the quest to locate and retain talent, these benefits make a difference as evidenced by successes with such programs as child care centers at Staples, Chevron, FedEx, and other companies.[7]

Also, there are a host of other perquisites that companies give to select employees that have a definite monetary value and, depending on the perquisite, psychological value. These may include such items as financial counseling, club memberships, gadgets such as cellular phones, and car allowances. Some companies believe that they get much more employee attraction-and-retention punch from a "prestige" benefit like a new car or club membership than they get from an equivalent dollar allocation. If the employee isn't desperate for cash, they are probably right.

Offsets

There are certain work experiences that may diminish or erode the perceived value of employees' tangible benefits from work. If not corrected, these may lessen the ability of the organization to hold on to its people. One class of experiences involves the psychological rewards associated with features of the job and the general working conditions in which the job is performed. Take two jobs with similar purposes — one that is more onerous (e.g., unlikable boss) and aversive (e.g., un-air-conditioned plant) than the other. The incumbent in the worse job would have to be compensated more to make up for the lower quality of work life in order to consider his or her net benefits from employment to be roughly equal to the benefits of the other job holder.

Shift work is another particular burden that some employees face that calls for the payment of wage differentials. In addition to the havoc shift work can inflict on employee health, employees who work other than the traditional day shift often feel more alienated from coworkers at the company and from family. Furthermore, often, there are fewer resources available for assistance (e.g., the company's day care center is closed) and less training and promotional opportunity. Again, additional compensation and benefits are needed to make up for the costs incurred — to keep people whole.

Some circumstances change employees' perceptions of the unit benefits of work. Specifically, the number of hours employees are asked to work affects their returns on an hourly basis. Thus, for example, many uncompensated hours beyond a standard workweek diminish the perceived benefits that employees are receiving.

Employees who are nonexempt (about two-thirds of the nation's workforce) from the provisions of the Fair Labor Standards Act must be paid:

- O   One and one-half times their regular rate of pay
- O   Above 40 hours worked per week

Overtime is a boon to some occupations. I have seen bus drivers and service repair people earn six-figure incomes through overtime. It also can be a bust: Companies, particularly in low-profit-margin industries (e.g., hotels, restaurants, retail), have been sanctioned for expecting employees to work off the clock. As long as the overtime is applied fairly, isn't extreme, and isn't always compulsory and last-minute (i.e., employees are not treated as just-in-time service providers), there ought not to be an erosion of perceived benefits.

There are, however, salaried or exempt employees who are not paid overtime. Yet, the hours can pile up and the calculation of an hourly wage would be frightening. Most workers these days expect to put in extra hours. As one managing partner of a major law firm said to me, though, "There are only so many hours a person can work before the engine begins to overheat." In addition to the stress of physically grueling schedules, there comes a time when the financial outcomes of work begin to lose luster.

Increasingly, employees work overtime without necessarily doing anything—they are on call. About 50 percent of organizations compensate employees for the lack of solace attributable to a beeper. The added on-call pay is used to entice employees to do what most would prefer not to do and to compensate them for their personal sacrifices, added responsibilities, and ongoing vigilance. You should be aware that on-call pay may not be an option. Hourly (nonexempt) employees who find the use of their personal time severely restricted (e.g., by having to remain on or near the employer's premises) must be paid for being on call. There is no similar requirement to pay exempt employees for being on call but, again, if a company doesn't want to erode the other benefits they offer employees, they will make up for the additional hours in some fashion.

It is important for companies to preserve the value of employees' benefits because:

- O   It is used by employees in the evaluation of fairness (i.e., "Am I treated equitably?").

- ○ It insulates a company from the competition by heightening employee dependence on the goods it delivers.

I'll have more to say about fairness and its ramifications in a later section.

When the Price Has to Be Right

A faint tap per se is not an interesting sound; it may well escape being discriminated from the general rumor of the world. But when it is a signal, as that of a lover on the window pane, hardly will it go unperceived.[8]

For the most part, employees don't perseverate on their economic benefits. Employees or relationship partners are not unduly distracted by the financial nature of the relationship. It goes on, undetected, like a faint tap. There are occasions, however, when the financial part of the relationship becomes its most salient aspect. I have observed certain features of organizations that make employees particularly attentive to money or, more generally, to the kind of returns they are getting. Like the lover on the window pane, there are organizational cues that divert employee focus in the direction of money. These are the following:

- ○ *Ability to count contributions.* For some employees, it is possible to quantify their contributions to the company (e.g., sales revenues for executives, salespeople, or consultants, or ticket revenues for athletes). Companies want to expressly pay for those contributions and employees want to get paid for them. Often, there is a weekly or monthly accounting of results. The exchange aspect of the relationship takes center stage with employees assessing the viability of the relationship by the company's effort and ability to pay for performance.

- ○ *The career structure of the organization.* Some companies have stringent policies around career advancement—only certain numbers of people will progress beyond a certain point. The remaining employees will either reside forevermore at a particular grade in the organization, or the losers will be asked to leave the organization. These "tournament" structures focus employer-employee relations on the shorter term, given the finiteness of the relationship:[9] It may end or stop growing. One key feature of short-term relationships is the emphasis on transactions and on staying even, especially financial transactions and getting one's due.

o *Relationships with nothing else to offer.* Some relationships are missing many of the other positive elements that we discussed in previous chapters. Thus, stripped of its socioemotional qualities, the weight of the relationship then teeters on economics — the ability of the relationship to be financially gratifying and equitable. The less there are of other interpersonal qualities, the more important the economic benefits become.

o *Use of money in relationships.* This is the organizational equivalent of parents repeatedly taking out their checkbooks and asking, "So how much will it take?" This is a company's attempt to buy happiness. Often, what emerges is a deal culture in which everything is for sale and everything can be bargained. Thus, the principal form of expression of feeling and value is through money. Investment banks are good examples of where money becomes the sum total of the relationship, but I have seen cultures in other industries where everything is assigned an economic value and negotiated.

o *Conditions of scarcity.* When there is not enough money to go around, companies can become quite preoccupied with it. There are daily calls on budget numbers, incessant and urgent requests to cut back, renewed and persistent emphasis on margins, and so forth. Everybody is talking about money. Employees begin to weigh their expectations and risks against the economic rewards that the company has to offer.

o *The fairness of the distribution.* If there is something notably wrong with one's benefits — if an employee feels short-changed in some way—then concern about money and related matters is heightened. That is, economic pain can draw an employee's attention to the financial nature of the relationship. Typically, the issue of justice is pursued until it is resolved one way or another.

Whenever employees begin to think about their level of economic benefits, there is a reason. It is not specifically the level of the benefit that really matters; rather, it is the fairness of the level of the benefit that matters. When employees take a careful look at their pay (and other economically related benefits), they want to know they are getting a fair deal. The equitableness of a relationship is one of the prerequisites for the relationship's healthy continuance.

Fairness[10]

The idea of getting one's just deserts is deeply ingrained in our culture. "That's not fair," is one of the most common utterances from preschool onward. Whereas our discussions of justice mature with age, at the root evaluations of fairness involve two things: (1) how goods are divided (distributive justice) and (2) the methods used to divide them (procedural justice).

Both distributive and procedural justice are uniquely important to employees' considerations of fairness regarding the rewards they receive, in which compensation often is the most pronounced reward in the total benefits basket. Consider a courtroom trial, as an example. The trial follows a process (procedural justice), which leads to a verdict, or trial outcome (distributive justice). Each aspect of the trial can be contested. Attorneys can argue for a mistrial if the procedures are biased in untoward ways, such as in kangaroo courts. Also, attorneys, plaintiffs and defendants, the broader legal community, and the public may question the outcome (the verdict) of a trial if it doesn't seem to fit the crime. Similarly, both aspects of the proceedings are important to employees when they render judgments of fairness about the payoffs of working for a given company.

In organizations, we tend to focus on the results of reward distributions, underappreciating the vital role played by process. Companies worry much more about what to give to employees instead of the procedures used to benefit employees for their efforts. Nonetheless, it can be argued that the procedural component is equally critical because it potentially tempers employees' discontent with less-than-expected outcomes—due process increases employees' acceptance of the results. Again, consider the analogy of a trial: The true results are seldom known, but they are more likely to be accepted as true if the procedures that were used to arrive at the verdict are considered fair. The process becomes progressively less consequential if everyone always gets what they believe to be the *right* amount. We'll discuss how employees make these determinations later in this section.

When employees aren't getting what they think they deserve, they not only begin to seek validation for their remuneration, but they begin to scrutinize the corporate procedures used to yield these results. If the process is to be viewed as fair, here's what employees should hope to find:

○ *Involvement in the process.* The procedures allow employee input; for example, encourage employees to document their various contributions and achievements. Companies may also use employee self-ratings as a proxy for involvement. As long as these ratings are accompanied by productive discussion, the process usually is viewed as worthwhile. If, on the other hand, employee input is ignored and unilaterally overridden by supervisors, employees become very cynical about these procedures, duly noting the immaterial nature of the ratings and their sham participation.

○ *Respect for the process.* Managers who preside over the process take their obligations seriously and reinforce corporate intentions to be fair. Managers who do not follow through on procedures to set goals, who do not review work and coach employees or submit evaluations in a timely manner (or at all), or worse, who publicly deride any attempt to do so, put the company at risk of losing their best performers. Employees who perform well do not want their contributions demeaned by managers who suggest through their actions that their performance is unimportant. In Figure 7.1, I show turnover patterns of employees who work for companies that either spend time on performance or who disregard it.[11]

o *Informed decisions makers.* People who are knowledgeable and informed about an employee's performance are involved in the process. Thus, employees are judged by others whose opinions they respect. Furthermore, the evaluators are close enough to the employee to furnish clear examples and explanations for their assessments.

o *Unbiased procedures.* There is an earnest attempt to limit contamination of results by instituting procedures that are evenhanded. This generally entails that the means of gathering performance-related information is viewed as objective and that there is sufficient oversight (checks and balances) in place to ensure comparability of results across the organization. Selection of reviewers, for instance, in 360-degree evaluations (evaluations in which supervisors, peers, and subordinates serve as reviewers) should proceed objectively and not be weighted by personal favorites or easy graders. Furthermore, evaluations

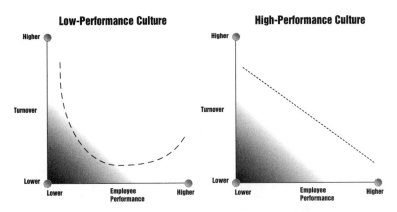

Figure 7.1 Turnover in high- and low-performance cultures. *Note:* Average performers tend to stay in organizations that conduct half-hearted assessments of performance; high performers tend to stay in organizations that encourage, rigorously measure, and reward performance excellence.

should undergo some companywide review to ensure consistency—that the same rules were applied to all.

The main goal with procedural justice in organizations is to give employees the best chance of making a best case in the most objective manner so that confidence can be placed in the results.

Two types of comparisons are important when employees evaluate their distributive share of pay, benefits, and so forth: intrapersonal and interpersonal comparisons. In both cases, it is implied that the question, "Is it fair?" can only be answered with reference to some standard. Intrapersonal comparisons are internal standards of fairness that employees develop over time that provide a gut feeling for what is just compensation. This gut feeling is produced, first, by one's living standards. Are the employees' basic needs covered, and do the benefits provide a modicum of creature comforts? When a Toyota plant recently was built in a small Indiana town, locals took up employment with Toyota not only because of the higher wages, but because of the higher standard of living that the wage afforded. Indeed, when employees were asked why they were leaving their current employers, the responses had more to do with "not enough" than "wanting more"—as one employee put it, "I'm living in a one-bedroom apartment and driving an '88 Ford van, for God's sake."[12]

Second, the gut feeling is produced through expectations about what constitutes a fair amount. These expectations are fed by personal goals for success, by past experiences with the company's pay system, by implicit or explicit promises made, and through awareness of the going rate for certain jobs. Many of the factors that we discussed earlier also inform employees' judgments of intrapersonal justice: Am I getting the rate I expected given the time I am putting in? Are my work-related costs higher than I anticipated? and so on. Employees put these facts together, which collectively fuel expectations about pay and other corporate benefits. An employee, for example, who expects more significant pay increases than he or she receives may become disaffected with the company.

Fairness, or equity, also demands that people get paid (or are benefitted) commensurately with the sum total of what they have to offer, relative to others—whether the others are inside or outside the company. Some companies discourage employees from making direct comparisons of pay and perquisites. Culturally, money tends to be a private matter that is not easily or openly discussed. This doesn't prevent employees from being immensely interested in the topic nor in making conjectures about their standing relative to others. Employees can certainly make reasonable assumptions about others' compensation. They assume, for example, that employees at the next highest grade level (e.g., their bosses) earn more and that employees who occupy similar jobs but who have been at the company much longer, also earn more (not less).

If employees feel that they don't benefit to the degree of their contributions compared with others, they will feel unjustly treated. The magnitude of this felt injustice will not only vary with the magnitude of the perceived or known discrepancies, but with the procedures used to determine those outcomes, as well as their personal expectations (i.e., feelings of intrapersonal justice). Again, the procedures used can mute or exacerbate employees' dissatisfaction with their rewards. Bad outcomes coupled with a capricious process lead to a heightened sense of unfairness. Employees want to know that a company is pursuing pay for performance and that it is doing what it can to get it right.

Also, employees who are getting what they expect react less strongly to violations of interpersonal justice. At least a portion of what composes their sense of fairness has been satisfied. The combination of these two forms of justice is neatly illustrated in the biblical story (Matthew 20:1–16) where laborers are hired throughout the day for the same price to work in the fields. Everyone gets precisely what they were promised, yet, comparatively, the rewards are unfair because the laborers worked for different periods of time. On the other hand, if employees believe they are being deprived of what they are due, then further injustices of the interpersonal variety pour salt on the wound.

Perceptions of fairness are important because there are behavioral consequences. These are illustrated in Figure 7.2. Employees who feel economically cheated in some fashion may pursue one of several options.

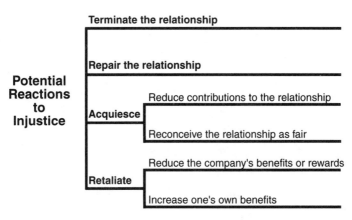

Figure 7.2 Reactions to injustice.

○   They may terminate the relationship—quit.

○   They may stay, pursuing one of three possible behavioral approaches to justice restoration.

   Repair. They may try to redress the inequity through candid discussions with their managers—arguing for greater pay.

   Acquiesce. They may reduce their inputs to the relationship—put in less effort, or justify the relationship as fair ("Maybe I'm really not that good").

   Retaliate. They may try to reduce the company's benefits and/or increase their own through illicit means as a way of making things even—for example, employees may steal from the company, leak secrets to the competition or engage in other conflicts of interest, sabotage or vandalize the company, or forget to do things or fail to see things (e.g., return petty cash or supplies that were borrowed, not report a quality control problem in a timely manner).

The method that employees use to restore justice depends on their personal character as well as the character of the relationship. If the relationship has other redeeming qualities and is worth saving, employees are more likely to approach the issues constructively. Whether employees retaliate or acquiesce should be of concern to companies, because each results in financial losses to the company.

Indeed, the cost of retaliation in the workplace is high, as revealed by a few facts culled from various sources:[13]

○ U.S. employers lose $400 billion annually to occupational fraud and abuse—about 6 percent of gross revenues.

○ About $40 billion to $100 billion is lost to employee theft, about $25 billion to $50 billion in the retail industry.

○ For every $1 stolen by shoplifters, $11 is stolen by employees—or approximately 1 percent of sales.

○ Theft by employees costs U.S. businesses an average of $9 per day per employee—about 20 to 30 percent of all new businesses fail because of employee theft.

Sabotage, too, is an issue. For example, the runaway Union Pacific train in Nebraska a few years ago was attributed to tampering by individuals who clearly understood railroad procedures.[14]

As illustrated in Figure 7.2, not everyone who feels wronged directly (e.g., steals) or indirectly (e.g., slows work pace) tries to even the score. There may be conditions that are likely to contribute to people's moral undoing, however. One such set of conditions are those that undermine employees' perceived self-determination. Every relationship has dependencies, but not everyone feels dependent—at least not until the carrot is used as a stick. The way in which benefits are conferred to another has a profound effect on the relationship. Benefits can be used as a means of control and as a way to underscore differences in power and status. Alternatively, they can be given in accordance with commonly accepted principles (e.g., need, equity) with no further strings attached. One way creates resentment, the other does not.

There are ways that people in relationships can use money that their partners may resent—which elicit negative and destructive reactions. Employers, too, may use money in these same ways—as weapons:

○ *Coercive/controlling.* For example, companies may exercise one-way discretion—make their own interpretations of performance and subsequent reward allocations.

○ *Manipulative.* For example, companies may design bonus plans that attempt to regulate all conceivable behaviors. Companies

may try to unobtrusively influence all kinds of behaviors (absenteeism, productivity, just being nice) through a system of rewards
and punishments, making everything overtly contingent.

o *Withholding.* For example, companies that don't make full payment on a bonus plan because, in retrospect, they believe the
plan is flawed; companies that delay reward payouts for an inordinate amount of time to make sure they absolutely get what
they paid for; companies that have one-sided gain-sharing
arrangements (e.g., 95 percent for me, 5 percent for you).

In the aggregate, a pattern emerges that suggests that the only way to
get what you want is to do precisely what I want. Furthermore, I (the
company) am the final arbitrator of all objections and differences of
opinion. Thus, employees may get their rewards at a very high price: by
working in an environment so confining it takes their breath away.
Employees who have no recourse feel trapped. The relationship
becomes more problematic if the benefits are perceived as unfair.
Injustice coupled with authoritarianism breeds contempt—and it
accounts for some of the employee-related losses that organizations
incur.

A good deal of research has been conducted on the motivational
properties of rewards, and there is considerable evidence that shows
that monies given in a manner that preserves people's sense of free
choice and self-determination increases intrinsic motivation (i.e., people will continue to do something even when the reward is removed or
is no longer apparent).[15] Contingencies between behaviors and
rewards that are administered in a way that undermine these values do
not. This distinction is important; any company can get some semblance desirable of behaviors if an adequate payoff is presented. However, that is not what makes companies successful or great. The true
test of corporate prowess and employee motivation comes when there
are no clear payoffs—when there is nothing material "in it" for the
employee. Do desirable behaviors persist or extinguish? I'll put it to
you: What do you think employees who feel trapped and forced into
acting a particular way will do when they find themselves in circumstances in which they don't have to do anything?

Summary and Final Thoughts

Many of the thoughts introduced in this chapter can be summarized by Figure 7.3.[16] People stay in relationships to the extent that they are uniquely dependent on them relative to the alternatives: The more attractive the alternatives and the lower the termination costs (i.e., the less one gives up by ending the current relationship), the less people are reliant on the existing relationship for the source of their satisfaction (however much or little). Companies frequently denigrate the products and work environments of the competition as a way of lowering the relative attractiveness of those companies, perhaps intuitively understanding that attractiveness to alternative relationships is a good predictor of relationship failure. As you might expect, persistent eyeballing of options is a sign that there are problems. Conversely, the less attractive the alternatives and the higher the termination costs, the greater the interdependence: the more the individual needs the relationship to obtain personal benefits and rewards.

Figure 7.3 also illustrates that even satisfying relationships can be

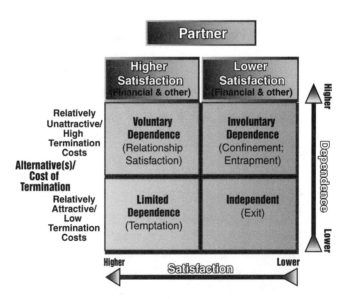

Figure 7.3 Forms of dependence.

susceptible to desirable options that opportunely present themselves. What the figure doesn't illustrate is that over time, as relationships mature, they *may* become more satisfying in many different ways (e.g., trusting, emotionally close), but they almost always become more complicated and entangled—very hard to extricate oneself without some losses. As commitment (and associated dependence) grows, people become less attuned to their alternatives and, when those alternatives become salient, more critical of them.

Companies believe that providing employees with economic benefits not only improves their chances of keeping them but that providing the right kind of benefit makes them better employees as well. Thus, it has become fashionable for companies to want to make the employees owners through the use of financial instruments (principally stock), because they believe employees as owners will be more responsible for the care of company property and interests. This is a mighty big claim and I'll not dissect all of the particulars here. For example, I think the main thesis that owners always take better care of their property than nonowners is itself debatable, given the state of many people's cars and houses. Similarly, there are fiduciaries and stewards who have no ownership stake who feel deeply responsible for others' property.

The theory is that by sharing wealth with, or by transferring property to, employees, they will feel and act as owners. This is particularly true if these exchanges and transfers are accompanied by instructions on how companies function and how employees specifically might be able to help (e.g., open-book management). Thus, many companies institute broad-based employee bonuses (e.g., profit sharing, gain sharing) and stock plans (e.g., employee stock ownership, stock options) with the intention of creating a high-performance workplace. However, the success of this strategy hinges on creating employees who feel like property holders and who believe they have a personal stake in the success of the company.

This raises a host of exciting and intriguing questions about property and ownership. The extent to which employees feel like owners largely depends upon whether they believe they are twentieth-century serfs and vassals working in a corporate feudal state or whether they are property owners with the rights of ownership. These bundles of rights typically include:[17]

- ○ The right of possession—determining who to include or exclude from that possession

- ○ The right to use and enjoy the possession

- ○ The right to manage the possession

- ○ The right to the income or profits from the use of the possession

- ○ The right to the capital in the possession (i.e., to consume, waste, sell, etc.)

- ○ The immunity from expropriation of the possession

- ○ The power to transmit by gift, bequest, or devise

Clearly, even if employees are given a piece of the company (i.e., stock), they do not enjoy all of the rights typically associated with ownership. Indeed, it might be argued that employees don't have any of these rights, because even the ones you might think they have are subject to conditions that accompany the transfer (e.g., you must hold the stock at least a year before selling; you must purchase stock options with previously owned stock; you cannot gift the stock to another, etc.). True ownership separates—it creates a boundary between public and private and the organization and the individual. That is precisely the opposite of what company programs are designed to do. In essence, they are designed to generate private wealth by encouraging allegiance to the public interest. A skeptic might suggest that these programs promote conformity rather than ownership.[18]

Employees are owners in a very limited sense. Whether they feel like owners depends on a variety of conditions outside of their participatory stake of cash or stock. That is, providing economic benefits may just be a catalyst for other organizational behaviors that instill a sense of responsibility to the corporate purposes. Paying a fair wage and benefits in a manner that preserves the personal dignity and autonomy of the employee would be a good start.

8

TO HAVE AND TO HOLD

Creating and Sustaining Commitment

If creating commitment isn't hard enough, maintaining it over the course of an employee's career is even harder. To say the obvious, relationships need ongoing attention, but then again, people don't always do the obvious. Often, it is only when a relationship is in trouble that time and resources are mustered to mend it. Managers who hadn't been spotted for some time suddenly reappear, money that was hard to find is found, assignments that were difficult to make now can be accommodated. For many employees, this rescue mission will be seen as too little, too late.

One of the many tasks of the corporation is to keep relationships with employees in good repair over time, as conditions and people change. This involves exercising preventative maintenance to keep the relationship moving in mutually desirable directions, as well as corrective maintenance to resurrect relationships that are faltering.[1] In the argot of this book, two of the goals of organizations are to keep commitment at satisfactory levels and to constructively rebuild relationship quality when it begins to break down. The following sections are devoted to further exploration of ways to instill commitment (commitment acts), mechanisms used to stabilize relationships over the longer term (maintenance acts), and prerequisite conditions and behaviors needed to resuscitate deteriorating employer-employee relations (regenerative acts).

Commitment Acts

The best way to promote the continuance of a healthy, productive relationship is to nurture those aspects of the relationship that build commitment: to reinforce the set of conditions that yield outcomes that the organization desires. Thus, fit and belonging, status and identity, trust and reciprocity, emotional reward, and economic interdependence all contribute to employees' sense of what it means to be an employee within your organization—and *commitment* serves as an appropriate and convenient organizing construct. The nature and degree of that commitment help to explain a host of employee behaviors associated with persistence, citizenship, and performance: employees' willingness to be present, to adhere to implicit and explicit organizational norms, and to expend effort.

It is unlikely, however, that each of the components of commitment individually, or in combination, has uniform effect on employee behaviors. A given component may have greater influence, for instance, on persistence than on citizenship. Also, it may have greater influence on certain aspects of citizenship, for example, than on others. I have placed these plausible, yet untested, ideas into Figure 8.1. The figure depicts what might be expected, in general, when high levels of a given element of commitment are present. I describe the major conclusions from the figure, concentrating the discussion on the ostensible, primary effects of each commitment component.

Fit and Belonging Affect Citizenship

Helping and cooperation is one of the hallmarks of this component of commitment, given its emphasis on interpersonal liking and positive group relations. Also, it is associated with a socially safe environment that enables employees to voice suggestions without fear of ridicule and to add new skills without fear of failure. Thus, employees in orga-

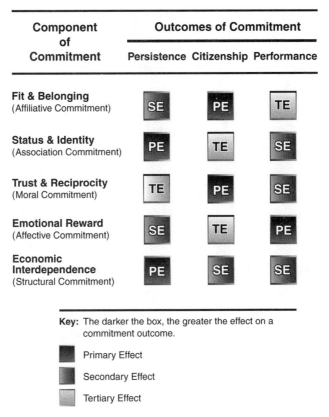

Component of Commitment	Outcomes of Commitment		
	Persistence	Citizenship	Performance
Fit & Belonging (Affiliative Commitment)	SE	PE	TE
Status & Identity (Association Commitment)	PE	TE	SE
Trust & Reciprocity (Moral Commitment)	TE	PE	SE
Emotional Reward (Affective Commitment)	SE	TE	PE
Economic Interdependence (Structural Commitment)	PE	SE	SE

Key: The darker the box, the greater the effect on a commitment outcome.

Primary Effect

Secondary Effect

Tertiary Effect

Figure 8.1 Effects of commitment components on behavior.

nizations with high fit and belonging may be more likely to undertake extrarole behaviors, such as those involving self-improvements that go outside the normal boundaries of the job.

Status and Identity Affect Persistence

This component implies interpersonal mergence; that the boundary between self and others is barely distinguishable. Union has such profound personal meaning to the employee that disengagement is extremely difficult (i.e., organizational persistence is important). Thus, a part of the binding power of commitment comes from the ability of a corporation to infuse employees with status. This creates an impetus to stay at work (e.g., not leave the company), return to work (e.g., following disability), and to keep on working (e.g., to one's retirement age, or beyond).

Trust and Reciprocity Affect Citizenship

Employees who are treated well by their employers often want to reciprocate employer considerations out of a sense of duty. These considerations may be repaid by subscribing to norms in which the needs and interests of the organization are equally attended to. Employees refrain from activities that will injure or harm the well-being of the company and seek ethical and prosocial ends, protecting the company against potential dangers and risks, making sacrifices, and spreading goodwill.

Emotional Reward Affects Performance

This component is central to creating an emotional attachment— giving a relationship its zest and appeal. Employees enjoy the activities in which they are engaged, feel effective in the exercise of their duties, and are satisfied with their vocational/career growth and progress. The relationship itself is fulfilling and intrinsically satisfying—people like what they do. Under the circumstances, employees keep at what gives them pleasure—the better their performance, the greater their pleasure.

Economic Interdependence Affects Persistence

Money (and its equivalents) have multiple uses, but its chief corporate use is to keep employees from straying from the fold: by providing something of value that is worth coming and staying for. That is, its primary function is to retain talent by fending off outsiders through competitive and equitable remuneration. Clearly, economic interdependence, like the other elements of commitment, are important in many ways. Money is used, for example, to incent performance, and rewards that are allocated to employees fairly may prevent them from restoring justice in their own way (e.g., through revenge).

Similarly, employees who are satisfied with their work are less likely to avoid it through absence or to escape it through turnover. Employees whose status is melded to the organization's history of innovation, for example, may feel compelled to prove their worthiness through creative endeavors requiring extra effort and perseverance. Employees who are given much (high trust and reciprocity), may feel obliged to give much with respect to performance, and so on.

The critical effects of each of the components of commitment are not confined to one area to the exclusion of others—but their effects are more focused in certain areas, which helps to explain what we observe in interpersonal as well as employer-employee relations. Depending upon the complexion of commitment, it is possible for people:

- To remain in relationships in which participants exert little effort and that are devoid of fidelity and fellow-feeling (i.e., to have persistence without citizenship or performance as when people feel trapped)

- To have relationships marked by mutual concern and caring but that do not grow or endure (i.e., to have citizenship without performance or persistence as when people have nice but boring and ineffective companions)

- To have immensely satisfying, burgeoning relationships that lack caring and moral tone and that come to an end (i.e., to have performance without persistence or citizenship as when infatuations eventually succumb to realities about the true qualities and offerings of one's partner)

This multifaceted nature of commitment is revealing of its fragility—if you want it all you have to have it all. This is complicated further by the fact that egregiously low levels on any commitment dimension may taint the other dimensions. For example, an employee who has no trust in the company will not interpret an unusually large pay increase in the same manner as a person who has trust in his or her employer. The former may be suspicious of the motives and question the seeming gesture of goodwill, believing there are undisclosed strings attached—and, consequently, ascribe less value to the money. The functional absence of any component may have a crippling effect on the relationship, first, in its own right and, second, because it potentially impairs the value of other commitment components. There are numerous possible interactions among the five commitment dimensions, but a few of the associations I have observed—as reflected in employee comments—are as follows:

- o *Fit and belonging is coincident with status and identity.* High fit and belonging doesn't ensure high status and identity, but low fit and belonging makes feelings of esteem derived from organizational membership difficult—if you feel you are surrounded by a bunch of half-witted slugs, it will be difficult to embrace corporate messages about the company's knowledge, success, wealth, and so on. On several occasions, I have seen organizations declare that they are the premium employer in the marketplace while being completely indifferent to who they hire—they are self-described as classy, but employees find themselves surrounded by slobs. It doesn't work.

- o *Trust and reciprocity is coincident with emotional reward.* Specifically, tenuous relationships built on a flimsy, moral foundation undercut other satisfactions one may gain from the relationship. The uncertainty and attendant watchfulness negate many of the pleasures of the job. I recently saw this within a major manufacturer: The area of the company with the best jobs and highest pay had the lowest morale. This confused the company until it was pointed out that there were rumors that the division, to which these employees belonged, was for sale. It is difficult to fully enjoy work activities and relationships that have a presumed, near-term end.

- o *Emotional reward is coincident with economic interdependence.* This, perhaps, is the most obvious connection between any two components of commitment. The rewards that employees receive are always made in the context of what they have to do to get them, and the conditions under which they are earned. Thus, a given level of compensation, for example, will have quite different meanings to a person who is satisfied with what he or she does versus a person who is not. Said differently, money has greater incremental value to employees who are emotionally rewarded through their work than to those whose work is perceived as onerous.

I am sure you have witnessed other trade-offs and interactions that illustrate the complexities of commitment. To be sure to reap the benefits of commitment, it is imperative to maintain wholesome levels on each of its precursory components. This involves conducting periodic reviews of commitment and assessing yourself on the five components.

Ideally, the assessment should focus both on employees' subjective experiences of commitment as well as on a company's internal practices, policies, procedures, and programs—and their likely effect on commitment. This is a daunting and detailed undertaking, but now that you know what to look for, you will have a structured way to inventory your actions. This review typically:

○ *Focuses on specific corporate audiences.* Companies do not treat all employee populations in precisely the same way.

○ *Includes an analysis of the recruitment process.* Commitment begins to form with the first meeting, not with entry into the organization.

○ *Examines evidence of commitment that is consistent or inconsistent with one's appraisals.* The company takes various measures of persistence, citizenship, and performance, and it relates those to commitment-instilling or commitment-destroying actions through a qualitative or quantitative analysis.

Based on the results of this review, it is possible to develop a commitment map that specifies major actions to be taken to inculcate a stronger sense of commitment among various populations of the organization. In essence, you develop a process flow that shows the specific actions you will take during the first two critical years of employment and the maintenance acts that are required thereafter. This provides an integrated, holistic approach to attracting, motivating, and retaining your talent.

Maintenance Acts

If we once again extrapolate from close relationships, we would find that there are five sets of behaviors that are instrumental in preserving or enhancing relationship quality (i.e., in keeping commitment at healthy levels).[2] I define each of these hereafter and discuss how they may manifest themselves within organizations.

Assurances

These are behavioral (including verbal) demonstrations of commitment in which the importance of the relationship is reiterated and the exchange focus remains fixed on the long run. These are acts that reaffirm an employee's value to the company and that suggest there is much more to be accomplished together. These may involve holding career discussions with employees and mapping out a likely career path or progression; asking an employee to participate in a special meeting or select project; recognizing an employee for meritorious contributions or for a history of solid performance; and so on. There are countless ways to express appreciation to employees which convey to employees that they are truly valued and are prognostic of a mutually rewarding future.

Joint Activities

This pertains to the joint participation among employees in work and nonwork activities that are enjoyable and that help solidify social bonds. These may involve joint projects that require varied skill sets and coordination of effort. These also may involve pleasurable interactions within corporate-sponsored events (e.g., training), clubs, or socials. Additionally, celebrations (e.g., birthdays, employees' corporate anniversaries, and retirements) and other community events (e.g., births, deaths) underscore employees' commonalities and linked histories and destinies, irrespective of organizational title—which bring them closer together. Some of these relations evolve from employees' natural affinities for one another and the attendant good fortune that brought them together. However, much of the continuing richness of environmental conditions depend on corporate efforts to develop positive social relationships in the workplace. Many times, new hires are warmly greeted and enthusiastically surrounded by well-wishers who soon go their own ways in the absence of the company's insistence on unity and teamwork.

Openness

For the most part, this refers to good old-fashioned communication that becomes more penetrating as the employee and the company become better acquainted. Employees progressively feel they are being brought deeper into the inner circle; this contrasts with employees who are "left in the dark," even though they may be long-service employees. One of the reasons managers like their jobs more than the rank and file and tend to be more highly committed is because corporate communications with them are more revealing—they are allowed to hear things that aren't divulged to others. Candor and open dialogue are instrumental in sustaining relationships, first, because of the feelings of privilege they engender, and second, because they foster an accurate mutual assessment of relationship status, positive or negative. People are made more aware, and become less speculative, of what's going on around them. Companies with multiple, credible forums of exchange will be better able to upkeep employer-employee relationships.

Positivity

This entails keeping the relationship on positive footing by displaying a congenial and cooperative social orientation. As starters, relationships should abide by politeness rituals and good manners that are consistent with the forms of expression extant in the organization (e.g., gratitude is shown as appropriate). Positivity also means that employers and employees are able to insert some levity into the purported seriousness of relationships that thrive on commerce and profit. Furthermore, relationships that are perceived as positive are those that the employer tries to keep enjoyable and interesting. Companies understand that relationships become worn and redundant, and that people get tired. Introducing novelty, change, or diversions that reinvigorate or restore their employees' warehouse of energy are ways of keeping employees enthusiastic, positive, stimulated, and productive. For instance, a company may work with employees to improve a process that will make jobs more fulfilling and work more efficient; it can add an interesting special assignment to employees' customary job domain, and so on.

Sharing Tasks

This means having a fair division of labor and agreement on roles and responsibilities. Employers and employees concur on what each needs to do to maintain a sense of balance in the relationship. Employees, for instance, are expected to be productive, to be giving of their extra time when needed, and such. Employers are expected to maintain the physical plant, provide direction and guidance, compensate employees, upgrade dated equipment, provide required training, and so forth: to offer a base level of services that keeps the relationship operational. Either party's neglect of its attributed roles and responsibilities will compromise the relationship as when employees aren't pulling their weight or when employers are perceived as exploitative—trying to get something for as close to nothing as possible. Thus, sharing tasks means that the functional needs of the relationship are duly attended to (e.g., metaphorically speaking, there is agreement on how the cooking, cleaning, child care, bill paying, money earning, etc., get done).

To a great extent, individual managers are responsible for ensuring that these routine maintenance behaviors, in fact, occur. Indeed, managers are the chief purveyors of commitment within the organization and, as such, much of the onus for organizational success lies with them. The most elegant corporate programs can easily break down at the point of transmission with poor management. However, companies may codify expectations through management development programs and make certain that managers are adequately trained for their duties and create tools/mechanisms that make the use of maintenance, and other commitment-related behaviors, easier to enact.

It is interesting to consider the degree to which managers attend to various subpopulations within the workforce. Specifically, are maintenance acts differentially applied to regular, full-time employees and part-timers? If so, this could partially explain why part-timers are more likely to separate from organizations, although there are many competing explanations:[3]

○ Part-timers may be assigned to more trying shifts or less convenient hours.

○ Part-timers often are paid a lower hourly wage and are ineligible for many corporate benefits.

○ Part-timers often work for different reasons than full-timers: to meet short-range financial needs or to afford greater flexibility in meeting responsibilities outside of the work place, for example.

Apart from these differences, however, part-timers also tend to be excluded from the organization's social systems. They don't register on management's radar screens like full-time employees. Joint activities may be precluded by logistical barriers such as scheduling and time availability. Managers may not provide assurances because the reduced time commitment of part-timers may be interpreted as lower employee interest and, consequently, result in reduced perceptions of part-timers' value. Additionally, openness and positivity may be applied sparingly with part-timers who tend not to be viewed as full-fledged partners in the enterprise. Overall, the things that companies think about doing with full-time employees to sustain sound employer-employee relations may not be considered appropriate or feasible with part-timers. In essence, part-time employees may leave because nobody tries to stop them.

Regenerative Acts

It is the exception for relationships to uniformly follow an upward emotional trajectory without interruption. There comes a time when the best of relationships are confronted with conflict, disinterest, or ill will. Some of these quickly spiral downward and break apart. Others are able to collect themselves and rise to new heights. Despite the seeming confusion that surrounds troubled relationships, the dissolution process follows a predictable pathway. It's one, upon reflection, that we have followed at one time or another in our lives.

The prototypical pattern moves through three stages. I'll discuss the standard course first, and then variations on this theme.[4]

Stage 1: Private Assessment

People privately begin to question the viability of the relationship—its strength and quality. They evaluate their commitment to the relationship based on feelings of acceptance, growth, pleasure, esteem, and so on. Predictably, people begin to lose interest, notice others, and act distant. Thus, employees in this stage may have reduced motivation, become more protective of their time, be less visible at work—withdraw physically and symbolically (e.g., take photos or reference books home, never unpack certain boxes), decrease communications with others within the company, take a cursory look at alternatives, and begin to heed the satisfaction of friends and acquaintances at other companies. The employee (or partner) psychologically steps back to assess the situation.

Stage 2: Public Expression

There is public expression of dissatisfaction with the relationship (or in cases of the more timid, strong hints). People vacillate between staying and leaving. There are attempts to remedy relationship problems—to patch things up—followed by experimentation and trial runs. It is an iterative, cyclical process: attempts at reconciliation followed by progressively greater physical distance, increased disinterest, and an escalation of thoughts about ending the relationship. Employees' attempts to revitalize the relationship through ongoing discussions with superiors or self-directed solutions in which they try to find ways to rev up their work lives, fail—perhaps more than once. Employees begin to look more seriously at their options. They field calls from recruiters, begin to network with associates, carefully peruse job listings, and update resumes.

Stage 3: Termination Planning (Grave Dressing)

This involves preparation for the impending break—seeking closure with the current relationship and separating. Employees justify why the relationship couldn't last and why it is best for all parties that the employee move on. Due notifications are proffered, farewells are said, and the relationship is formally concluded. In the final weeks, employees once again feel replenished and unburdened. Discussions more frequently turn to joyous topics of the future—to the new job, the new company, changes in lifestyle, and so on—and of completing unfinished business.

This standard dissolution process is illustrated by the middle wave in Figure 8.2. It depicts the gradual downward trend and cyclicity of attempts and failures to spark renewed interest and regain commitment lost. Most separations run this uneventful course of steady decline, undisturbed by extreme passions one way or another. They slowly fizzle out.

We have not devoted much time to managers' reactions to quit announcements from their staff. They range the gamut of human response from resigned, to perturbed, to betrayed. In some instances, where corporate conditions are ripe for flight (e.g., serious decline in corporate fortunes accompanied by refocusing of work on less interest-

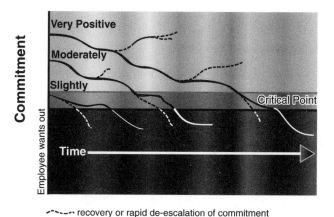

--·-·-·· recovery or rapid de-escalation of commitment

Figure 8.2 The innoculating effects of commitment.

ing projects), managers understand that they are assured of losing people and try the best they can to manage the outflow. In other instances, managers spend considerable time attending to the pay and careers of individuals on their staffs, and to developing them accordingly—and feel personally betrayed when anyone leaves. Managers sometimes are duly angered by departures that they did not suspect and perturbed when they believe they were not given ample opportunity by an employee to remedy a problem. On such occasions, the two-week notice, often the procedural staple that is outlined in companies' management handbooks, probably serves as a worthwhile cooling-off period in which everyone can emotionally adjust to the separation. It also prevents managers from acting impulsively—against the better wishes of legal departments. For example, when being rejected, it always is tempting to counterreject (*Employee:* "I'm giving my two weeks' notice." *Manager:* "Why don't you leave now!?"). In this scenario, it is possible to inadvertently change a quit into a discharge, which has legal ramifications as well as implications for unemployment insurance benefits.[5]

Let's return to Figure 8.2. The three lines in the graph depict different relationship starting places: higher commitment, moderate commitment, and slight commitment. All are initially positive as would be expected for a relationship just starting out. The chart then illustrates that the higher the quality of the relationship in its formative months, the more resistent it is to decline and the more enduring it is over the longer run. Some may think this graphic to be counterintuitive, because it appears that those whose relationships are initially better have more room to drop and, consequently, are more susceptible to decline. This is a mistaken belief held by those who are unaware just how far a relationship can fall—and how fast.

Thus, Figure 8.2 shows what can happen when one's reserve of commitment is depleted. When a relationship reaches the critical point of not having much left, it becomes vulnerable to single, even minor, events—the last straw that broke the camel's back. Without much commitment, marginal slights and innuendos can snatch the final vital signs from a relationship.

One of the best ways, then, to sustain employer-employee relations is to inoculate them. By making sure that employees are highly committed from the start of the relationship (e.g., because they were hired and joined for the right reasons) and by building a solid basis for commitment early on, relationships are more resistant to potential damage because participants are:

- More likely to openly communicate difficulties
- More likely to engage in maintenance acts
- More likely to make benign interpretations of motives and intentions
- More likely to use constructive conflict resolution strategies

Constructive, communicative principles and devices used to handle differences include those that follow.[6]

Face Conflict

Differences of opinion are natural outgrowths of social life, not aberrations within communities. Most people are relieved when conflict is addressed because it removes uncertainty from ambiguous situations and allows the relationship to proceed without the weight of unresolved issues.

Distinguish between Interests and Positions

Most of us develop points of view and solutions based upon our assumptions of the underlying problems. Indeed, most of us jump to conclusions too quickly. Positions are finite and often present either-or choices that are in conflict and that cannot easily be reconciled. Thus, parties lose the benefit of discussing interests by readily fixating on answers. In contrast, a broader discussion of interests is a more wholesome and productive avenue of discourse: Interests may not be opposed when positions are.

Explore Mutual Interests

Those in healthy relationships approach disagreements as problems to be solved rather than fights to be won. Thus, there is a thorough examination of mutual needs and interests confined to the area of dispute. Constructive problem-solvers do not allow the issues to get away from them and to devolve into discussions of problematic personalities or troublesome behaviors that occurred in the distant past. If a person begins to move away from the subject, a constructive manager (or employee) will nudge them back to the here-now-this with gentle prompting, wit and humor, and such.

Listen

Listening well entails empathy, role reversals, and perspective taking. Each party needs to feel understood, needs to fully understand the other person's thoughts and feelings, and how what one says or does potentially affects the other person ("I know what you want, and I know that you know what I want"). Most of us have felt the frustration of dealing with a person who simply did not listen—someone who didn't know what we really wanted and who acted with indifference to our wishes.

Be Aware of Bias

Sometimes we make false judgments. For instance, we tend to view things in all-or-nothing terms, to catastrophize little problems (e.g., imagine the worst), to believe we have more limited options than we actually do (e.g., there's nothing that can be done), and to commit errors in judgment. One error we are prone to make is called the *fundamental attribution error* in which we attribute others' behavior to personality traits and dispositions (e.g., someone who makes a mistake is seen as an idiot) and describe our own behavior in terms of the situational context (e.g., the reason we screwed up was because we misread a smudged number on the report). Reflecting upon potential overgeneralizations, misrepresentations, and so on, can rein in dialogue that is not helpful to relationship stability or quality.

Understand Interpersonal Tendencies

It is helpful to know one's predispositions in conflict situations to monitor one's reactions and responses for reasonableness and appropriateness. Often, people who consider themselves adversaries do not have the self-discipline to reflect on how their own behavior may be contributing to their problems. Typically, people have different tendencies toward conflict, particularly with regard to the degree of approach-avoidance and methods of dealing with anxieties.[7]

- ○ *Approach-avoidance.* Some people relish conflict (to paraphrase Samuel Johnson's quip, these might be people whose idea of a balanced personality is having a chip on each shoulder), whereas others avoid it, suppress it, deny it, and so forth (i.e., these people may be passive and indirect, so you have to be a mind reader to know what they are thinking).

- ○ *Anxiety.* People interpret their anxieties resulting from conflict in different ways. Some view it as a harmless, natural consequence of differences of opinion; some think it portends threat and loss of control, instigating aggressive reactions or attempts to gain the upper hand; others may feel overwhelmed and withdraw.

People's mental models of the world (e.g., their characteristic ways of seeing themselves and others) differ and, accordingly, their actions and reactions will vary.

Develop Effective Means for Handling Conflict

Again, drawing from Morton Deutsch (from the same article cited above), constructive discussion of differences is characterized by the three F's:

- ○ *Firm.* Resist people who use deceptive, exploitative, or underhanded tactics, or who try to intimidate or bully you into agreement on their own terms.

- ○ *Fair.* Stick to your moral principles and avoid attacking another despite obnoxious behavior and provocation.

- ○ *Friendly.* Acknowledge and reciprocate gestures of goodwill and cooperative behaviors.

Not all employer-employee differences will have easy resolution. In such instances, it is important to have procedures to which everyone can agree as a method of relief. Many companies have instituted alternative dispute resolution programs such as mediation as a formal means to deal with seemingly intransigent issues. Corporate ombudsmen often have the role of chief mediators and they review a wide variety of cases, many of which are germane to our discussion on commitment (e.g., issues regarding demotions, working with problem employees, etc.).

The problem with commitment-challenged relationships is that constructive communication and processes either do not occur or occur badly. As problems are encountered, either nothing is done or attendant employer-employee interactions are destructive and hasten employees' exit. Befuddled onlookers (including the relationship participants) watch the relationship go up in flames without serious attempts to directly intervene. There are widely circulated suspicions about reasons and causes, and managers retreat to the command center where discussions of potential improvements take place. Nothing happens, though. Absent mutual commitment, the relationship quickly devolves because no one is able to put the brakes on its descent through mature and constructive interventions.

In addition, relationships with sparse supply of commitment and goodwill often have problem-solving strategies that are characterized by criticism, defensiveness, contempt, stonewalling, and belligerence.[8] These are attempts to get one's way, or to prevent someone else from getting theirs. Clearly, these are behaviors that prompt conflict escalation.

Employees (and employers) with low commitment play a different game than those who have an ample store of commitment. There are essentially three basic game play orientations that employers and employees (or couples) may adopt:

  o *Cooperation.* Maximize our (mine and yours) joint outcomes (i.e., benefits).

  o *Competition.* Maximize my outcomes relative to yours (i.e., maximize our differences — win).

  o *Individualism.* Maximize my outcomes irrespective of yours.

With low commitment, there is a proclivity to use the latter two moves. To understand why, we need to return to our basic conceptions of commitment and consider the intentions and motives of the players and the anticipated time horizon of play.[9]

Intentions and Motives

Employees make decisions about the kind of players with whom they are engaged. Think about what lower commitment potentially implies: dissimilarity of attitudes and values, interpersonal detachment, suspiciousness and distrust, relationship dissatisfaction, and feelings of inequity. Employees begin to think that this is an exchange relationship that the employer wants to win at their expense. The employer is seeking indivisible victory in a zero-sum game: trying to take maximum advantage while doing the minimum to keep the relationship alive. Employees think that their employer is uncooperative, or worse.

Time Horizon

Now, think about the subjective probabilities of relationship dissolution as imagined by those in low- versus high-commitment relationships. People with less commitment don't think the relationship will last. Either they or the company will end it. People with high commitment, on the other hand, believe the relationship will go on indefinitely. These two different time perspectives dramatically change the complexion of the game and one's maneuverability within it—so many possible solutions are closed off by reducing the time frame: making an infinite game finite. In essence, the short-term perspective heightens one's wariness of what the other might do and of being disadvantaged without opportunity for recourse.

Now, you are in a relationship with someone whose motives you question and that you believe has a high probability of ending. Furthermore, the stakes, one's livelihood, are quite high. What do you do? First, you are likely to develop a "long memory." With substantive consequences and no longer-term opportunities at play, you will want to make sure each of your moves is a good one. To do that, you will need to reflect on the behaviors in which the employer has engaged in the

past to predict what it might do in the future. Given lower commitment, the company will not fare well. Your recollections only will confirm what you now believe to be true: that your employer will "get you"
if he or she can.

Second, you will seek to protect yourself against potential end game
strategies: You will want to minimize your worst possible outcome.
What's the worst possible outcome? How about giving your heart and
soul to the company and then getting canned—and stuck with skills
that few other companies want at an age when no other companies
want them? Under the circumstances, there will be a strong predilec-
tion to follow self-interest and feign allegiance to the collectivity until
a time comes when those interests are no longer served.

Once an employee has determined that he or she is involved with a
competitive, self-interested partner, and vice versa, it becomes very difficult to make the cooperative moves that can stabilize the relationship
for fear that the other party will not reciprocate and that the relationship will end—that there will be no further opportunities for punishment and redemption. Every action is made as if it's the last. The
relationship sputters or plummets, and when a more satisfying alternative is found, is abandoned.

Relationships do not flicker out without organizational consequence. Not only does the organization progressively lose the useful
services of an employee who it felt once had promise, but uncooperative behaviors have a way of spreading. Certain choices that an
employee makes may be confined to their personal relationship with
their employer, but other choices may have more systemic influence.

For example, many organizational activities require the coordinated
effort of a group of employees.[10] The more people who elect to pursue
their private interests, however, to the exclusion of the group, the more
compromised the organizational results will become. These are public
goods' dilemmas where social loafing and free ridership are possibilities. If a sufficient number of people are unwilling to actively participate and/or contribute, the joint enterprise will fail. The problem is
that noncooperative responses feed upon themselves—my own full
participation becomes questionable if I know that others will not be

sufficiently engaged. Why would I devote time and resources to a project, for example, that will never be fully developed or come to fruition for lack of mutual employee interest? It's like a stag hunt:[11] If you want to capture a stag, you have to surround it. If I think, however, that some of the members of our team will not be in place, the stag will escape no matter what I do. Therefore, I don't bother—although I may have a rich array of good reasons why I couldn't make it. I don't want anyone to think that I am not a team player.

There are many social dilemmas that pit employee interests against the collective interest—from engaging in individualistic, self-serving behaviors to greedily harvesting from a pool of resources (e.g., merit increases, capital budgets) without due consideration for the greater good. The choices that employees ultimately make occur within a social context that can be perceived as nasty, brutish, and short, or friendly, stimulating, trusting, and long lasting. The choice of context is yours.

NOTES

Chapter 1

1. *HR Magazine* (January, 2000): 21.

2. According to a survey by Worthlin Worldwide. See the *Wall Street Journal* (May 10, 1999): A1.

3. See *Management Review* (July-August 1999): 16–23; the *Wall Street Journal* (July 12, 1999): A1.

4. See *Barrons* (September 6, 1999): 27–29.

5. *Workplace Visions*, 5 (1999).

6. See "Labor Forecast" in *HR Magazine*'s special issue on HR in the twenty-first century.

7. *New York Times* (February 1, 1998): Business Section, 12.

8. *HR Magazine* (August, 1998): 20; *The McKinsey Quarterly*, 3 (1998): 48.

9. *Fortune* (October 26, 1998): 206–226.

10. *Fortune* (January 11, 1999): 122.

11. The following duties are based on research conducted by *Management Review*; see *Management Review* (April 1999): 16–26.

12. The concept of transactional versus relational psychological contracts is described by various authors. See N. Anderson and R. Schalk, "The psychological contract in retrospect and prospect," *Journal of Organizational Behavior*, 19 (1998): 637–647; D. M. Rousseau, *Promises in Action: Psychological Contracts in Organizations* (Newbury Park, CA: Sage, 1995).

13. For definitions of motivation, see R. A. Katzell and D. E. Thompson, "Work motivation: Theory and practice," *American Psychologist*, 45 (1990): 144–153; F. K. McSweeney and S. Swindell, "General-process theories of motivation revisited: The role of habituation," *Psychological Bulletin*, 125 (1999): 437–457.

14. J. C. Collins and J. I. Porras, *Built to Last: Successful Habits of Visionary Companies* (New York: HarperCollins, 1994).

15. This example is adapted from E. Hyland, "Motivational control theory: An integrative framework," *Journal of Personality and Social Psychology*, 55 (1988): 642–651.

16. *Forbes* (November 18, 1996): 164–170.

Chapter 2

1. See the work of Rusbult for definitions of commitment: C. E. Rusbult, "A longitudinal test of the investment model: The development (and deterioration) of satisfaction and commitment in heterosexual involvement," *Journal of Personality and Social Psychology*, 45 (1983): 101–117; C. E. Rusbult, J. M. Martz, and C. E. Agnew, "The Investment Model Scale: Measuring commitment level, satisfaction level, quality of alternatives, and investment size," *Personal Relationships*, 5 (1998): 357–391.

2. B. Fehr, "Lay people's conceptions of commitment," *Journal of Personality and Social Psychology*, 76 (1999): 90–103.

3. Also see the following for discussions on the multidimensional nature of commitment: M. P. Johnson, J. P. Caughlin, T. L. Huston, "The tripartite nature of commitment," *Journal of Marriage and the Family*, 61 (1999): 160–177; J. E. Mathieu and D. Zajac, "A review and meta-analysis of the antecedents, correlates and consequences of organizational commitment," *Psychological Bulletin*, 108 (1990): 171–184; J. P. Meyer and N. J. Allen, "A three-component conception of organizational commitment," *Human Resources Management Review*, 1 (1991): 61–89.

4. The ensuing ideas are based on the work of Sternberg. See R. J. Sternberg, "A triangular theory of love," *Psychological Review*, 93 (1986): 119–135.

5. The relationship between cognitions and attitudes about the organization and employee persistence (propensity to stay with or withdraw from a job or work) is described by K. A. Hanisch, C. L. Hulin, and M. Roznowski, "The importance of individuals' repertoires of behaviors: The scientific appropriateness of studying multiple behaviors and general attitudes," *Journal of Organizational Behavior*, 19 (1990): 463–480.

6. The ensuing discussion on organizational citizenship was informed by J. W. Graham, "An essay on organizational citizenship behavior," *Employee Responsibilities and Rights Journal*, 4 (1991): 249–270; D. Organ, "Personality and organizational citizenship behavior," *Journal of Management*, 20 (1994): 465–478.

7. The following list is adapted from the following sources: J. M. George and A. P. Brief, "Feeling good—doing good: A conceptual analysis of the mood at work-organizational spontaneity relationship," *Psychological Bulletin*, 112 (1992): 310–329; D. Katz, "The motivational basis of organizational behavior," *Behavioral Science*, 9 (1964): 131–146.

8. For recent discussions on commitment-performance linkages, see J. P. Meyer, S. V. Paunonen, I. R. Gellatly, R. D. Goffin, and D. N. Jackson, "Organizational commitment and job performance: It's the nature of the commitment that counts," *Journal of Applied Psychology*, 74 (1989): 152–156; M. J. Somers and D. Birnbaum, "Work-related commitment and job performance: It's also the nature of the performance that counts," *Journal of Organizational Behavior*, 19 (1998): 621–634.

9. L. I. Langbein and A. J. Lichtman, *Ecological Inference* (Beverly Hills, CA: Sage Publications, 1978).

10. Most organizational studies on the evolution of commitment examine a short time frame. See, for example, J. P. Meyer, D. R. Bobocal, and N. J. Allen, "Development of organizational commitment during the first year of employment: A longitudinal study of pre- and post entry influences," *Journal of Management*, 17 (1991):

717–733; R. J. Vandenberg and R. M. Self, "Assessing newcomers' changing commitments to the organization during the first 6 months of work," *Journal of Applied Psychology*, 78 (1993): 557–568. The following section owes much to the longitudinal model developed by Karney and Bradbury, and to the conceptual account of commitment processes offered by Surra and Hughes—particularly the distinction between event-driven and relationship-driven relationships: B. R. Karney and T. N. Bradbury, "The longitudinal course of marital quality and stability: A review of theory, method and research," *Psychological Bulletin*, 118 (1995): 3–34; C. A. Surra and D. K. Hughes, "Commitment processes in accounts of the development of premarital relationships," *Journal of Marriage and the Family*, 59 (1997): 5–21.

Chapter 3

1. This is a position advanced by B. Schneider—organizations tend to be composed of homogenous groups with a modal personality. See B. Schneider, "The people make the place," *Personnel Psychology*, 40 (1987): 437–454; B. Schneider, H. W. Goldstein, and D. B. Smith, "The ASA framework: An update," *Personnel Psychology*, 48 (1995): 747–773; also see J. A. Chatman, "Improving interactional organizational research: A model of person-organization fit," *Academy of Management Review*, 14 (1989): 333–349.

2. *Fast Company* (January 1999): 100–108.

3. I present interpersonal attributes that researchers believe are essential to the nurturance of budding relationships. See E. Berscheid, M. Snyder, and A. M. Omoto, "Issues in studying close relationships: Conceptualizing and measuring closeness," in C. Hendrick (ed.), *Close Relationships* (Newbury Park, CA: Sage, 1989, pp. 63–91); M. R. Parks and K. Floyd, "Meanings for closeness and intimacy in friendship," *Journal of Social and Personal Relationships*, 13 (1996): 85–107.

4. For examples of scripts in relationships, see S. Rose, and I. H. Frieze, "Young singles' scripts for a first date," *Gender & Society*, 3 (1989): 250–268.

5. *USA Today* (June 29, 1998): B1.

6. These are sample questions that recruits reported being asked. See *HR Magazine* (April 1995): 57–61. Also, there is a report from Bernard Holdan & Associates on the experiences of over 400 job applicants. See the *Wall Street Journal* (September 28, 1999): A1.

7. For a discussion of relationship continuity, see J. Gilbertson, K. Dindia, and M. Allen, "Relational continuity constructional units and the maintenance of relationships," *Journal of Social and Personal Relationships*, 15 (1998): 774–790.

8. Quoted by La Rochefoucauld, cited in F. Heider, *The Psychology of Interpersonal Relations* (New York: John Wiley & Sons, 1958).

9. *Workforce* (April 1999): 92.

10. This point has been made elsewhere; see, for example, S. L. Rynes and A. E. Barber, "Applicant attraction strategies: An organizational perspective," *Academy of Management Review*, 15 (1990): 286–310.

11. See S. L. Rynes, R. D. Bretz, and B. Gerhart, "The importance of recruitment in job choice: A different way of looking," *Personnel Psychology*, 44 (1991): 487–520.

12. For a summary discussion on the advantages of brands, see P. Berthon, J. M. Hulbert, and L. F. Pitt, "Brands, brand managers, and the management of brands: Where to next?" *Marketing Science Institute* (1997): 97–122; S. J. Garone, "Managing reputation with image and brands," *The Conference Board* (New York: 1998); K. Troy, "Managing the corporate brand," *The Conference Board* (New York: 1998).

13. See T. A. Judge and D. M. Cable, "Applicant personality, organizational culture and organization attraction," *Personnel Psychology*, 50 (1997): 359–394.

14. See, for example, F. L. Schmidt and J. E. Hunter, "The validity and utility of selection methods in personnel psychology: Practical and theoretical implications of 85 years of research findings," *Psychological Bulletin*, 24 (1998): 262–276; W. C. Borman, M. A. Hanson, and J. W. Hedge, "Personnel selection," *Annual Review of Psychology*, 48 (1997): 299–337.

15. For research on reactions to selection procedures, see T. N. Bauer, C. P. Maertz, Jr., M. R. Dolen, and M. A. Campion, "Longitudinal assessment of applicant reactions to employment testing and test outcome feedback," *Journal of Applied Psychology*, 83 (1998): 892–903; S. Gilliland, "The perceived fairness of selection systems: An organizational justice perspective," *Academy of Management Review*, 18 (1993): 694–734; S. L. Rynes and M. L. Connerley, "Applicant reactions to alternative selection procedures," *Journal of Business and Psychology*, 7 (1993): 261–277.

16. *Wall Street Journal* (May 4, 1999): B1.

17. *Wall Street Journal* (July 13, 1999): A1.

18. M. Gilley, "Don't the girls all get prettier at closing time?" in *Ten Years of Hits* (New York: Sony/Columbia, 1987).

19. For a discussion on fatal attraction, see D. H. Felmlee, "Fatal attractions: Affection and disaffection in intimate relationships," *Journal of Social and Personal Relationships*, 12 (1995): 295–311.

20. See E. E. Lawler, III, *Motivation in Work Organizations* (Monterey, CA: Brooks-Cole, 1973).

21. *Wall Street Journal* (August 1999): B1.

22. See M. R. Buckley, D. B. Fedor, J. G. Veres, D. S. Wiese, and S. M. Carraher, "Investigating newcomer expectations and job-related outcomes," *Journal of Applied Psychology*, 83 (1998): 452–461; J. P. Wanouus, "Installing a realistic job preview: Ten tough choices," *Personnel Psychology*, 42 (1989): 117–134.

23. The collective works of Kahneman and Tversky provide a discussion of the many complexities and irrationalities of decision making under conditions of uncertainty. See, for example, D. Kahneman and J. Snell, "Predicting utility," in R. M. Hogarth (ed.), *Insights in Decision Making* (Chicago: University of Chicago Press, 1990, pp. 295–311); A. Tversky, "Intransitivity of preferences," *Psychological Review*, 76 (1969): 31–68.

24. See J. Nunnally, *Psychometric Theory* (New York: McGraw-Hill, 1978).

25. *HR Magazine* (May 1998): 49–57.

26. See R. F. Baumeister and M. R. Leary, "The need to belong: Desire for interpersonal attachments as a fundamental human motivation," *Psychological Bulletin*, 117 (1995): 497–529.

27. *New York Times* (September 6, 1999): A12.

28. P. Cappelli, "A market-driven approach to retaining talent," *Harvard Business Review* (January-February, 2000): 103–111.

29. *Wall Street Journal* (January 12, 2000): B1.

30. N. J. Shumsky, "Repatriation: Effectively bring expatriates home," *ACA News* (September 1999): 89–92.

Chapter 4

1. L. K. Acitelli, S. Rogers, and C. R. Knee, "The role of identity in the link between relationship thinking and relationship satisfaction," *Journal of Social and Personal Relationships*, 16 (1999): 591–618; A. Aron and E. N. Aron, *Love as the Expansion of Self: Understanding Attraction and Satisfaction* (New York: Hemisphere, 1986); A. Aron, E. N. Aron, M. Tudor, and G. Nelson, "Close relationships as including other in self," *Journal of Personality and Social Psychology*, 60 (1991): 241–253.

2. Whenever the term *membership* is used in this chapter, I am referring to the psychological experience, not a social or legal fact.

3. For a review of the sociocognitive processes that are associated with identification, see M. A. Hogg, D. J. Terry, and K. M. White, "A tale of two theories: A critical comparison of identity theory with social identity theory," *Social Psychology Quarterly*, 58 (1995): 255–269.

4. A number of social researchers have addressed the issue of organizational identification. I am indebted to the following authors for their views on organizational identification: B. E. Ashforth and F. Mael, "Social identity theory and the organization," *Academy of Management Review*, 14 (1989): 20–99; M. B. Brewer, "The social self: On being the same and different at the same time," *Personality and Social Psychology Bulletin*, 17 (1991): 475–482; M. B. Brewer and W. Gardner, "Who is this 'we'? Levels of collective identity and self representations," *Journal of Personality and Social Psychology*, 71 (1996): 83–93; K. Deaux, "Reconstructing social identity," *Personality and Social Psychology Bulletin*, 19 (1993): 4–12; D. M. Rousseau, "Why workers still identify with organizations," *Journal of Organizational Behavior*, 19 (1998): 217–233; H. Tajfel, "Instrumentality, identity and social comparisons," in H. Tajfel (ed.), *Social Identity and Intergroup Relations* (Cambridge, U.K.: Cambridge University Press, 1982); J. C. Turner, *Rediscovering the Social Group: A Self Categorization Theory* (Oxford, U.K.: Basil Blackwell, 1987).

5. See the *Wall Street Journal* (May 5, 1999): A1.

6. See the *Wall Street Journal* (April 21, 1999): B1.

7. See the *Wall Street Journal* (September 8, 1997): A1A.

8. *Fortune* (January 10, 2000): 96.

9. See the *Wall Street Journal* (August 25, 1998): A1.

10. The distinction between company reputation and employees' perception of that reputation has been made by J. E. Dutton, J. M. Dukerich, and C. V. Harquail, "Organizational images and member identification," *Administrative Science Quarterly*, 39 (1994): 239–263; V. N. Wan-Huggins, C. M. Riordan, and R. W. Griffeth,

"The development and longitudinal test of a model of organizational identification," *Journal of Applied Social Psychology*, 28 (1998): 724–749.

11. See *Business Week* (November 2, 1998): 64.

12. See the *New York Times* (February 4, 1999): G1.

13. *Fortune* (July 5, 1999): 93–98.

14. This example comes from G. Dessler, "How to earn your employees' commitment," *Academy of Management Executive*, 13 (1999): 53–67.

15. *New York Times* (June 27, 1999): Money & Business, 1.

16. See *Industry Week* (December 10, 1998).

17. Institutional socialization tactics (as well as other forms of socialization) have been discussed by B. E. Ashforth and A. M. Saks, "Socialization tactics: Longitudinal effects on newcomer adjustment," *Academy of Management Journal*, 39 (1996): 149–178; J. Van Maanen, "People processing: Strategies of organizational socialization," *Organizational Dynamics*, Summer (1978): 19–30; J. Van Maanen and E. H. Schein, "Toward a theory of organizational socialization," in B. M. Staw (ed.), *Research in Organizational Behavior*, Vol. 1, (Greenwich, CT: JAI Press, 1979, pp. 209–264).

18. For more information, see *HR Magazine* (April 1998): 99.

19. See the *New York Times* (February 14, 1999): Business Section, 4.

20. For an engaging discussion of dirty work from which the ensuing definitions are taken, see B. E. Ashforth and G. E. Kreiner, " 'How can you do it?': Dirty work and the challenges of constructing a positive identity," *Academy of Management Review*, 24 (1999): 413–434.

Chapter 5

1. *Management Review* (July/August 1998): 11–16.

2. *Fortune* (December 4, 1989): 56.

3. These benefits of trust are summarized by R. M. Kramer, "Trust and distrust in organizations: Emerging perspectives, enduring questions," *Annual Review of Psychology*, 50 (1999): 569–598; also see F. Fukuyama, *Trust: The Social Virtues and the Creation of Prosperity* (New York: Free Press, 1998), from whom I lifted the concept of spontaneous sociability.

4. For a recent discussion, see R. C. Leana and H. J. Van Buren, III, "Organizational social capital and employment practices," *Academy of Management Review*, 24 (1999): 538–555.

5. I am indebted to the following authors for their definition and clarifications of trust: K. D. Alpern, "What do we want trust to be? Some distinctions of trust," *Business & Professional Ethics Journal*, 16 (1997): 29–45; A. Baier, "Trust and antitrust," *Ethics*, 96 (1986): 231–260; L. C. Becker, "Trust as noncognitive security about motives," *Ethics*, 107 (1996): 43–61; G. G. Brenkert, "Marketing trust: Barriers and bridges," *Business & Professional Ethics Journal*, 16 (1997): 77–98; F. L. Flores and R. C. Solomon, "Rethinking trust," *Business & Professional Ethics Journal*, 16 (1997): 47–76; K. Jones, "Trust as an affective attitude," *Ethics*, 107 (1996): 4–25; R. Hardin, "Trustworthiness," *Ethics*, 107 (1996): 26–42; L. T. Hosmer, "Trust: The connecting

link between organizational theory and philosophical ethics," *Academy of Management Review*, 20 (1998): 403; D. Koehn, "Trust and business: Barriers and bridges," *Business & Professional Ethics Journal*, 16 (1997): 7–28; R. C. Mayer, J. H. David, and F. D. Schoorman, "An integrative model of organizational trust," *Academy of Management Review*, 20 (1995): 709–734; P. Pettit, "The cunning of trust," *Philosophy & Public Affairs* (Summer 1995): 202–225.

6. For definitions of trust, see the seminal works of Deutsch: M. Deutsch, "A theory of cooperation and competition," *Human Relations*, 2 (1949): 129–151; M. Deutsch, "Trust and suspicion," *Journal of Conflict Resolution*, 2 (1958): 265–279; M. Deutsch, *The Resolution of Conflict* (New Haven, CT: Yale University Press, 1973); M. Deutsch, *Distributive Justice: A Social Psychological Analysis* (New Haven, CT: Yale University Press, 1985).

7. *Wall Street Journal* (January 27, 1999): B1.

8. Others have proposed key attributes of managers that are instrumental in inculcating trust. For a review, see R. C. Mayer, J. H. Davis, and F. D. Schoorman, "An integrative model of organizational trust," *Academy of Management Review*, 20 (1995): 709–734.

9. *Wall Street Journal* (June 16, 1999): B1.

10. *USA Today* (February 4, 1998): 48.

11. *Wall Street Journal* (January 26, 2000): B1.

12. *Wall Street Journal* (July 2, 1999): C1; (September 20, 1999): A1.

13. *USA Today* (September 8, 1997): 30.

14. *USA Today* (July 15, 1998): 43.

15. *Wall Street Journal* (February 10, 1999): B1.

16. The *New York Times* (February 28, 1999): Business Section, 11.

17. This is one of the central tenets of the attachment theory. See J. Bowlby, *A Secure Base* (London: Routledge, 1988), p. 11.

18. There are other exceptions; Dunford and Devine provide a nice review of the origins and history of the employment-at-will doctrine and discuss typical challenges to the doctrine under principles of contract and tort law (*Personnel Psychology*, 51 (1998): 903–934).

19. *Fortune* (April 15, 1996): 140–141.

20. *Sales and Marketing* (September 1996): 118–123.

21. *Business Week* (April 28, 1997): 26.

22. See the *New York Times* (August 15, 1999): Business Section, p. 4, for commentary on divided loyalties during layoffs.

23. *Economist* (January 30, 1999): 55–56.

24. R. M. Kanter, *Wall Street Journal* (July 21, 1997): A22.

25. *Wall Street Journal* (February 23, 1999): A6.

26. *Fortune* (November 11, 1996): 201.

27. *Fortune* (February 11, 1999): 142.

28. *Personnel Journal* (March 1996): 50.

29. This example comes from G. Fine and L. Holyfield, "Secrecy, trust and dangerous leisure: Generating group cohesion in voluntary organizations," *Social Psychology Quarterly*, 59 (1996): 22–38.

30. The *New York Times* (February 15, 1999): A14; (February 11, 1999): A1.

Chapter 6

1. See M. T. Iaffaldano and P. M. Muchinsky, "Job satisfaction and job performance. A meta-analysis," *Psychological Bulletin*, 97 (1985): 251–273.

2. The ensuing ideas are from R. E. Sanders, "Find your partner and do-si-do: The formation of personal relationships between social beings," *Journal of Social and Personal Relationships*, 14 (1997): 387–415.

3. The following list is from T. Butler and J. Waldroop, "Job sculpting: The art of retaining your best people," *Harvard Business Review* (September-October 1999): 144–152.

4. See, for example, N. D. Glenn, "The course of marital success and failure in five American 10-year marriage cohorts," *Journal of Marriage and the Family*, 60 (1998): 569–576; C. O. Vaillant and G. E. Vaillant, "Is the u-curve of marital satisfaction an illusion? A 40-year study of marriage," *Journal of Marriage and the Family*, 55 (1993): 230–239.

5. See P. M. Senge, *The Fifth Discipline: The Art and Practice of the Learning Organization* (New York: Doubleday, 1990).

6. For representative readings on career commitment, see K. D. Carson and A. G. Bedeian, "Career commitment: Construction of a measure and examination of its psychometric properties," *Journal of Vocational Behavior*, 44 (1994): 237–262; J. E. Wallace, "Professional and organizational commitment: Compatible or incompatible," *Journal of Vocational Behavior*, 42 (1993): 333–349.

7. The following ideas on self-efficacy belong to A. Bandura. See A. Bandura, "Self-efficacy: Toward a unifying theory of behavioral change," *Psychological Review*, 84 (1977): 191–215; and A. Bandura, "Self-efficacy mechanism in human agency," *American Psychologist*, 37 (1982): 122–147.

8. See M. E. P. Seligman, *Helplessness: On Depression, Development and Death* (San Francisco: Freeman, 1975).

9. *Business & Health* (April 1998): 16.

10. The following studies are reported in *HR Magazine* (June 1997): 110–114.

11. *Employee Benefit News* (April 15, 1998): 14.

12. The ensuing discussion owes much to the following authors: R. C. Barnett, "Toward a review and reconceptualization of the work/family literature," *Genetic, Social, and General Psychology Monographs*, 124 (1998): 125–182; S. D. Friedman, P. Christensen, and J. DeGroot, "Work and life: The end of a zero-sum game," *Harvard Business Review* (November-December 1989): 119–129; D. T. Hall and J. Richter, "Balancing work life and home life: What can organizations do to help?" *The Academy of Management Executive*, 2 (1988): 213–233; R. M. Kanter, *Work and Family in the United States: A Critical Review and Agenda for Research and Policy* (New York: Russell Sage Foundation, 1977).

13. *Forbes* (March 9, 1998): 26.

14. See, for example, *U.S. News & World Report* (May 12, 1997): 64–73.

15. *Business Week* (September 15, 1997): 102–104.

16. For the seminal work on stress, see R. S. Lazarus, *Psychological Stress and the Coping Process* (New York: McGraw-Hill, 1966).

17. Collected by the Commerce Clearing House as reported in *Business & Health*, 15 (1997): 45–46.

18. See the special report on stress produced by the National Institute for Occupational Safety and Health.

19. *USA Today* (June 22, 1999): 56.

20. *Wall Street Journal* (July 6, 1999): A1.

21. Following is a modified version of Weiss' social provisions. See R. S. Weiss, "The provisions of social relationships," in Z. Rubin (ed.), *Doing onto Others* (Englewood cliffs, NJ: Prentice-Hall, 1974, pp. 17–26).

22. For a superb review of control, see S. C. Thompson, "Will it hurt less if I can control it? A complex answer to a simple question," *Psychological Bulletin*, 90 (1981): 89–101.

Chapter 7

1. The economics of relationships are described in detail in the works of Gary Becker. See, for example, G. S. Becker, "A theory of marriage: Part I," *Journal of Political Economy*, 81 (1973): 813–846; G. S. Becker, "A theory of marriage: Part II," *Journal of Political Economy*, 82 (1974): S11–S26; G. S. Becker, E. M. Landes, and R. T. Michael, "An economic analysis of marital instability," *Journal of Political Economy*, 85 (1977): 1141–1187.

2. See the works of B. M. Staw for reviews and applications of sunk costs. Representative writings include B. M. Staw, "Knee deep in the big muddy: A study of escalating commitment to a chosen course of action," *Organizational Behavior and Human Performance*, 16 (1976): 27–44; B. M. Staw, "The escalation of commitment to a course of action," *Academy of Management Review*, 6 (1981): 577–587.

3. See H. R. Arkles, and P. Ayton, "The sunk cost and Concorde effects: Are humans less rational than lower animals?" *Psychological Bulletin*, 125 (1999): 591–600; J. Brockner, "The escalation of commitment to a failing course of action: Toward theoretical progress," *Academy of Management Review*, 17 (1992): 39–61.

4. For an excellent discussion on the constraints against leaving a relationship, see M. P. Johnson, J. P. Caughlin, and T. L. Huston, "The triparate nature of marital commitment: Personal, moral, and structural reasons to stay married," *Journal of Marriage and the Family*, 61 (1999): 160–177.

5. *Wall Street Journal* (June 30, 1999): B1.

6. The Conference Board and the American Compensation Association offer excellent reviews of long-term compensation programs through their publication series.

7. *Business Week* (April 26, 1996): 32.

8. W. James, *Psychology: A Briefer Course* (London: MacMillan, 1892).

9. The purest forms of tournaments often can be found in law firms; for a thor-

ough analysis of tournament structures, see the *Virginia Law Review*, 84 (November 1998): 1581–1681.

10. Much of the ensuing discussion is based on the works of Gerald Greenberg and Joel Brockner. See J. Greenberg, "Organizational justice: Yesterday, today and tomorrow," *Journal of Management*, 16 (1990): 399–432; J. Brockner and B. M. Wisenfeld, "An integrative framework for explaining reactions to decisions: Interactive effects of outcomes and procedures," *Psychological Bulletin*, 120 (1996): 189–208.

11. See C. R. Williams and L. P. Livingstone, "Another look at the relationship between performance and voluntary turnover," *Academy of Management Journal*, 37 (1994): 269–298. The relationship between performance and turnover is a complex area of study and there are lingering disputes about its true nature.

12. *Wall Street Journal* (April 6, 1999): A1.

13. *Business Perspectives* (June 1998): 9; *HR Magazine* (November 1998): 10; *Success* (August 1998): 24.

14. *Railway Age* (January 1997): 22.

15. E. L. Deci, R. Koestner, and R. M. Ryan, "A meta-analytic review of experiments examining the effects of extrinsic rewards on intrinsic motivation," *Psychological Bulletin*, 125 (1999): 627–668.

16. The following discussion draws on concepts of interdependence as discussed by H. H. Kelley and J. W. Thibaut, *Interpersonal Relationships: A Theory of Interdependence* (New York: Wiley, 1978); C. E. Rusbult and B. P. Buunk, "Commitment processes in close relationships: An interdependence analysis," *Journal of Social and Personal Relationships*, 10 (1993): 175–204; J. W. Thibaut and H. H. Kelley, *The Social Psychology of Groups* (New York: Wiley, 1959).

17. J. Oakes, "Property rights in constitutional analysis today," *Washington Law Review*, 56 (1981): 537.

18. There are skeptics who liken corporations to private governments that dispense entitlements in exchange for certain liberties. See, for example, the seminal paper by Charles Reich on *new property*: C. A. Reich, "The new property," *The Yale Law Journal*, 73 (1964): 733–787.

Chapter 8

1. The distinction between preventative and corrective maintenance has been made elsewhere. K. Dindia and D. J. Canary, "Definitions and theoretical perspectives on maintaining relationships," *Journal of Social and Personal Relationships*, 10 (1993): 163–173.

2. The following are based on the works of M. Dainton and L. Stafford, "Routine maintenance behaviors: A comparison of relationship type, partner similarity and sex differences," *Journal of Social and Personal Relationships*, 10 (1993): 255–271; L. Stafford and D. J. Canary, "Maintenance strategies and romantic relationship type, gender, and relational characteristics," *Journal of Social and Personal Relationships*, 8 (1991): 217–242.

3. See T. N. Martin and J. C. Hafer, "The multiplicative interaction effects of job involvement and organizational commitment on the turnover intentions of full- and

part-time employees," *Journal of Vocational Behavior*, 46 (1995): 310–321; C. Tilly, "Reasons for the continuing growth of part-time employment," *Monthly Labor Review*, 114 (1991): 10–18.

4. The following stages are based on S. W. Duck, "A topography of relationship disengagement and dissolution," in S. W. Duck (ed.), *Personal Relationships 4: Dissolving Personal Relationships* (London: Academic Press, 1982, pp. 1–29); D. M. Battaglia, F. D. Richard, D. L. Datteri, and C. G. Lord, "Breaking up is (relatively) easy to do: A script for the dissolution of close relationships," *Journal of Social and Personal Relationships*, 15 (1998): 829–845.

5. See *HR Magazine* (April 1999): 124–128.

6. The following list is adapted from M. Deutsch, "Sixty years of conflict," *The International Journal of Conflict Management*, 1 (1990): 237–263.

7. I based these on characteristic ways in which people approach interpersonal relations, as described by attachment theorists. See C. Hazan and P. R. Shaver, "Romantic love conceptualized as an attachment process," *Journal of Personality and Social Psychology*, 52 (1987): 511–524; M. C. O. Tidwell, H. T. Reis, and P. R. Shaver, "Attachment, attractiveness, and social interaction: A diary study," *Journal of Personality and Social Psychology*, 71 (1996): 729–745.

8. These attitudes are predictive of relationship dissolution. See J. M. Gottman, *What Predicts Divorce?* (Hillsdale, NJ: Lawrence Erlbaum Associates, 1994).

9. The following discussion draws on concepts from game theory. See E. C. Fink, S. Gates, and B. D. Humes, *Game Theory Topics: Incomplete Information, Repeated Games, and N-Player Games* (Thousand Oaks, CA: Sage Publications, 1998); F. C. Zagare, *Game Theory: Concepts and Applications* (Thousand Oaks, CA: Sage Publications, 1984).

10. For a review of the different types of social dilemmas that may occur in organizations, see S. S. Komorita and C. D. Parks, "Interpersonal relations: Mixed-motive interaction," *Annual Review of Psychology*, 46 (1995): 183–207.

11. Many social dilemmas are pertinent to organizations such as Prisoner's Dilemma and Chicken. For a recent discussion of stag hunt, see S. J. Guastello and D. D. Guastello, "Origins of coordination and team effectiveness: A perspective from game theory and nonlinear dynamics," *Journal of Applied Psychology*, 83 (1998): 423–437.

INDEX